FUN
BOD
T0022608

20 FUN FACTS ABOUT THE SKELETAL SYSTEM

BY THERESA EMMINIZER

Gareth Stevens
PUBLISHING

Please visit our website, www.garethstevens.com. For a free color catalog of all our high-quality books, call toll free 1-800-542-2595 or fax 1-877-542-2596.

Library of Congress Cataloging-in-Publication Data

Names: Emminizer, Theresa, author.
Title: 20 fun facts about the skeletal system / Theresa Emminizer.
Description: New York : Gareth Stevens, [2019] | Series: Fun fact file: body systems | Includes index.
Identifiers: LCCN 2018032237| ISBN 9781538229262 (library bound) | ISBN 9781538232828 (pbk.) | ISBN 9781538232835 (6 pack)
Subjects: LCSH: Human skeleton–Juvenile literature.
Classification: LCC QM101 .E46 2019 | DDC 611/.71–dc23
LC record available at https://lccn.loc.gov/2018032237

First Edition

Published in 2019 by
Gareth Stevens Publishing
111 East 14th Street, Suite 349
New York, NY 10003

Copyright © 2019 Gareth Stevens Publishing

Designer: Sarah Liddell
Editor: Meta Manchester

Photo credits: Cover, p. 1 (main) Life science/Shutterstock.com; file folder used throughout David Smart/Shutterstock.com; binder clip used throughout luckyraccoon/Shutterstock.com; wood grain background used throughout ARENA Creative/Shutterstock.com; p. 5 qualitystocksuk/Shutterstock.com; p. 6 GSK/Shutterstock.com; p. 7 Carlos Horta/Shutterstock.com; p. 8 Sergey Novikov/Shutterstock.com; p. 9 PRESSLAB/Shutterstock.com; p. 10 NoPainNoGain/Shutterstock.com; p. 11 udaix/Shutterstock.com; p. 12 Dmitry Naumov/Shutterstock.com; p. 13 Suttha Burawonk/Shutterstock.com; p. 14 logika600/Shutterstock.com; p. 15 Kjetil Kolbjornsrud/Shutterstock.com; p. 16 CSA Images/Vetta/Getty Images; p. 17 Vecton/Shutterstock.com; p. 18 CLIPAREA | Custom media/Shutterstock.com; p. 19 Andrew Sutton/Shutterstock.com; p. 20 videodoctor/Shutterstock.com; p. 21 ilusmedical/Shutterstock.com; p. 22 Blamb/Shutterstock.com; p. 23 Cherry-Merry/Shutterstock.com; pp. 24, 25 Double Brain/Shutterstock.com; p. 26 creativemarc/Shutterstock.com; p. 27 Art_Photo/Shutterstock.com; p. 29 Fotokostic/Shutterstock.com.

All rights reserved. No part of this book may be reproduced in any form without permission in writing from the publisher, except by a reviewer.

Printed in the United States of America

CPSIA compliance information: Batch #CW19GS: For further information contact Gareth Stevens, New York, New York at 1-800-542-2595.

CONTENTS

Words in the glossary appear in **bold** type the first time they are used in the text.

THE SKELETON DANCE

You couldn't dance without your skeleton! In fact, you couldn't even sit, stand, or walk. The skeleton is your body's framework. It helps you move. It also protects your body's most important **organs**, like your brain and heart.

What exactly is the skeletal system? It's the bones, **joints**, and **cartilage** that form a skeleton. All these parts work together to help you live your life. There's a lot to learn about the skeletal system. Let's bone up on these fun facts!

As the song goes: the foot bone's connected to the ankle bone, the ankle bone's connected to the leg bone! Now shake those skeleton bones!

TEETH VS. BONES

YOUR TEETH ARE PART OF YOUR SKELETAL SYSTEM!

Are teeth bones? You might think so because they're hard and white. But they aren't! They're made of different matter than bones, but they're part of the skeletal system. Like bones, teeth store **calcium**, which the skeletal system needs.

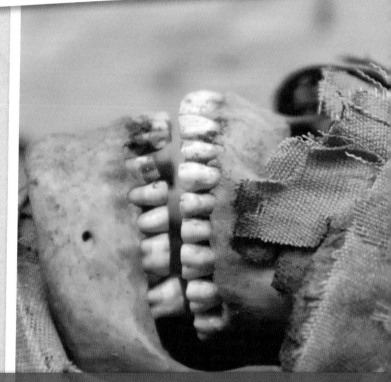

After death, teeth are the slowest part of the body to decay, or break down. Scientists are able to learn about ancient people by studying their teeth!

Unlike bones, teeth can't heal themselves when they're broken.

FUN FACT: 2

TEETH ARE STRONGER THAN BONES!

Teeth are the hardest part of your body because they're covered in enamel. Enamel is a hard **tissue** that protects teeth from being hurt by chewing hard food or eating things that are too hot or cold.

7

BUILDING STRONG BONES

FUN FACT: 3

BONES GET STRONGER UNDER PRESSURE!

Human bones are built to last, but they become weaker if they're not used enough. Doing weight-bearing activities that use the body's weight and **gravity** puts pressure on bones and makes them stronger.

Lifting weights, running, and doing jumping jacks are weight-bearing activities that help your bones grow strong!

In the United States, about 6.8 million people are treated for broken bones each year. Most broken bones take about 6 to 12 weeks to heal.

BONES CAN HEAL THEMSELVES!

When a bone breaks, a **blood clot** forms around it.

Then, a callus, or lump of healing tissue, forms and holds the broken pieces together. The callus hardens as new bone cells are created.

WHAT'S IN A BONE?

BONES ARE ALIVE!

Looking at a skeleton, it looks like bones are dry and lifeless. But inside your body, your bones are living and changing. They grow and heal themselves all the time. Bones are made of living cells, **proteins**, **vitamins**, and **minerals**.

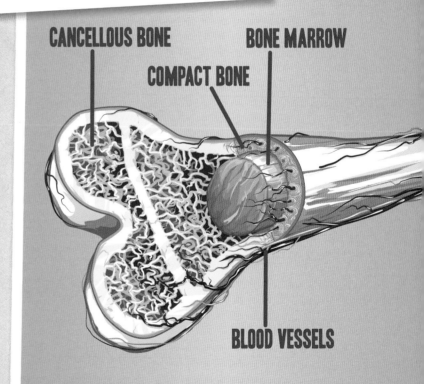

CANCELLOUS BONE

COMPACT BONE

BONE MARROW

BLOOD VESSELS

Bones have a hard outer layer called compact bone and a spongy inner layer called cancellous bone.

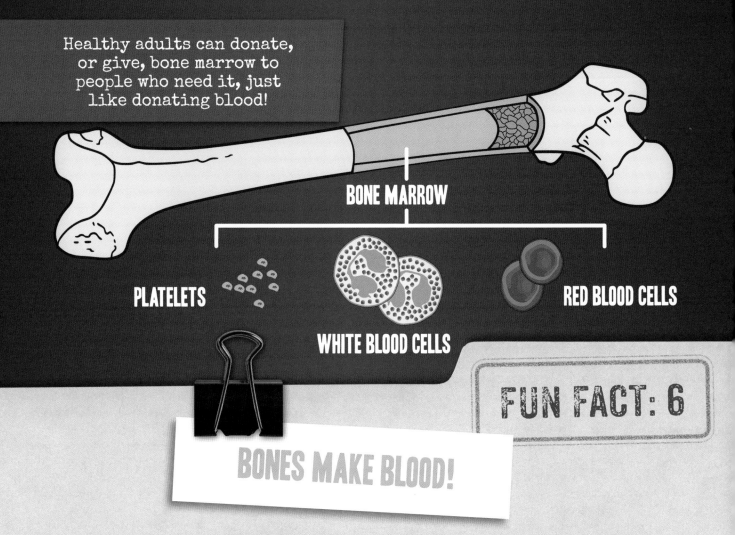

Healthy adults can donate, or give, bone marrow to people who need it, just like donating blood!

BONE MARROW

PLATELETS

WHITE BLOOD CELLS

RED BLOOD CELLS

FUN FACT: 6

BONES MAKE BLOOD!

Bone marrow is a jellylike matter inside bones. It makes three parts of blood: red and white blood cells and **platelets**. We need blood cells in order to live. They carry oxygen, the gas we breathe in. They also keep us from getting sick and help heal us when we're hurt.

11

BONES AS YOU GROW

BABIES HAVE MORE BONES THAN ADULTS.

Babies are born with about 300 bones, but adults only have 206 bones. This is because some bones fuse, or join together, as you grow! Babies also have more cartilage than adults. Some of this cartilage becomes bone through a process called ossification.

Baby skulls are softer than adult skulls. That's because the skull bones haven't grown together yet!

Bones grow at different rates in different people. Bone mass is gained until about age 30. After that, more bone begins being lost than gained.

CHILD

TEEN

ADULT

THE BONES YOU HAVE TODAY WILL BE NEW BONES IN ABOUT 10 YEARS!

Bones are made of proteins, mostly one called collagen.

Collagen is organic, or living, and is always being renewed.

Your body always has a mix of old and new bone. It takes

about 10 years for bone to be completely replaced.

TINY BONES, BIG BONES

THE TINIEST BONE IN YOUR BODY IS JUST 0.1 IN (3 MM) LONG!

The stapes is a tiny, stirrup-shaped bone in your middle ear. It works with two other little bones called the malleus and incus to carry sound from the outer ear to the inner ear.

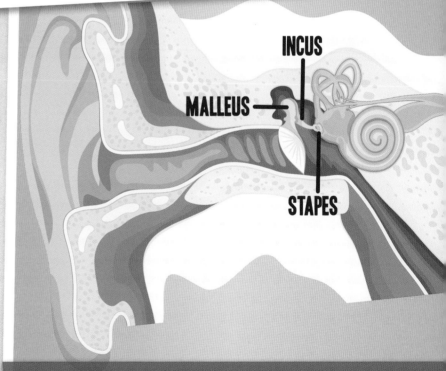

INCUS

MALLEUS

STAPES

Together, the stapes, malleus, and incus are called the ossicles. They're the only three bones in the ear!

A healthy femur can support 30 times a person's bodyweight—or more, if you're active!

THE FEMUR, OR THIGHBONE, IS THE BODY'S STRONGEST, LONGEST BONE!

It's so big because it carries the weight of your whole body! The femur stretches from the hip to the knee. An adult's femur is about 18 inches (46 cm) long.

BONES IN YOUR BODY

MORE THAN HALF YOUR BONES ARE IN YOUR HANDS AND FEET!

Of your 206 bones, 106 are found in your hands and feet! You have 27 bones in each hand and 26 bones in each foot. These small bones work together so you can do challenging tasks such as playing a guitar or dancing ballet.

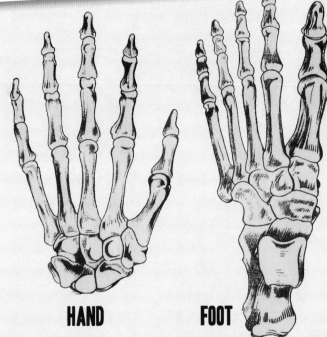

HAND   **FOOT**

It may not look like it from the outside, but the bones in your hands and feet are arranged very similarly.

THE SKELETAL SYSTEM

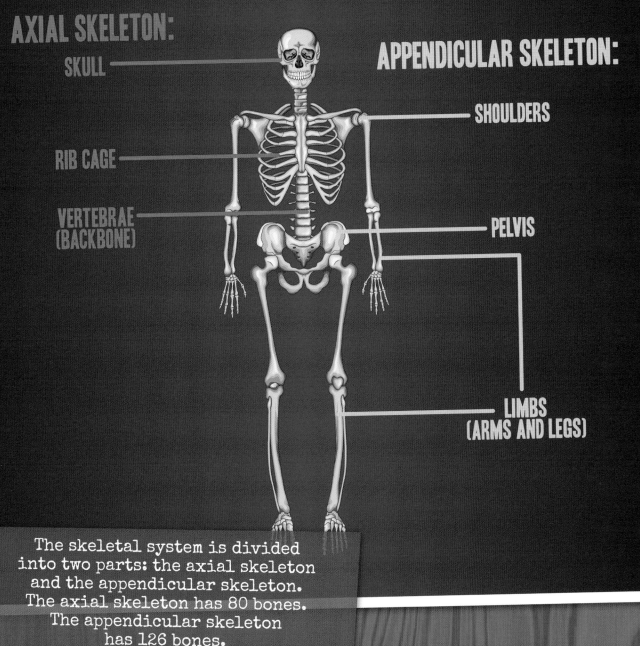

AXIAL SKELETON:

SKULL

RIB CAGE

VERTEBRAE
(BACKBONE)

APPENDICULAR SKELETON:

SHOULDERS

PELVIS

LIMBS
(ARMS AND LEGS)

The skeletal system is divided
into two parts: the axial skeleton
and the appendicular skeleton.
The axial skeleton has 80 bones.
The appendicular skeleton
has 126 bones.

SPECIAL SKELETONS

THERE ARE 33 BONES IN YOUR SPINE!

The bones in your spine are called vertebrae. That's why creatures with spines are called vertebrates! Each vertebra is ring-shaped. Cartilage is found between the vertebrae.

The cartilage between vertebrae absorbs, or takes in, the shock of jumping.

From tiny mice to huge blue whales, all mammals are vertebrates. Mammals are warm-blooded animals with backbones that have hair, breathe air, and feed milk to their young.

FUN FACT: 13

THERE AREN'T MANY VERTEBRATES IN THE WORLD!

Having an internal skeletal system is special! Less than 10 percent of the world's animals are vertebrates. Invertebrates, or animals without spines, must use their **muscles** to move. Some invertebrates have an exoskeleton, or a skeleton outside their body.

ALL ABOUT JOINTS

YOUR SKELETON WOULDN'T MOVE WITHOUT JOINTS!

Joints connect parts of the skeleton. Some joints, such as the elbows and knees, are hinges and allow movement like a door opening. Some are ball-and-socket joints, such as the shoulders and hips. Ball-and-socket joints can move in a full circle.

Joints are connected by tough tissue called ligaments. Tendons are the stretchy tissue that connect bones to muscles and allow you to move!

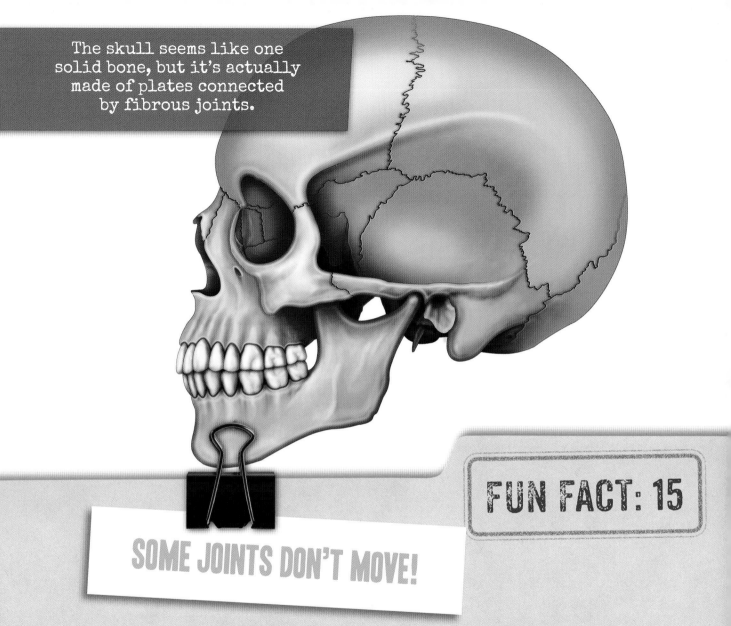

The skull seems like one solid bone, but it's actually made of plates connected by fibrous joints.

FUN FACT: 15

SOME JOINTS DON'T MOVE!

Joints that don't move are called fibrous joints. Fibrous

joints are made of collagen. The joints that connect the teeth

to the jawbone are fibrous. So are the joints in the skull.

TYPES OF SYNOVIAL JOINTS

A. BALL-AND-SOCKET JOINT: A BALL-SHAPED BONE MOVES IN A SOCKET, OR HOLLOW-SHAPED BONE, TO ALLOW MOVEMENT IN ALL DIRECTIONS.

B. HINGE JOINT: ALLOWS SWINGING, BACKWARD AND FORWARD MOVEMENT.

C. PIVOT JOINT: ALLOWS TURNING AND TWISTING MOVEMENT.

D. GLIDING (PLANE) JOINT: BONES THAT MEET AT A FLAT OR NEARLY FLAT SURFACE THAT ARE ABLE TO SLIDE PAST EACH OTHER ALONG THE FLAT SURFACE IN ANY DIRECTION.

E. SADDLE JOINT: A SADDLE-SHAPED BONE SLIDES ALONG ANOTHER BONE, ALLOWING MOVEMENT IN MOST DIRECTIONS.

F. CONDYLOID JOINT: ALLOWS BACKWARD AND FORWARD MOVEMENT LIKE HINGE JOINTS, AND ALSO ALLOWS SOME SIDE-TO-SIDE MOVEMENT.

Most of the joints in the body are called synovial joints. These joints allow for the most movement.

THERE'S ONE BONE THAT'S NOT CONNECTED TO ANY OTHERS!

There's only one bone that isn't connected to a joint: the hyoid bone! This bone is in your throat, and its job is to keep your tongue in place.

The hyoid bone makes it possible to talk!

FEMALE OR MALE?

MALE SKELETONS ARE BIGGER THAN FEMALE SKELETONS!

Women's skeletons and men's skeletons are slightly different. How can you tell if a skeleton belonged to a man or a woman? One way is to look at bone density, or the amount of minerals in bone tissue, which is often greater in males.

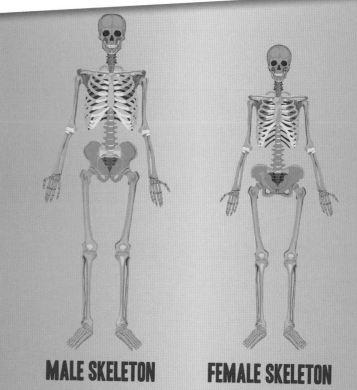

MALE SKELETON   **FEMALE SKELETON**

Male bones are commonly thicker and longer than female bones.

Scientists can study a skeleton's pelvis to figure out if it belonged to a man or a woman.

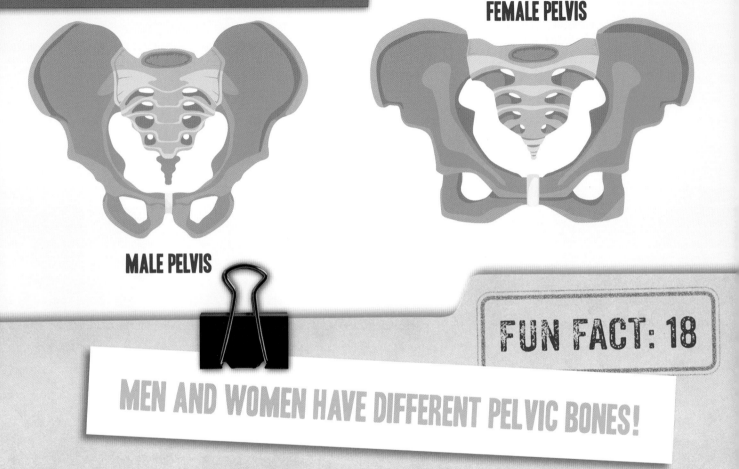

FEMALE PELVIS

MALE PELVIS

FUN FACT: 18

MEN AND WOMEN HAVE DIFFERENT PELVIC BONES!

The biggest difference between male and female skeletons is the pelvis. Women's pelvic bones are wide and rounded, but men's are narrower and heart shaped. This is because women's bodies are specially made for childbirth.

FUN FACT: 19

OUR SKELETONS DON'T LOOK LIKE THOSE OF OUR ANCESTORS!

A skeleton's size is affected by what someone eats, how much they exercise, and their age. Americans today eat better and live longer than our ancestors did, so our bodies and bones have become bigger over time.

Scientists know that human ancestors' skulls looked different than ours do today!

The study of the
human skeletal system
is called osteology.

FUN FACT: 20

MANY PEOPLE'S SKELETONS HAVE MAN-MADE PARTS!

Metal, plastic, and other **materials** are used to make

implants, which are parts put into the body to allow people

to move normally. Bones can be fused together, or fixed using

pins, screws, and metal plates. Even entire hip joints can

be replaced!

CARING FOR YOUR SKELETON

Every day, your skeleton works hard to help you walk, talk, move, and live your life! As you get older, your bones lose density and weaken. It's important to give your skeleton the care it needs to keep it healthy.

You can make your skeleton strong by eating foods with lots of calcium in them. Getting outside helps, too! Spending time in the sun boosts vitamin D, which helps your body absorb calcium. Exercise makes your joints and bones stronger. With a strong skeleton, you can do anything!

Don't be a lazybones. Get out there and move your skeleton!

29

GLOSSARY

ancestor: a relative who lived long before you

blood clot: a thick, sticky clump of dried blood that stops blood from flowing

calcium: a type of mineral stored in bones and teeth

cartilage: tough, bendable tissue that makes up part or all of a skeleton

gravity: the force that pulls objects toward Earth's center

joint: a point where two bones meet in the body

material: matter from which something is made

mineral: a substance important in small quantities for the nutrition of animals

muscle: one of the parts of the body that allow movement

organ: a part of the body (such as the heart or liver) that has a certain job

platelets: tiny cells that stick together and help blood clot

pressure: a force that pushes on something else

protein: a structural material made by the body

tissue: matter that forms the parts of living things

vitamin: a natural matter that is often found in foods and helps a body be healthy

FOR MORE INFORMATION

BOOKS

Kenney, Karen Latchana. *Skeletal System*. Minneapolis, MN: Jump!, Inc., 2017.

Manolis, Kay. *The Skeletal System*. Minneapolis, MN: Bellwether Media, 2009.

Morgan, Ben, and Steve Parker. *The Skeleton Book*. New York, NY: DK Publishing, 2016.

WEBSITES

How the Body Works

kidshealth.org/en/kids/center/htbw-main-page.html?WT.ac=k-nav-htbw-main-page
Learn more about how your body works with these fun activities!

Skeleton & Bones Facts

www.sciencekids.co.nz/sciencefacts/humanbody/skeletonbones.html
Discover more fun facts about the skeletal system!

Publisher's note to educators and parents: Our editors have carefully reviewed these websites to ensure that they are suitable for students. Many websites change frequently, however, and we cannot guarantee that a site's future contents will continue to meet our high standards of quality and educational value. Be advised that students should be closely supervised whenever they access the internet.

INDEX

21 Aug	**Prom 48** 8.00pm • Jules Buckley Orchestra Jules Buckley Orchestra/Buckley		28 Aug	**Prom 57** 7.00pm • Fantasy, Myths and Legends BBC CO/Helsing		4 Sep	**Pro** 7.30pm • Bruckner: Symphony No. 8 BBC SO/Bychkov	
22 Aug	**Prom 49** 7.30pm • Schumann: Das Paradies und die Peri Crowe, De Bique, Kožená, Staples, Vrielink, Boesch, London Symphony Chorus & Orchestra/Rattle		29 Aug	**Prom 58** 8.00pm • Jon Hopkins with the BBC Symphony Orchestra and Jules Buckley Hopkins, BBC SO/Buckley		5 Sep	**Prom 66** 7.30pm • Rufus Wainwright: Want Symphonic – Want One Wainwright, BBC CO/Hicks	**Prom 67** 🌙 10.15pm • Rufus Wainwright: Want Symphonic – Want Two Wainwright, BBC CO/Hicks
23 Aug	**Prom 50** 7.00pm • Handel: Samson Soloists, Philharmonia Chorus, Academy of Ancient Music/Cummings		30 Aug	**Prom 59** 7.30pm • Beethoven, Tchaikovsky, Dvořák Hadelich, Tonhalle Orchestra Zurich/Järvi		6 Sep	**Prom 68** 7.30pm • L. Auerbach, Corelli, Tippett, M. Richter Britten Sinfonia/Gould	
24 Aug	**Prom 51** 7.30pm • J. Weir, Schumann, Elgar Tetzlaff, BBC SO/Oramo		31 Aug	**Prom 60** 7.30pm • Weill, T. Adès, Rachmaninov Gerstein, Berlin Radio SO/Jurowski		7 Sep	**Prom 69** 7.30pm • Anon., Mozart Morley, Mingardo, Kilsby, Rosen, Pygmalion/Pichon	
25 Aug	**Prom 52** 6.30pm • J. Adolphe, R. Strauss, Prokofiev Boston SO/Nelsons	**Prom 53** 🌙 10.15pm • J. S. Bach I. Davies, The English Concert/Bezuidenhout	1 Sep	**Prom 61** 7.30pm • V. Coleman, Coleridge-Taylor, Haydn, Perkinson, Beethoven Akugbo, Chineke! Orchestra/Parnther		8 Sep	📍**P@GY** 6.00pm • Vaughan Williams, Khachaturian, Stravinsky, S. Rodgers, R. Rodgers/Walker Frank, BBC CO/Helsing	**Prom 70** 7.30pm • Honegger, Rachmaninov, G. Ortiz, Bernstein Tsujii, RLPO/Hindoyan
26 Aug	**Prom 54** ☀ 2.00pm • Wagner/I. Demers, R. Laurin, J. S. Bach/Dupré, Coleridge-Taylor, Reger, Still, Prokofiev/I. Demers Demers	**Prom 55** 7.30pm • C. Simon, Stravinsky, Gershwin, Ravel Thibaudet, Boston SO/Nelsons	2 Sep	**Proms 62 & 63** ☀ 3.00pm & 7.30pm • The Rite by Heart Aurora Orchestra/Collon		9 Sep	**Prom 71: Last Night of the Proms 2023** 7.00pm • R. Strauss, Coleridge-Taylor/S. Parkin, Bruch, J. B. Wilson, Wagner, Mascagni, Verdi, Kálmán, Wood, Arne/Sargent, Elgar, Parry/Elgar, Trad./Campbell Davidsen, S. Kanneh-Mason, BBC SC & SO/Alsop	
27 Aug	📍**P@T** ☀ 2.00pm • Schubert, Coleridge-Taylor, Gershwin/T. Poster Kaleidoscope Chamber Collective	**Prom 56** 7.30pm • Mahler: Symphony No. 9 London Symphony Orchestra/Rattle	3 Sep	📍**P@P** ☀ 2.00pm • Haydn, Tippett, Shostakovich Osborne, Heath Quartet	**Prom 64** 4.00pm • Berlioz: The Trojans Soloists, Monteverdi Choir, Orchestre Révolutionnaire et Romantique/Gardiner		📍 'Proms at' venues P@A Proms at Aberystwyth P@D Proms at Dewsbury P@GY Proms at Great Yarmouth P@L Proms at Londonderry P@P Proms at Perth P@SG Proms at Sage Gateshead P@T Proms at Truro	

At a Glance

For Season Listings, see pages 107–143 • For Contents, including details of feature articles, see pages 4–5

Mahler Symphonies

'The symphony must be like the world. It must embrace everything.' Mahler believed that all of human experience should be poured into a symphony: life and death, love and angst, nature and destruction. For many, his daringly autobiographical works in the genre represent the high point of the repertoire – a reimagining of what the orchestra could do. Four of his symphonies appear this season, including the 10th, left incomplete at the composer's death.

PROM 6 • 18 JULY
See also Proms 35, 45 & 56

Proms Around the UK

Following last year's series of Proms around the UK, this summer sees chamber-music programmes in Aberystwyth, Dewsbury, Londonderry, Perth and Truro, as well as a special weekend series at Sage Gateshead featuring the Royal Northern Sinfonia – plus a first Proms visit to Great Yarmouth, with a concert of colourful classical favourites performed by the BBC Concert Orchestra.

PROMS AROUND THE UK
See pages 140–143

Horrible Histories

Don't know your Carmen from your Carmelites or your fivers from a tenor? Fret not. The devilish devisers at *Horrible Histories* have created 'Orrible Opera – an irreverent whistlestop trample through the history of opera, presented by your favourite *Horrible Histories* characters, joined by the Orchestra and Chorus of the English National Opera.

PROMS 10 & 11 • 22 JULY

NYO Jazz and Dee Dee Bridgewater

Grammy- and Tony-Award-winning singer Dee Dee Bridgewater joins NYO Jazz (USA) on its European tour. Carnegie Hall's national youth jazz orchestra is made up of some of the most talented 16- to 19-year-old players from across America.

PROM 23 • 1 AUGUST

The Trojans

Fifty-five years after his Proms debut, and having conducted more than 60 concerts at the festival, Sir John Eliot Gardiner presides over Berlioz's magnum opus, *The Trojans*. The composer never saw a complete performance of this grand operatic treatment of the fall of Troy and the love of Dido and Aeneas, based on Virgil's *Aeneid*. For Gardiner, the music is 'heart-rendingly truthful and ageless in its epic sweep'.

PROM 64 • 3 SEPTEMBER

From Boston, Full of Beans

The Boston Symphony Orchestra under Music Director Andris Nelsons returns for the first time in five years to give two concerts, each combining sizzling orchestral showpieces with an exciting European premiere. The Bostonians join other visiting orchestras from Berlin, Budapest, Zurich and elsewhere, complementing the rich array of the UK's own first-rank groups.

PROMS 52 & 55 • 25 & 26 AUGUST
See also Proms 4, 23, 37, 38, 39, 47, 59, 60 & 69

Contents

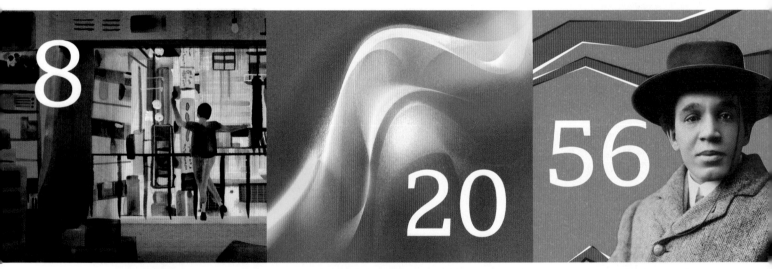

Welcome
to the 2023
BBC Proms

Creating each Proms season feels a little like trying to solve a massive, musical 3-D jigsaw puzzle – the result of many years of conversations with orchestras, conductors, agents and artists. It's a huge challenge, but also immensely rewarding. Our 2023 edition includes an eclectic mix of old favourites and new talents, and continues to broaden our view of orchestral music in the 21st century. This musical range is matched by a broad geographic reach, with chamber concerts from Perth to Truro, a BBC Concert Orchestra Prom in Great Yarmouth and a whole festival weekend at Sage Gateshead with its resident orchestra, the Royal Northern Sinfonia.

While we treasure our growing partnerships around the UK, the Royal Albert Hall remains at the centre of the BBC Proms. This unique building and its possibilities define the scale and ambition of our festival. This year, that includes an adventurous opera programme featuring Berlioz's epic masterpiece *The Trojans*; the UK premiere of an opera based on Samuel Beckett's *Endgame* by celebrated composer György Kurtág; and an affectionate spoof of the whole operatic artform with the team from *Horrible Histories*. We also take the Aurora Orchestra's tradition of memorised performances to the ultimate level when, boosted to around 100 players, it performs Stravinsky's ferociously challenging *The Rite of Spring* without the safety net of printed music. And running through the season is the familiar thread of epic symphonies and huge choral works, which are so ideally suited to this magnificent venue.

The uniquely relaxed atmosphere at the Proms owes much to the engagement of our audiences, and this year their role is even more significant – entrusted with choosing the programme of the Budapest Festival Orchestra's Audience Choice concert from a repertoire of over 250 pieces. The BFO is just one of eight international orchestras visiting the Proms this summer, bringing us a glorious palette of orchestral colour from around the world. They are joined by some of our finest UK-based ensembles: the Proms is, as ever, a showcase for their prowess, and a reminder of how lucky we are to live in a country with such a rich and vibrant musical life.

This year our composer anniversary celebrations include that most celebrated of early English masters, William Byrd; 20th-century pioneer of the avant-garde György Ligeti; and one of classical music's most popular composers, Sergey Rachmaninov, represented by (among other works) his three symphonies, each written during a different stage of the composer's career. Less familiar will be the work of Croatian pioneer Dora Pejačević, who died 100 years ago, and that of Samuel Coleridge-Taylor, a contemporary of Holst and Vaughan

Williams who died tragically young at 37. The BBC orchestras and choirs play a crucial role in bringing lesser-known works to a wider audience, and the Proms is proud to reflect the imagination of their year-round programming.

Each year we aim to explore genres new to the Proms. This summer we celebrate the music of Bollywood, with a tribute to one of the leading playback singers, Lata Mangeshkar, who died last year, aged 92. We also present our first ever fado Prom and, closer to home, a concert celebrating Northern Soul – a phenomenon of the 1960s and 1970s, originating in clubs in the North of England, that has enjoyed a revival in recent years. Rufus Wainwright and Jon Hopkins, two distinctive musical personalities, feature in their own special concerts, giving audiences a chance to hear their work in an orchestral setting.

Sir Ian McKellen has described the Proms as 'one of the nation's cultural glories' and the tradition of Promming – just £8.00 (including booking fee) to stand a few feet away from the performers – makes this a uniquely democratic and accessible glory. If you have never been to a Prom, may 2023 be the year in which you discover the thrill of being a part of the audience. And, as ever, you can enjoy every concert on BBC Radio 3 and BBC Sounds – whenever and wherever you like – and a selection on BBC TV and iPlayer.

David Pickard Director, BBC Proms

Hello and welcome to the 2023 BBC Proms – the last I will be associated with in my role as Controller of BBC Radio 3. Again, we are looking forward to welcoming audiences for the communal experience of joy and intensity that live music brings. The Royal Albert Hall remains the unique focus of this festival, but this year we continue to spread our Proms wings ever wider around the country.

As ever, at the heart of the Proms is the fact that every lovingly crafted programme is broadcast on BBC Radio 3 and on BBC Sounds, captured by our dedicated engineers, with production and presentation by our Radio 3 team. Many will be broadcast across the European Broadcasting Union, allowing millions to experience the special atmosphere of the Proms. And many will also be available on BBC TV and on BBC iPlayer.

It has been a privilege to be part of the great mission of Proms founder-conductor Henry Wood – to bring great music to everyone, both in the Hall and to those who listen and watch. Welcome to another great year at the BBC Proms.

Alan Davey Outgoing Controller, BBC Radio 3

The **Mothers**

A short story by Madeleine Thien

Illustrations by Marc Martin

Prelude

In Hong Kong, when I was a child, we had two mothers. Big Mom lived on the 10th floor with my brother and me. Little Mom lived on the third floor with my three half-sisters and half-brother. This was in the 1960s. The Mothers never tired of exchanging gossip, secrets, food and even insults; and, since I was their messenger, I was forever running up and down stairs. Going between them was like flying between heaven and earth.

My older brother and I were the children of Big Mom. Our home was airy, with a panoramic view of the harbour. Big Mom spent her days reading, writing and listening to music, especially Chopin, Mussorgsky and anything by Debussy.

We rarely saw Father. He ran a hugely successful restaurant and was forever dealing with staff, suppliers and clients. Our dad was an ambitious, handsome man. 'I inherited nothing,' he always said. 'I relied on my own two hands.' When he married our mother, the daughter of a Shanghai industrialist, he rose high.

Meanwhile, Little Mom's third-floor apartment was cramped and noisy. She had a view of walls, honking cars and shouting neighbours. My three half-sisters slept on fold-out mats, while Little Mom and Baby Brother slept on the couch. Little Mom was compact and expressive, with a laugh like a firecracker.

In 1962, when our neighbours on the 10th floor left Hong Kong for Canada, I advised Little Mom to move her family upstairs. The air was cleaner and I wouldn't have to run up and down the stairs so much.

She laughed. 'What a bunch of problems that would cause.'

'What do you mean?'

'The root of a tree is below ground but it's closer to the heart.'

She always teased me like this. In the hierarchy of things, as the eldest daughter of Big Mom, I ranked above her. Yet her love for me was real and reassuring, and felt to me like true mothering.

Little Mom's family came from the Red Boats. In the 1930s the Pearl River Delta had hundreds of these travelling opera troupes. They would build a stage in two days, put on a big show with singers, kung fu fighters, acrobats, clowns and eye-popping costumes, and then sail away. Her dad was a set-builder and scene-puller, and her ma was the wardrobe-keeper.

As a child, Little Mom was the opera troupe's Local Ghost. Her job was to remind performers to get on stage. She knew every role and every phrase of music, and developed a deep, generous memory. Their troupe was hugely popular, but then the war started and the old world came crashing down.

After the war Little Mom found work in a dress shop in Hong Kong. One day my father took Big Mom to have a gown fitted and he saw her. He fell in love. She was just a teenager but she became his second wife.

As much as my father loved her, Little Mom's children were always left behind. In our two households, it was a mystery to me how love and opportunity were afforded or refused.

Reflets dans l'eau

As a child, Big Mom studied literature, mathematics and music with private tutors. When Japanese soldiers invaded Shanghai, her father sent her to Hong Kong, accompanied by only a nanny. She was just 12 when they arrived at Kowloon harbour. She saw sun glinting on water and heard 'Danseuses de Delphes' as if Debussy's ethereal yet majestic chords were a voice within her. They were fragments cut loose from the fullness of sound. They climbed like ivy before rotating down like a ball of glass sinking into the sea.

The Emperor's Daughter

In the lower floors of our building the radios were always on, usually tuned to the same broadcast. Arias from the Cantonese operas *The Emperor's Daughter* or *Summer Snow* rang through the hallways. Everyone knew the words and gestures, the *zuo*, but Little Mom taught us kids the meticulously choreographed fight scenes, called *da*. She had a glorious voice and often performed from the balcony, which was really for hanging laundry.

Back then, everyone was crazy for Cantonese opera. People like Tong Tik-San and Yam Kim-Fei were putting out one hit after another. Our district theatre could seat 1,400 people but even then it was standing room only. The past clings to me in such images. We used to watch the neighbourhood TV while old people took their caged birds for a walk or joined a sidewalk game of chess, or savoured a bowl of hot noodles from the corner grandma, who knew exactly how to make heaven out of nothing.

Red Boats

While my half-siblings worked in our father's restaurant, I went to school. I was the only one of my father's daughters to be given this opportunity. My school in Tsim Sha Tsui was run by Catholic nuns, and classes were in Cantonese and English. By the time I was 14 everything was in English. At the time Hong Kong was a British colony and China was under Mao. We lived in a carved-out space between two powers, between uncertainties, between languages, beliefs and ways of dreaming.

When I was 18, Father sent me to Canada for university. I ended up in medical school in Montreal. Eventually I sponsored Little Mom's immigration, swearing she was my birth mother – but that's another story. Now both mothers have passed away I find myself thinking of the Red Boats. Each opera troupe had two: an Earth Boat and a Sky Boat. Little Mom told me they were interlinked. The Earth Boat had the water boiler, while the Sky Boat had the stove. The Earth Boat had kung fu masters and acrobats, while the Sky Boat had singers and clowns. If either went down, the troupe was finished. You had to learn, Little Mom taught me, to love the other side, the accompaniment, the reply, the difference.

Le palais du silence

One day, a man named Sun moved into a small room on the fifth floor of our building. Our neighbours whispered that he was a famous man, born in Heilongjiang, or maybe Paris, or maybe Warsaw. The day after his arrival, an expensive piano was moved into his room.

The first time I saw him was in the stairwell. He wore a soft green vest, grey trousers, and carried two bags of groceries. Because I was pretending to kick enemies down the stairs, I nearly punched him. He was old and swung his cheap cane at me.

'You,' he said. 'Impossible.'

I felt guilty and carried his groceries up to the fifth floor. His room was bare except for a piano which seemed to come from another galaxy. There were no photos, no trinkets, nothing to put a life to him. I set the groceries on the windowsill and turned to go.

'Is it possible you don't know me?' he said.

I took a second look at the piano. It was a Blüthner. 'Are you famous?'

He laughed.

A few days later Big Mom announced we were going to visit family. I put on a dress and nice shoes and carried the Maxim's bakery box and cut fruit she had prepared, but all we did was go to the fifth floor.

Mr Sun, dressed in a Western suit, let us in. We sat on a sofa which had not been there before. He gave us a handwritten programme. Big Mom clutched hers like a little girl, and the light sliding through the room seemed to curve around her waist. Mr Sun played from the opening of *Le palais du silence.* The notes made the walls shimmer as if they breathed, they made the ground roll beneath my feet. Why was Debussy disguised as a Chinese grandfather? Through the walls I could hear honking horns, kids crying and a radio playing. I felt my soul rising out the top of my head. I felt as if my whole body was made of ears.

Afterwards, as we sat in our lonely apartment, Big Mom surprised me by saying, 'He's a foreigner. That's why I feel close to him.'

'He's Chinese.'

'He's been a guest his whole life. He'll be a guest until the day he dies. You're too young to understand.'

Handover

My father and Big Mom grew old together. They lived wealthy, comfortable lives, barely saying a word to one another. Father suffered a fatal heart attack two months after Big Mom died of pancreatic cancer, and they were buried side by side. That was the year that Hong Kong was returned to China.

By then, I was taking care of Little Mom in Montreal. One night I asked if she had regrets about her marriage. My father had been rapturously, painfully in love with her – we all knew it. But, for reasons I never understood, Father denied my half-siblings a life of comfort. My eldest brother inherited millions and I was given an education, but Little Mom and her children were left to scatter to the four winds. Employed as garment workers, cleaning ladies, clerks and taxi drivers, they lived precariously.

'If it were me,' I said, 'I would be bitter.'

'These kinds of arrangements are common. They haven't disappeared, even in your generation. They just go by different names.'

I didn't argue. The older generation seemed to have entirely different expectations of love. Through the windows I watched our neighbours' kids sword-fighting with rolled-up newspapers. One pretended to die.

'Anyway, you've got it upside down. It was Big Mom who encouraged your father to find a second wife.'

I was so startled I laughed.

'Big Mom came from a very rich family. Her fortune gave your father opportunities. She could have stopped it if she wanted.'

'Her life revolved around him. Why would she do that?'

'She's your mother. You tell me.'

Appoggiare

One night, Big Mom pointed to a bag on the table. 'Take that food downstairs while it's still hot.' As usual, she'd arranged dinner for Mr Sun. I glimpsed three egg tarts glowing like miniature suns.

My curiosity was overwhelming. 'Did Mr Sun move to Hong Kong because of you?'

'Of course not.' She knew that I knew she was lying. What hold did this old man have on her?

In the stairwell I brooded. I was the product of an arranged marriage, while my half-siblings were the product of passion. I was the daughter of cold practicality.

I knocked angrily at Mr Sun's door.

'Go away,' he said, but I ignored him and barged in.

'It's me,' I said, setting the food down.

'No kidding.'

We smiled at one another sadly.

My eyes fell on the Blüthner, which cost as much as a fancy car. 'Are you rich?' I asked.

'Do I look rich?'

'What did you do with your life?'

'I was a household musician.'

> 66 As she listened to her mother play, daylight moved across the floor like something alive, patterns of shadow and sun reinventing the ground. She connected silence to her mother's happiness. 99

'In Paris?'

'None of your business.' He began playing. 'Do you know this piece? You can have that pineapple bun if you guess right.'

'It's Couperin and I don't want your leftovers.'

'So you do study music. With which mother?'

'Neither. I'm going to be an oncologist. Why did you come to Hong Kong?'

He shrugged, tickled a note. 'My heart turned grey.'

'Your heart?'

'I can teach you piano,' he said.

'No, thank you.'

Annoyed, he kept playing. The notes seemed to condense and hold their breath. 'These are blue-orange chords, see?'

'Obviously.'

'Progression is fragmentary. Can you hear that? This kind of music has a quality that we call situational.'

'What does that even mean? Anyways, you're not my teacher.'

'*Appoggiare*, to lean. So an appoggiatura is a note which displaces a main note and changes its colour. It may not resolve, the added note may keep the character of intrusion, but their shared sonority grants it an equal citizenship.'

I let his words sink in. 'That's beautiful.'

'It's Messiaen. All breaks from tradition find their source in tradition. Don't stand right behind me. It's irritating.'

I took a bite of the pineapple bun. 'Why don't you have a family?'

'Who says I don't?'

The household musician

In 1918 a boy named Sun presented himself to a wealthy family in Shanghai. He told my grandparents that he was 21 years old, a recent graduate of the Paris Conservatoire and a former student of Claude Debussy. It seemed that he lied about his age, but the rest was true.

Teacher Sun became my grandmother's piano teacher. He arranged concerts, delivered talks on music theory and spoke passionately about how Debussy was devoted to the piano's true nature.

'Some people wish above all to conform to the rules,' Debussy said. 'I wish only to render what I can hear. There is no theory. You have only to listen. Pleasure is the law.'

In fact, I knew too much about Debussy and nothing about my own mother's life. So I peppered Mr Sun with questions. 'What was my grandmother like? What happened to her?'

He studied my face as if it could unlock a memory. 'Your mother never told you?'

'Never.'

'I lived in your grandmother's house for 30 years.'

I was shocked. He had lived like a servant for 30 years?

'When Shanghai was invaded, I left. I was part of the Communist underground and was ordered out. That was 1937. A few months later the house burnt down.'

'And my grandmother …'

'It was an accident. Your grandfather survived. But afterwards he sent your mother away. She was 12 years old. I didn't think I would ever see her again.'

En bateau

I tried to make myself invisible as Big Mom and Teacher Sun reminisced about Shanghai. She used to listen from behind the door as her mother and Teacher Sun played, side by side, the two parts of 'En bateau' from Debussy's *Petite suite*. Chords unfolded and turned over, making another kind of relation. One set of hands floated beneath the other in call-and-reply. Big Mom had been amazed that a piano could sing with two separate voices.

Or had she been mistaken? The piano itself was both a harp and a bell. It contained side-by-side diverging forms.

From the time Big Mom was born, Teacher Sun's music had filled the rooms like a painting which dissolved at each brushstroke. Sometimes she envied his importance to her mother. Yet she couldn't imagine home without his presence. Was this inability to imagine a world without him its own kind of love?

Her mother played fragments from *Le palais du silence*. Debussy's ballet was based on a French fairy tale that he transposed to China: a prince decrees that, in his palace, words have failed. The prince's beloved, 'the only light in all this sadness', is forced to be mute, yet she is music itself. Debussy loved this composition, Teacher Sun said, yet he never finished it. The story is about music that draws from the well of silence. As she listened to her mother play, daylight moved across the floor like something alive, patterns of shadow and sun reinventing the ground. She connected silence to her mother's happiness.

After the fire she was certain her mother had gone in search of Teacher Sun. She held onto this image, even though everyone told her that Mother was gone forever.

Nocturnes: Nuages

'Sometimes I think music matters most to the one who doesn't play it,' Little Mom said to me.

'What do you mean?'

'Big Mom was happiest when she was

in the company of musicians. She liked to hear stories of the Red Boats, about my parents and all the composers and singers. Don't you remember?'

I shook my head. Sometimes I could barely recall my birth mother. She was a stillness almost imperceptible to me.

'Your mother searched for Teacher Sun. When she found him, he was old and poor. She promised to take care of him.'

I had guessed the same. 'She felt responsible for him.'

> ❝ If you keep the door closed, she believes, the room stays intact and nothing burns away. Open it, and all the colours escape, they flicker and dissolve. ❞

'Family is unexpected,' Little Mom agreed. 'Even when people can't escape certain roles, they rearrange the pieces in their own way.'

I had an image of my mother sitting on the other side of a closed door, yearning for happiness for people other than herself.

'Take you, for example,' Little Mom continued. 'Here you are in a completely different country, taking care of a woman who isn't your mother. Two households can lean against one another.'

I smiled.

'And where do you live?' she teased.

'Upstairs.'

'And where do I live?'

'Downstairs, at the heart of things.'

'A daughter with two mothers is lucky,' she said. 'We tried to teach you that intellect and imagination should always touch. Big Mom and I used to talk and talk. I miss her.'

Mother

When I was a child, my siblings and I adored Cantonese opera. The stories had everything we desired: catastrophe, fight scenes, unrequited love, power, folly. Its sons and daughters, thwarted at every turn by mistaken identities, doomed love affairs and wild dreams, heard the gods whispering in their ears and saw gold and eternal happiness flickering, unreachable, before their eyes.

Once, on the phone with Big Mom, we got into a heated argument. She was angry that I refused to sponsor Little Mom's immigration. How could she ask me to lie and jeopardise my whole life?

'Little Mom's children have burdens of their own,' she told me. 'You are the lucky one. You have responsibilities.'

'Father and eldest brother should support the second household,' I said.

My mother, always so reserved, laughed.

For years, I'd thought she resented my loyalty to Little Mom and my half-siblings. I wished always to be on their side and not hers. But now she said, 'You're my daughter. You know what's right.'

I gave in. By then she was ill, but she didn't tell me. After her death I dreamt

we met on the fifth floor in a room that held only a piano. Did I ever know you? I wondered.

'What is there to know?' She said it lightly but there was pain in her voice.

I woke in the night and reached for my phone. I searched for Debussy's *Préludes* and opened a link. Sviatoslav Richter played and the world around me slipped apart. Pictures arranged and rearranged themselves. I saw mother arriving in Hong Kong as a child accompanied by the nanny who would become her family. The child looks at the sun on the water and hears Debussy. 'Danseuses de Delphes' was written in a single day: 7 December 1909. The chords are a figure turning in the air, a microcosm that opens outwards even as it closes. I try to reach that child standing on the harbour but no words come. I see her leaning against a doorway, listening to music coming from a room she chooses not to enter. She wonders if she ever knew her mother. She wonders what she guessed right, and what she guessed wrong. If you keep the door closed, she believes, the room stays intact and nothing burns away. Open it, and all the colours escape, they flicker and dissolve.

My mother leans against the door, and I lean against the opposite side, listening. ●

Madeleine Thien lives in Montreal. She is the author of four books, most recently *Do Not Say We Have Nothing*, which was shortlisted for the 2016 Booker Prize.

Marc Martin is an artist, illustrator and author based in Melbourne, Australia. He works with watercolour, pencil and digital manipulation across a range of commercial projects, editorial, picture books and fine art for gallery shows and commissions.

Welcome Back,
Mr Rachmaninov

Skewered by the critics during his lifetime for his sweeping lyricism, warm nostalgia and popular touch, Rachmaninov has tended to be disparaged by the history books. Old news, says **MARINA FROLOVA-WALKER**: 150 years after his birth his star has risen again – and audiences have never needed convincing

Portrait of Rachmaninov by
Boris Grigoriev (1886–1939)

South Korean scientists recently created a computer model to calculate the level of musical innovation in the work of different composers. The result? Rachmaninov was judged to be the most innovative composer of the 18th and 19th centuries. This might have given the composer a certain grim satisfaction: after his emigration to the US following the Russian Revolution of 1917, the highbrow critics there dismissed him as a has-been. Each new piece was greeted with derision. The Fourth Piano Concerto? 'Super-salon music.' The *Rhapsody on a Theme of Paganini*? 'Isn't philosophical, significant or even artistic.' And the general verdict: 'From [his music], there flows a sadness distilled by all things that are a little useless.' It's no surprise that Rachmaninov wrote so little in those years after arriving in America.

British critics of the 1930s and 1940s were hardly any kinder. The UK's gatekeeper of classical music, Eric Blom, in his waspish *Grove's Dictionary of Music and Musicians*, roundly dismissed Rachmaninov a decade after his death: 'His music is well constructed and effective, but monotonous in texture, which consists in essence mainly of artificial and gushing tunes accompanied by a variety of figures derived from arpeggios. The enormous popular success some few of Rachmaninov's works had in his lifetime is not likely to last.' But Rachmaninov had the last laugh. His music is still going strong, 70 years later.

How could the critics have failed to see that Rachmaninov was a classic in the making? And is there anything in the Korean scientists' verdict that Rachmaninov was actually an innovator? To shed some light on this, let's take a look at his career – which embraced not only composing but also parallel careers as a world-famous pianist and a conductor.

His family was aristocratic, but little Sergey was not surrounded by wealth. His parents divorced and his father frittered away the family fortune. At an early age, Rachmaninov clearly had talents, but he had to work round the clock to turn himself into the kind of musician who could bring in enough money to keep his family afloat. All the time, he was practising, performing, composing and giving piano lessons. On one occasion he was on a train journey when a thief stole his money. To make up for the loss, he published his first great solo piano pieces, the *Moments musicaux*, Op. 16, in 1897. The same year he became an opera conductor at the age of only 24, and he soon had the orchestra of Moscow's hallowed Bolshoi Theatre under his command. He was an exceptional conductor and might have continued along that path, were it not for a perfectionism that led to tensions and created more stress than Rachmaninov could take.

His early career as a composer was a roller-coaster ride. He wrote his First Piano Concerto while he was still a student at the Moscow Conservatory –

one of the most amazing pieces ever to be published as an 'Opus 1'! He became a protégé of Tchaikovsky just before the elder composer met his sudden and early death. This association helped Rachmaninov bring his graduation piece, the opera *Aleko*, to the Bolshoi stage in 1893. Now the public sat up and paid attention to this up-and-coming composer. But trouble lay ahead.

Rachmaninov's next big project was his First Symphony, a stunningly ambitious piece that made great demands of musicians and listeners alike. But, when it came to the work's 1897 premiere, instead of a home game in Moscow, he was playing away in St Petersburg. The two cities have an intense rivalry, music included. Moscow was dominated by Tchaikovsky's international outlook and heart-on-sleeve style. St Petersburg was dominated by Rimsky-Korsakov, Russian nationalism and a highly polished, often emotionally neutral style. Rachmaninov's symphony was enormous, complex, emotionally intense and a tough task for any orchestra – not to mention its theme, which was the Last Judgement. St Petersburg was already casting a jaundiced eye on this upstart from the rival city. Added to this, the conductor was to be Alexander Glazunov, a disciple of Rimsky-Korsakov. And a key reviewer? César Cui, an old friend and colleague of Rimsky-Korsakov. Already, the cards were stacked against the First Symphony.

The first performance was not an auspicious occasion. The usual story blames this on the conducting of a

Have emoter, will travel: Rachmaninov – a fan of cars and boats – on his Russian country estate, Ivanovka, in 1910; in a newspaper interview some years later he explained: 'When I conduct, I experience much the same feeling as when I drive my car – an inner calm that gives me complete mastery over myself and of the forces, musical or mechanical, at my command.'

drunken Glazunov. But alcohol was no stranger to Glazunov's bloodstream and hadn't stopped him from maintaining a successful career. Glazunov simply wasn't interested in any of Rachmaninov's tendency to complicate and emote. He didn't do his homework on the score, so little wonder that the piece didn't make sense when he performed it. Cui's review took up the Last Judgement theme and joked that this was truly the symphony from hell. Even a thicker-skinned composer would have had trouble salvaging his confidence after this.

The deeply depressed Rachmaninov lost interest in the symphony, and the score itself was lost during the chaos of the Revolution. Fortunately, the orchestral parts survived, and the score was reconstructed from them after the composer's death. Rachmaninov's First Symphony has now finally been accepted as a masterpiece and there are many superb recordings. Be that as it may, the symphony's failure back in 1897 most likely turned Rachmaninov into a more cautious composer. He also began to cultivate the popular touch that would endear him to musicians and audiences, instead of bewildering and repelling them.

With the help of hypnosis and other psychotherapies, Rachmaninov returned to the concert hall four years later, as both composer and soloist, with his Second Piano Concerto. It begins with fateful bell-like chords in the piano, and passes through storms and dreams, ending in triumph, almost like the story of his recovery after the First Symphony's

failure. He was now adulated, especially by women, who flocked to him – he was bemused, but received them kindly. Audiences felt that there was real blood flowing through his music, at the opposite end of the spectrum from the wispy mysticism of Scriabin, the other rising Russian star of the day. Part of the enchantment was Rachmaninov's stage presence – he was lanky, with a serious demeanour and long slim fingers that could stretch and bend abnormally. The Third Piano Concerto, composed in 1909, begins soberly and modestly, but soon proves much more difficult again than the Second, and Rachmaninov wrote it to show off his own strengths – including those unique hands.

In 1907 a female music student had sent Rachmaninov an anonymous letter, telling him that he should read Edgar Allan Poe's *The Bells*. She felt sure the poem would inspire a masterpiece. Rachmaninov followed the advice and, completed six years later, a majestic choral symphony was the result. He was proud of the piece, but even some of his musical friends failed to show up to congratulate him after the premiere. He had set the text with directness, but the fashion of the time was with the mysterious suggestions of the Symbolists, such as Scriabin. The ravishing score, though, was fully up to date, borrowing recent tricks of orchestration from Richard Strauss's modernist (and scandalous) *Salome*.

Even early on, Rachmaninov's talents and hard work had won him a comfortable life. He had a fast car for touring around and a tractor for his country estate … until October 1917 came, and his way of life was swept away by revolution. Rachmaninov left Russia on a cold December night, supposedly to go on tour, so he could take little with him. He never returned. We like to spin sentimental fantasies about the aching nostalgia for Russia that we hear in his music. In reality, he was a spectacularly successful émigré. He reinvented himself as an American-style concert pianist, recouped his losses and regained his status as a musical celebrity. He even built a villa on the shores of Lake Lucerne, filled with all the latest mod cons. When his thoughts turned to home, it wasn't so much sadness that he felt, but anger. His *Three Russian Songs* (1926) are tinged with darkness, oppression and violence. After he signed a letter in 1931 accusing the Soviet government of atrocities, his music was banned in Russia. But the boycott lasted only two years – pianists couldn't seriously be asked to stop playing it. There were approaches from Soviet envoys, but he rebuffed them, softening his position only during the Second World War.

A modest, gentle, introverted man, he never chased popularity but was constantly chased by it. In 1898 his cousin Anton Siloti launched the Prelude in C sharp minor on a tour of the USA and Britain. Twenty years later, one G. L. Cobb turned it into the 'Russian Rag' and so began Rachmaninov's other life as a popular-culture icon. Around a decade

after that, the silent film *Prelude* linked the piece to Poe's gruesome story *The Premature Burial*. This paved the way for myriad film and pop-song adaptations, including David Lean's *Brief Encounter* and the young Sinatra's hit 'Full Moon and Empty Arms', both in 1945. Rachmaninov heard and saw several of these popular adaptations, not only tolerating but enjoying them.

All this jazzing-up and filming introduced him to a worldwide audience far beyond the concert hall, but it sounded his death knell among the highbrow critics. The situation worsened in the 1920s and 1930s, when anti-Romantic modernism became the mainstream, with Schoenberg, Stravinsky and Bartók vying to create the harshest new sounds. The critics stopped listening to Rachmaninov with any care and failed to notice any of the modernism in the *Paganini Rhapsody* or its steely edge and caustic humour.

Today, these are all the half-forgotten squabbles of our great-grandparents. We happily stream both Stravinsky and Rachmaninov to our phones. We enjoy the popular versions of the 1930s and 1940s for their quaint antique mood, while the Rachmaninov originals sound fresh. Pianists and orchestras have upped their game to meet all of Rachmaninov's challenges. Those Korean scientists mentioned earlier underlined the tonal richness and variety in Rachmaninov's music but, even if we don't believe he was the most innovative composer of the 18th and 19th centuries, we don't

> 66 No, the critics are not helpful. When my First Symphony was first played, they said it was so-so. Then, when my Second was played, they said the First was good, but that the Second was so-so. Now that my Third has been played – just this fall – they say my First and Second are good but that my … oh, well, you see how it is.

Rachmaninov in an interview with the San Francisco *Call-Bulletin*, 6 February 1937

care, since composers are not a form of technology like laptops or video games. International fame and the test of time have revealed that Rachmaninov's pieces are anything but simplistic or 'monotonous' – they are tightly knit, intricate, resilient constructions, giving performers scope for an array of interpretations and keeping listeners intrigued. ●

Marina Frolova-Walker is Professor of Music History at the University of Cambridge and Fellow of Clare College, Cambridge. She is the author of *Russian Music and Nationalism from Glinka to Stalin* (2007, Yale UP) and *Stalin's Music Prize: Soviet Culture and Politics* (2016, Yale UP).

Piano Concerto No. 1
PROM 6 • 18 JULY

Five Études-tableaux (orch. Respighi)
PROM 7 • 19 JULY

The Bells
PROM 16 • 26 JULY

Symphony No. 2
PROMS 24 & 25 • 2 & 3 AUGUST

Rhapsody on a Theme of Paganini
PROM 27 • 4 AUGUST

Vocalise (arr. R. Wallfisch); **Cello Sonata**
PROMS AT DEWSBURY • 6 AUGUST
(see pages 140–141)

Piano Concerto No. 2
PROM 30 • 6 AUGUST

Symphony No. 1
PROM 33 • 9 AUGUST

Symphony No. 3
PROM 60 • 31 AUGUST

Piano Concerto No. 3
PROM 70 • 8 SEPTEMBER

First Contact

Sir Stephen Hough recalls his initial encounter with Rachmaninov's Piano Concerto No. 1.

When Rachmaninov wanted to make a mark as a student at the Moscow Conservatory, what better way than with a piano concerto, that form that, by the end of the 19th century, had become the calling card for all composer-pianists? (Prokofiev did the same with his First Piano Concerto around a decade later.) And yet, after its first performance, Rachmninov's Piano Concerto No. 1 was hardly played, by the composer or others, as the years passed. He had moved on, and eventually moved continents. In 1917, more than a quarter of a century after the First Concerto's premiere and years after the successes of the Second and Third Concertos, Rachmaninov decided to revisit his first work. What wonderful tunes there were! What a dramatic opening! What memories of youthful promise now so fulfilled!

But in the early years of the 20th century this piece was pretty much unplayable – too many thick chords for the pianist, heavy, ungainly orchestration, and a structure that barely hung together. Perhaps there was a better piece inside, waiting to be (re)born? Rachmaninov thought so, and he settled down to reshape and rework the concerto in a brilliant revision retaining a youthful flare but now with a structure of supreme sophistication, and with his quicksilver pianism showcased alongside his trademark inner-voiced counterpoint and rich, chromatic harmonies.

He was a more experienced composer by this stage, but, more to the point, he was a more experienced pianist. He had played his Second and Third Concertos numerous times and had gradually realised what works and what doesn't with a full orchestra in a large concert hall: the constant danger of the piano fighting to be heard as the orchestral strings swell and the brass blare. The Third Concerto added (many!) more notes for the piano and fewer for the orchestra, but in the revised First the whole fabric was thinned out, top to bottom. The crinolines have become a smart trouser suit.

He was proud of this reincarnation and begged two of his closest friends in America to play it: Vladimir Horowitz and Gitta Gradova. The former never did and regretted it. The latter promised she would but retired early to have a family, hardly ever performing in public. But towards the end of her life, though she was old and frail, she agreed to play it with her hometown orchestra, the Chicago Symphony, at the Ravinia Festival under James Levine. In 1985 I got a call from the festival's director, Edward Gordon. 'Stephen, Gitta has agreed to come out of retirement to play Rach 1 this summer. If for some reason she can't do it, could you be on standby?' I was thrilled, learnt the piece and (tragically, as she died before the concert) got to play it. So, indirectly, it felt as if I was fulfilling the composer's dream. I never met Gitta Gradova but I feel I meet Rachmaninov every time I play this evergreen concerto.

Sir Stephen Hough plays Rachmaninov's Piano Concerto No. 1 in Prom 6 (18 July)

I: Help Musicians

We've been a charity supporting professional musicians in times of crisis and opportunity for over 100 years.

With the cost of living crisis, the ongoing impact of the pandemic and the new restrictions on touring, it is hard to imagine any point since the Second World War when it has been tougher to be a professional musician.

Almost half of the musicians we've surveyed have said they are concerned about having to leave the industry. We cannot afford to lose this musical talent if we want to continue enjoying the music that inspires us all.

Visit **helpmusicians.org.uk** to donate today to help musicians across the UK.

Registered Charity No.228089
Help Musicians is the working name of the Musicians' Benevolent Fund

◀ Suspended in mid-air: György Ligeti is perhaps best remembered for his groundbreaking studies in blurred orchestral and choral colour

Hungary's *Caterpillar*

Initially cocooned from the advances of new music in Western Europe, György Ligeti later forged a unique musical language that embraced all manner of influences. As we celebrate the centenary of his birth, **GILLIAN MOORE** charts Ligeti's musical development, from the censorship of his early years to the unapologetic pluralism that followed

here's footage on the internet showing Pierre Boulez collapsing in giggles while conducting a Prom at Camden's Roundhouse in 1971. The music was *Aventures/Nouvelles aventures*, György Ligeti's 1966 absurdist mini-opera. There are no words, just nonsense syllables and vocal gestures: whispering, tongue clicks, panting, laughing and neurotic switches between extreme emotional states, all common currency in the 1960s with the vocal experiments of Pauline Oliveros, John Cage and Luciano Berio. But Boulez was right to corpse, because this music was actually meant to be humorous. Ligeti was a composer who could pull off that rare trick of being laugh-out-loud funny.

Take the Prelude to his 1974–7 opera *Le Grand Macabre*, played entirely on car horns, a mischievous re-imagining of the trumpets in Monteverdi's *L'Orfeo*. Or the trick he uses in several of his pieces, from

Atmosphères (1961) to the Piano Concerto (1985–8), where the music climbs up and up as high as it can possibly go, and then seems to fall off the top of itself only to reappear immediately, right at the bottom of the orchestra. We, the audience, have the giddy feeling of being picked up and flipped over. Later in life Ligeti was drawn to the topsy-turvy world of Lewis Carroll. He died before he could write his planned opera *Alice in Wonderland*, though we do have the hilarious *Nonsense Madrigals* (1988–93), which include a version of 'The Lobster Quadrille' complete with a Ligetian 'God Save the King'.

But Ligeti's humour has a dark side. Born a Hungarian-speaking Jew in Romanian-speaking Transylvania, he was an outsider from the start. The nonsense language and exaggerated gestures of *Aventures/ Nouvelles aventures* were a flashback to early childhood memories of Romanian border guards barking in a language he couldn't understand. And Ligeti's life, as

with so many Europeans of his generation, was torn apart by the catastrophes of the mid 20th century. Much of his family died in Nazi death camps. 'I did not choose the tumults of my life,' he said. 'Rather, they were imposed on me by two murderous dictatorships: first by Hitler and the Nazis, and then by Stalin and the Soviet system.'

After the war Ligeti walked a perilous tightrope as a young composer in communist Budapest. He devoured what information he could find about musical developments in the West, while using his knowledge of folklore as a cloak of disguise against the censors who demanded Socialist Realism. The *Concert Românesc* ('Romanian Concerto', 1952), for example, is full of folk tunes and innocuous humour – but with the modernist Ligeti bubbling just beneath the surface. In the riotous finale we have Keystone Cops meets Khachaturian's 'Sabre Dance' meets Gypsy fiddle music with scurrying, insect-like textures

Ligeti pictured in 1996 at The Hague's Royal Conservatoire, where he was Composer-in-Residence

Frances Bourne and Rebecca Bottone as Amando and Amanda in English National Opera's 2009 production of *Le Grand Macabre*, whose Prelude is written exclusively for car horns

underneath. Close to the end a trumpet fanfare bursts through the jollity, landing on a brazen clash between neighbouring semitones. Ligeti recalled how censors, on hearing this, barred the piece from public performance.

When the Soviet tanks rolled into Budapest to quash the 1956 uprising, Ligeti escaped across the border and ended up in the nerve centre of Western European new music: Cologne's Electronic Music Studio. Here he made up for lost time. Electronic music, serialism, jazz and, later, pop and American Minimalism were quickly absorbed and re-formed through the prism of his formidable intellect and outsider imagination.

Although he worked with Stockhausen and others in the studio, Ligeti composed little in the way of electronic music himself. Instead, the sounds he heard in the studio suggested a new kind of purely acoustic orchestral and choral music. The cloudy, clustery masterpiece *Atmosphères* is a study in blurred orchestral colour, as if Ligeti is sat at an imaginary mixing desk, filtering orchestral sound from near-white noise to recognisable harmonies, allowing a succession of sonic veils of different densities to float past our ears. Later we hear startling effects such as the trembling sound masses of ocarinas and slide whistles in the Violin Concerto (1989–93); or the unearthly vibrations produced by four differently tuned natural horns in the *Hamburg Concerto* (1998–2002). Both owe much to Ligeti's knowledge of folk and non-Western music. But they also show

how his imagination had been liberated by his time at the electronic studio.

As he explored the possibilities of sound itself, Ligeti was also preoccupied with the pulse and flow of life and matter. As a Jew, he had been barred from becoming a scientist in his youth. Instead, music became its own form of scientific exploration. Sometimes his fascination with the way things move is heard in fantastical, Heath Robinson-style musical machines – what Ligeti called 'meccanico' style. In the third movement of the 1969–70 Chamber Concerto we seem to be inside a giant clockwork mechanism with cogs of different sizes whirring at different speeds. Deep study of Central African rhythm and the frenzied piano rolls of Conlon Nancarrow helped Ligeti imagine ever more dynamic and mind-expanding rhythmic games heard in works such as the Piano Concerto and two books of Études for solo piano (1985, 1988–94).

Ligeti, an arachnophobe, recounted a recurrent childhood dream in which his bed was surrounded by a tangled web full of knots and networks of fibres. Each tiny movement in one part of the web would send shudders through the whole system. This provided Ligeti with a metaphor for how his music pulsates and grows, a more organic starting point than the 'meccanico' approach. He called it 'micropolyphony': music branching out from a single sound, nervously circling around a few notes, gradually expanding, replicating and changing itself to create a complex mass of sound. Later study of fractal geometry gave Ligeti another way of understanding and expanding this idea which, in musical terms, also has roots in the polyphonic webs of Renaissance composers Tallis and Ockeghem. In the Kyrie of Ligeti's 1963–5 *Requiem*, a post-Holocaust Mass for the dead, instruments and voices begin on a low B flat, then gradually creep outwards from this sound, the music cautiously spreading and bifurcating. In no time we are enveloped by a huge, unsteady lament, a cry of pain seeming to come from all humanity – a fierce confrontation with the terrors of the 20th century.

When Ligeti escaped to the West in 1956, he had no time for the 'isms' and factions of European mid-century music. A true pluralist, he devoured whatever he could find. Indeed, his whole life as an artist was a dedicated exploration of *everything*: science, numbers, nature, beauty, tragedy, catastrophe. He moulded and filtered it all into his miraculously imagined music and, somehow, helped us see in ways we never could have imagined. ●

Gillian Moore is Artistic Associate at Southbank Centre. Her book *The Rite of Spring* was named by the *Financial Times* as one of the best music books of 2019. She regularly contributes to BBC Radio 3 and 4 and has written for *The Guardian*, among other publications.

On the Silver Screen

Stanley Kubrick and György Ligeti were two titans of 20th-century culture whose work collided in films such as *2001: A Space Odyssey (pictured below)*. Writer and broadcaster Matthew Sweet explores their fruitful – and oftentimes strained – artistic relationship

The fear of flying, the 400-day schedules, the Xanadu-sized personal archive: mythology made Stanley Kubrick a man apart. But he was no cultural hermit. Irreverant comedian and DJ Kenny Everett's Capital Radio show had few more avid listeners. He watched *Doctor Who* and enquired earnestly about its special effects. And his exposure to the music of György Ligeti came through a chance encounter on the wireless.

Jan Harlan, Kubrick's executive producer, remembers how it happened. On a Friday afternoon in August 1967, Kubrick's wife Christiane was painting in her studio when Ligeti's *Requiem* came rushing through her radio speakers. It was the British broadcast premiere of the work. 'She ran over to the cutting room and told Stanley: "Listen to Radio 3, I think this is it!"' With that, *2001: A Space Odyssey* had a language to convey a time-bending journey to the edge of the universe and the cold, restless power of an extraterrestrial intelligence.

Ligeti never left Kubrick's headspace. For psychological horror *The Shining* (1980), he deployed the textured harmonies of *Lontano* to suggest the workings of paranormal power. In *Eyes Wide Shut* (1999), a fragment of *Musica ricercata* (1951–3) clangs away like a warning of doom. But this is not evidence of a long and beautiful creative relationship.

When Kubrick heard the *Requiem* on Radio 3, he wrote to the broadcaster Melvyn Bragg, hoping that he had sufficient influence to borrow the BBC's tape of the piece. Bragg passed him on to the record label Deutsche Grammophon – who insisted that only Ligeti could give permission. When producer Jan Harlan rang Ligeti's home, the housekeeper told him he was away and uncontactable.

Here's where it gets knotty. A deal was done, but Ligeti believed that he was licensing a modest amount of music – until a friend in the Bavarian Radio Chorus brought news of Kubrick's expansive use of his work. Ligeti bought a ticket for *2001* and sat in the dark with a stopwatch, his resentment gathering with every click. 'I have been compromised,' he declared. 'I am now fighting against it.' A lawsuit was settled out of court – though war between director and composer loomed again in 1982, when Kubrick listened to Ligeti's *Desert Island Discs* and heard himself accused of theft.

Ligeti and Kubrick are now entwined as thoroughly as any director and composer. It's hard to hear those haunted strings and voices without thinking of the oil-black smoothness of an alien monolith. Despite the lack of warmth between them, they understood their mutual debt. So did the woman who brought them together. When Christiane Kubrick attended the German premiere of *Eyes Wide Shut*, her husband was already in his grave. She took another companion: György Ligeti.

'STILL THE BEST SHOW IN LONDON,
BY A FLIPPING MILE'

DOMINIC CAVENDISH, DAILY TELEGRAPH

★ ★ ★ ★ ★

DAILY TELEGRAPH, EVENING STANDARD, INDEPENDENT, FINANCIAL TIMES, METRO, TATLER

CABARET
THE MUSICAL AT THE KIT KAT CLUB

book by
Joe Masteroff

music by
John Kander

lyrics by
Fred Ebb

based on the play by **John van Druten** and stories by **Christopher Isherwood**

TICKETS AVAILABLE NOW AT **WWW.KITKAT.CLUB**

Photography by Dan Kennedy

BY APPOINTMENT TO
HER MAJESTY QUEEN ELIZABETH II
PIANOFORTE MANUFACTURERS
STEINWAY & SONS

MASTERPIECE

COLLECTION

To honour and celebrate the natural beauty of the earth's most precious woods, Steinway & Sons has created the MASTERPIECE 8X8 collection, a limited edition of eight grand pianos and eight upright pianos in its hand-crafted veneer, designed to showcase the quality and unique personality of each wood and bring it to life.

MASTERPIECE 8X8 pianos are issued as model B 211cm grand and model K 132cm upright. The model B is equipped with **SPIRIO** | **r**, the most modern technology Steinway currently has to offer.

Availability is limited to:
1 Oak Model B
1 Figured Walnut Model B
1 Macassar Ebony Model K

For more information or to arrange a private appointment at our London showrooms, please call: **0207 487 3391** or email info@steinway.co.uk

Steinway Hall London W1U 2DB www.steinway.co.uk

STEINWAY & SONS

RHS

Hampton Court Palace
Garden Festival

Tue 4 – Sun 9 July 2023

Press play on a spectacular
day out packed with gardening,
music and entertainment

rhs.org.uk/shows

*Your visit supports
our work as a charity*

BOOK NOW 〉

BECHSTEIN HALL

22 Wigmore Street

London's newest concert venue

Opening in 2024

SOUTHBANK CENTRE

THIS IS

CLASSICAL MUSIC

IN THE 21ST CENTURY

ABOMINATION: A DUP OPERA
PRESENTED BY CONOR MITCHELL
& BELFAST ENSEMBLE
FRI 5 – SUN 7 MAY

**ABEL SELAOCOE, SECKOU KEITA
& CHINEKE! ORCHESTRA**
FRI 12 MAY

**BUDAPEST FESTIVAL
ORCHESTRA: MAHLER 9**
WED 17 MAY

**DENNIS & GNASHER:
UNLEASHED AT THE ORCHESTRA**
SAT 3 JUN

**ANNE-SOPHIE MUTTER,
MAXIMILIAN HORNUNG
& LAMBERT ORKIS**
SUN 4 JUN

CURATE YOUR OWN EXPERIENCE
WITH OUR MULTI-BUY OFFER

LOTTERY FUNDED

Supported using public funding by
ARTS COUNCIL
ENGLAND

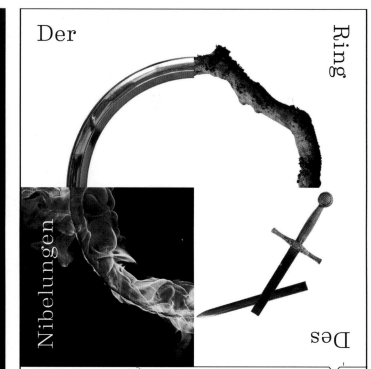

Der   Ring

Nibelungen   Des

"Regents Opera's lean and mean Wagner packs a punch"
The Guardian

"Is this slimmed down Wagner the future of opera?"
The Times

Der Ring des Nibelungen

**At the Grand Temple, Freemasons' Hall,
Covent Garden, London WC2B 5AZ.**

Die Walküre .... May 2023: 21st, 23rd & 27th
Siegfried .... Feb 2024: 4th, 7th & 10th
Full Cycles .... Nov 2024: 10th, 12th, 15th & 17th
.... Nov 2024: 24th, 26th, 29th & Dec 1st

ticketsource.co.uk/regents-opera
REGENTSOPERA.COM

REGENTS OPERA

Events at
Freemasons' Hall

ROYAL PHILHARMONIC ORCHESTRA

Join the journey
rpo.co.uk

2023–24 Season

Tchaikovsky's *Iolanta*, Verdi's *Requiem*, Wagner's *Grand Festival*.

Music by composers from **Dorothy Carwithen** to **Rachmaninov**, **Ethel Smyth** to **Elgar**, **John Williams** to **Poulenc**.

Featuring: **Vasily Petrenko, Louis Lortie, Sophie Bevan, Alexander Shelley, Nikolai Lugansky, Felix Klieser, Jennifer Johnston** and more.

"pretty much perfection"
The i on Vasily Petrenko and the RPO, October 2022

Full season announced Monday 24 April 2023
RPO Club Members get priority booking and access to exclusive ticket discounts, join today and book your tickets at **rpo.co.uk**

ARTS COUNCIL ENGLAND

Supported using public funding by
ARTS COUNCIL ENGLAND

My First *Prom*

Seven Prommers – six veterans and a novice – recount
their first Proms experience, reflecting on what the festival
means to them and how it has impacted their musical lives

Thomas Adès *composer*

My first Prom featured Stravinsky's *Perséphone*, conducted by David Atherton, in 1983; I was 12. I wanted to discover things I didn't know, new places, new noises; not the same old familiar children's stuff. I wanted adult music and here I got it. I'll never forget the shock of the opening xylophone, like ice cracking, plunging me instantly into another world, the primordial mystery of winter and spring, presented as an extraordinary mythical drama. The jolt was amplified by the echo: where I was standing, near the front of the Arena, the whip-crack of the xylophone pinged back from the dome a half-second later, creating a startling, thrilling effect of perspective. To me, it was time-travel. I'll always retain the impact of that moment. I can still see as well as hear it: in my memory, it was as if someone threw a switch, and on went the light. For the next three years I had a season ticket and went to every Prom I could. The tenor part in *Perséphone* was sung by Philip Langridge, who, at Covent Garden just over 20 years later, sang the role of the King in the first production of my opera *The Tempest*.

◀ The cavernous auditorium of the Royal Albert Hall, home of the BBC Proms since 1941

Dame Sarah Connolly *mezzo*

How lucky are the children who are taken to see a Prom at the Royal Albert Hall! I wish I had had my daughter's experience (at 15 years old) of seeing Berlioz's *Symphonie fantastique* performed – from memory – by the incredible Aurora Orchestra with conductor Nicholas Collon. The Royal Albert Hall was the elevated backdrop during my studies over the road at the Royal College of Music, looming proudly, daring us to aspire. I saw countless Proms there during that time and was beguiled by how small-scale chamber music also works in that acoustic. In 1983 I heard my first live *Rite of Spring*, performed by the BBC Symphony Orchestra under Dennis Russell Davies, and wondered how anyone could play those explosive rhythms – much less conduct them. That same season, I remember hearing tenor Anthony Rolfe Johnson's performance of Britten's song-cycle *Les illuminations* with Neville Marriner and the Academy of St Martin in the Fields, and thinking that this was the most beautiful voice I had ever heard. It's such a thrill to be a part of this precious festival and we must strive to protect it.

Katie Derham *broadcaster*

Mahler's Fifth Symphony, 1992. I blame *Educating Rita*. Don't get me wrong, the Proms had always been part and parcel of my childhood, but I grew up in the North-West, so we would watch Richard Baker perched precariously on the edge of a Grand Tier box on the TV, and marvel at the pastel colours worn by the BBC Symphony Chorus. It wasn't until I'd left university and was firmly settled into London life that I had the chance to get along to the Royal Albert Hall and experience a Prom properly. And, as my friends and I thought we would 'die without Mahler' (to borrow Maureen Lipman's phrase in *Educating Rita*), we got tickets to see the London Symphony Orchestra under Michael Tilson Thomas perform Mahler's Fifth Symphony. We had Stalls seats (we hadn't yet realised that Promming in the Arena is miles more fun). And, looking back, I had absolutely no idea, aged 22, what a hot ticket it was. It made an enormous impression. The venue, the crowd, the sheer scale of the music and the experience. Not my first classical concert, but the first one with such a sense of occasion. It's fair to say that night I caught the Proms Bug.

> 66 My Prom years were the late 1940s and early 1950s. Some of my outstanding memories are of composers conducting their own works. Among them were Vaughan Williams conducting his 'London' Symphony and Constant Lambert conducting his *Rio Grande*. Most thrilling of all was William Walton conducting *Belshazzar's Feast* with the peerless Dennis Noble as narrator.

The late Brendan Sadler, from Street in Somerset, reflecting on his early Proms experiences as part of the 2020 Proms Time Capsule

Nubya Garcia *saxophonist*

I've been going to the Royal Albert Hall in one way or another throughout my life, and have attended many Proms. Often I would sit up in the Gallery, not being able to see much, or down in the Arena, standing, but with a much better view! The performances I heard at those concerts still inspire me to this day. As does the building itself: I've spent many years walking all the way around it, getting lost and hearing incredible music. You can really feel the history of all those musicians who came before … I have very special memories of the Hall from when I was a teenager, playing with the Camden Youth Jazz Band and some of the other Camden Music ensembles. Those concerts were an important part of the connection that I've had with that building. Then to play my own music at the 2021 Proms with my band: so many emotions went through me as I stepped onto that stage, both surreal and exciting at the same time. Reconnecting with audiences after lockdown at the iconic Royal Albert Hall is something that I will never forget. It will always remind me why I love what I do, and it continues to inspire me to reach greater heights musically.

Sam Jackson *Controller, Radio 3*

My first encounter with the BBC Proms was in the summer of 2002, a season I shall never forget. Aged 19, I'd never been to the Proms before – but that year I was lucky enough to secure work experience as a 'runner' for BBC TV. In practice, this meant navigating the labyrinthine backstage corridors of the Royal Albert Hall with various musicians in tow, hoping we'd arrive at the 'studio' box in time for that crucial post-performance interview. One Prom from that season will forever remain in my memory. The centrepiece was a performance of Rachmaninov's *The Bells* with the BBC Scottish Symphony Orchestra and Huddersfield Choral Society. I can vividly recall the wall of sound, the remarkable artistry and the packed hall of audience members ranging from seasoned Prommers to those who, like me, were attending for the first time. Sitting in the Hall, immersed in the most captivating music, I caught the Proms Bug. Now, over two decades later, it is the greatest privilege to once again be working on the Proms. This season, there will be people in the audience who, like my 19-year-old self, will experience live music like never before. I can't wait to hear about the memories they will make.

Reuben *violin student*

Last July I went to the First Night of the Proms at the Royal Albert Hall. The trip was part of the Awards for Young Musicians mentoring partnership with the BBC Symphony Orchestra. My mentor, Peter, was playing the viola and it was great to watch him perform. I had been to one small classical concert before, but this was the first that I had experienced on this scale. I hadn't realised the Royal Albert Hall would be quite so big. I sat near the top, in the Circle: the view was amazing from up there – and the drop was very steep! The piece being performed was Verdi's *Requiem*. It has several loud, dramatic moments which really stood out. The music made me shiver at first but, once I got used to those loud moments, it just became a nice listening experience. By the end I felt relaxed, calm and peaceful. I managed to spot where Peter was and stood up and waved just in case – though I don't think he saw me! The day before the Prom, he had taught me a slow passage from the *Requiem*, which I recognised during the performance. It made me really happy being surrounded by so many different people, all of them watching the orchestra play.

John Wilson *conductor*

My first visit to the Proms was in July 1992, shortly after I'd finished my first year at the Royal College of Music. In those days the college would have a couple of free tickets for each Prom and, if you got to the library quickly enough, you could put your name down for the concert of your choice. I saw that Vaughan Williams's *A Sea Symphony* was to be played that season by the Royal Philharmonic Orchestra, and so I bagged a couple of tickets. I had recently fallen in love with the symphony, having performed it myself as part of the RCM Chorus. It's the perfect piece for the Royal Albert Hall, so I'm sure l must have loved it – but the memory that stays with me from that evening is Tasmin Little and Raphael Wallfisch's performance of Delius's Concerto for Violin and Cello, a work I'd never heard before and one which absolutely intoxicated me. It was a magical experience and led to a lifelong love of Delius. Looking through the online Proms Performance Archive, I see that this concert was dedicated to the memory of Charles Groves – a fine conductor and tireless champion of British composers and of new work, and one who added so much to the musical life of the country.

Family-Friendly Proms

Every year the Proms offers half-price tickets for under-18s. Why not bring the whole family to one of the concerts below, perfect for classical starters.

'Orrible Opera

The English National Opera Orchestra and Chorus/Keri-Lynn Wilson

PROMS 10 & 11 • 22 JULY

Orff: Carmina burana

City of Birmingham Symphony Orchestra/ Kazuki Yamada

PROM 17 • 27 JULY

Relaxed Prom: Walton, Mozart, Skoryk & Rachmaninov

Bournemouth Symphony Orchestra/ Kiril Karabits

PROM 25 • 3 AUGUST

Hindemith, Strauss & Copland

National Youth Orchestra of Great Britain/ Carlos Miguel Prieto

PROM 28 • 5 AUGUST

Ligeti & Strauss

London Philharmonic Orchestra/ Edward Gardner

PROM 36 • 11 AUGUST

Audience Choice

Budapest Festival Orchestra/Iván Fischer

PROM 38 • 13 AUGUST

Fantasy, Myths and Legends

BBC Concert Orchestra/Anna-Maria Helsing

PROM 57 • 28 AUGUST

The Rite by Heart

Aurora Orchestra/Nicholas Collon

PROMS 62 & 63 • 2 SEPTEMBER

The Nightingale *of India*

In the first Proms Bollywood celebration for over a decade, the City of Birmingham Symphony Orchestra and guests honour Lata Mangeshkar, whose voice adorned countless Indian movies before her death last year at the age of 92. JAMEELA SIDDIQI celebrates the revered singer and her unrivalled legacy

For almost seven decades, Lata Mangeshkar (1929–2022) defined what it meant to be the best. Accolades such as the 'Melody Queen' and 'Nightingale of India' were already piling up for this film playback singer while she was still in her early twenties. Following her death last year, having recorded some 50,000 songs in 14 languages while lending her voice to five generations of female actors, she was given a state funeral. By this time, commentators and critics had simply run out of superlatives to describe her unique talent and lifetime achievements.

Indian film music is not only an integral part of the musical culture in India (and Pakistan and Bangladesh), but has a vast following among Indians settled abroad, as well as a cult following among Western listeners and movie-goers.

Indian film songs are written and arranged for orchestra by composers credited as 'Music Director'. The lyrics are penned by poets in Urdu and Hindi. But the songs are almost never sung by the actors themselves. Playback singers pre-record the tracks which are later mimed by the stars of the film. Typically the composer and lyricist go through the tune and words with the singer before the recording. Mangeshkar was said to often get it right in one take.

◀ Lata Mangeshkar: according to film composer A. R. Rahman, 'not just a singer, not just an icon, but part of India's consciousness, Indianness and Hindustani music'

The songs can range from Indian classical and semi-classical to traditional folk styles, also featuring any number of foreign influences, including Western classical and pop as well as Latin American, Caribbean, Middle Eastern and Central Asian, all the way to Indonesian gamelan and Chinese court music. Similarly, traditional Indian string instruments such as the sitar and sarod sit comfortably alongside guitar, clarinet, saxophone, piano and keyboards. This kind of instrumental 'fusion', often assumed to be a trend of modern times, was already the norm in Indian film music by the late 1940s.

Playback singing is not considered 'high art' by Indian classical music purists, but a film song can make even greater demands on its singer. Apart from a perfect singing voice, as well as flawless diction in any number of Indian languages, a successful playback singer also needs to have a full understanding of the emotions expressed by the song's lyrics.

Ever since the end of the silent era and the arrival of sound in 1931, songs have been an indispensable part of Indian movies. With a minimum of six (and in one instance even 42) songs in a single soundtrack, such films often do good business at the box office based on song sequences alone. The same playback singer might sing for literally scores of actors of all ages and in all situations: romantic, comic or tragic. Most good singers are in fact voice-actors, adjusting their tone and pitch according to the speaking voice of the relevant actor.

By happy coincidence, Lata Mangeshkar's long career coincided with songs by extremely talented musicians and lyricists who created many immortal numbers between the 1940s and early 1970s, the period known as the Golden Age of Indian film music. It was also a time during which some highly respected poets of Urdu often doubled as lyricists for film songs, turning out some heavy-duty Urdu poetry that might have proved difficult to sing, but Mangeshkar (whose native tongue was Marathi) went that extra mile and made a serious study of the language, so much so that diehard purists were dumbfounded at her pristine diction and pronunciation in a language that was foreign to her. At least one Urdu poet is known to have confessed that he got fresh insights into his verses when he heard them sung by Lata Mangeshkar. But the ultimate praise came from one of the heavyweights of the classical arena. The revered singer Bade Ghulam Ali Khan confessed to remaining glued to his radio in the hope of catching a mistake. 'I have known the greatest of classical maestros to occasionally hit a false note,' he observed wryly. 'She never ever hits a wrong note!'

The daughter of classical singer Dinanath Mangeshkar, Lata initially disappointed her father by wanting to sing for films. The cinema still carried a somewhat unsavoury reputation, both in moralistic terms and in its trends towards diluting the classical music of India. But her father's sudden death left the family in dire financial straits, forcing her, the oldest of five siblings, to seek paid work,

The Nightingale's swansong: crowds gather on the streets of Mumbai at the funeral procession for Lata Mangeshkar in February last year; the Indian government announced two days of national mourning followng her death, and the country's Prime Minister, Narendra Modi, attended her last rites

and cinema was the only game in town. But not even her own father (also her first music teacher) could have guessed that she would go on to become *the* voice of the Indian cinema. Strangely enough, her voice was not initially welcomed and was considered too thin and squeaky compared to the voices of other female vocalists – many descended from a courtesan tradition of song – who had become the stalwarts of the talkies alongside the handful of singing stars who could both sing and act. But, despite her being considered somewhat 'lightweight' in tone, some were quick to realise that her voice – with its amazing clarity ranging over three and a half octaves – embodied a kind of innocence and chasteness that epitomised the ideal woman in South Asian culture.

In 1948 she was still virtually unknown, struggling from song to song, supplemented by a few small acting roles. But by 1949, with the almost simultaneous release of films including *Mahal* and *Barsaat*, both of which featured landmark songs in her still very young voice, she was the talk of the town. Her haunting 'Ayega aanewala' from the former and playful 'Hawa mein udta jaaye' from the latter are cherished to this day. By the time the iconic film *Awaara* was released in 1951, soon proving a major success in China as well as the Soviet Union and all over the Middle East, Lata Mangeshkar was already India's favourite singer. After that, she sang for almost every film composer or music director from the early 1950s right up to A. R. Rahman in the 2000s.

While many leading female actors would have it written into their contracts that their singing voice would be provided by Lata Mangeshkar alone, Lata herself often refused point-blank to sing a song if she thought the lyrics were in any way vulgar or sexually suggestive. In this way, Lata indirectly helped her younger sister, Asha Bhosle, to establish her own career as a playback singer, since Asha would be approached as second choice by music directors if Lata had turned down a song.

Lata Mangeshkar was indeed famously choosy about the songs she would sing. Devotional and patriotic songs were among her favourites. Her live performance of 'Aye mere watan ke logo', an ode to the sacrifice of soldiers who died in the war with China in 1962, penned by the poet 'Kavi' Pradeep and composed by C. Ramchandra, is said to have reduced India's first Prime Minister, Jawaharlal Nehru (a lifelong fan) to tears.

India's current Prime Minister, Narendra Modi (another self-confessed fan), described Lata Mangeshkar's death as leaving 'a void in our nation that cannot be filled'. Apart from cricket (of which she was an ardent follower), Lata's voice was perhaps the only other undisputed embodiment of Indian national unity. ●

Jameela Siddiqi is an award-winning broadcaster, novelist, journalist and lecturer in the history of Indian classical music and poetry. She is a former presenter of BBC Radio 3's World Routes programme and writes for Songlines magazine.

Lata Mangeshkar: Bollywood Legend
PROM 18 • 28 JULY

EDINBURGH INTERNATIONAL FESTIVAL

4–27 AUGUST

·EDINBVRGH·
THE CITY OF EDINBURGH COUNCIL

CREATIVE SCOTLAND
ALBA CHRUTHACHAIL

Charity No SC004694

Agony *and* **Ecstasy**

TOM SERVICE interrogates the mysterious art of conducting, and two Proms conductors, New Zealand-born **GEMMA NEW** (making her Proms debut) and **MARK WIGGLESWORTH** (making his 25th appearance) swap notes on the challenges and rewards of life on the podium

The conductor – as phenomenon, as musical leader, as public figure – has never been more familiar nor more controversial in our culture. The questions of how their authority is wielded with those silent sticks carving shapes in the air are just as urgent as they have been ever since the 'Maestra' of the convent of St Vito in Ferrara used a baton to keep her nuns in musical order in the late 16th century, the first reference to the use of a conducting baton as we understand it in Europe – even if the use of sticks in other ways, banged on the ground to mark musical time, already had a long history, from Ancient Greek armies to massive outdoor entertainments. And that's if our conductors even use batons, since some of the conductors you'll see on the podium at the Proms prefer the flexibility of baton-less open hands to the inanimate limb of the baton.

But whether they're stick-free conjurors or magus-like alchemists of musical wands, all of our Proms conductors share the same problem, which is how to lead the groups of instrumentalists and singers in front of them, how to connect with their audiences – even though their backs are turned to the majority of us in the Royal Albert Hall – and how to make their performances fly into the stratosphere of expression and emotion, whether they're leading a first performance of music by Grace-Evangeline Mason, an opera by György Kurtág or a concerto by Samuel Coleridge-Taylor.

And there's an even more basic question before we get to how they do it – which is: who are they? Who gets to be a conductor at the Proms? Is it a self-selecting group of wannabe musical leaders (for some), or tin-pot musical tyrants (for others); or is it a meritocratic selection process of talent and drive? What are the criteria not only for what makes a successful conductor, but for who gets to enter the field of conductors' dreams?

Conducting has a major diversity and inclusion problem, if you measure the profession by who's at the helm of major symphony orchestras: in terms of women in chief conductor roles with major orchestras, in the USA, Nathalie Stutzmann leads the Atlanta Symphony Orchestra – and that's it; in the UK, after Mirga Gražinytė-Tyla steps down at the City of Birmingham Symphony Orchestra, there will be none. There's much work to do.

Yet, historically, conducting has never been quite as mono-cultural or mono-gendered as it's often thought to have been, it's just that the lives and careers of conductors such as Antonia Brico (1902–89) or Ruth Gipps (1921–99) haven't received the same attention in history as their male counterparts: it's also true that they didn't receive the same opportunities of major

Conductors as collaborators: Gemma New *(top)* and Mark Wigglesworth *(below)* share a view that performances are forged as a collective with orchestral players

music directorships, which has been the yardstick by which the success of careers in conducting has usually been judged. There are signs that's changing: Alice Farnham's recent book, *In Good Hands: The Making of a Modern Conductor*, shows how the range of what conductors actually do – whether in opera houses and film sessions or on video game soundtracks, or in amateur and community ensembles – is much wider than the image of the singular conductor in raptures on the podium leads us to believe. Along with every other kind of area of diversity that needs to be addressed, it's our image of the conductor that needs to develop too.

Most radically, Farnham's idea is that conducting should belong to everyone who learns music, that having the chance to co-ordinate your classmates singing or playing should be something that every musical child experiences. If as many of us as possible had the chance to try out this unique role in music-making for ourselves, its mysteries and its magic would belong to all of us.

That's a conducting utopia that might seem a long way off but, away from the podium, conducting is a job that requires skills that can be learnt, honed and crafted. Reading this Proms Festival Guide this year, conducting at the Proms in a future season: for some of you, that's a reality. Make your dreams come true! ●

Tom Service presents *The Listening Service, Music Matters, The New Music Show* and other programmes for BBC Radio 3, and has also presented Proms broadcasts and documentaries on BBC TV. Among his books is *Music as Alchemy: Journeys with Great Conductors and their Orchestras* (Faber, 2012).

The conductor as leader

GEMMA NEW: I think, these days, we're moving into a more collaborative style. One of the reasons I love conducting is that we're never alone. We are always creating something together that is more powerful than us as individuals. That two-way communication between conductor and players is really important. So I don't think of it as being 'the' leader. I think we all need to lead, we all have that responsibility.

MARK WIGGLESWORTH: Yes, it's the same as in any other field, whether in the theatre, business or sport. Your job is to inspire the people you're working with to express themselves, and to unify that expression into something coherent. Of course, there's the contradiction of asking people to express themselves in a specific way, but that's the challenge of leadership. I agree: ultimately, it's the players who are creating the sound. So, actually, you are *only* a leader.

But it's also true that some players *want* to be told what to do, and believe the conductor's job is to lead every decision. That's problematic, because the idea of working collaboratively is only viable if people want to work with you in that way. Trying to create a unity among 100 individuals is complex. And the dynamic is often further complicated by the historically entrenched hierarchy in the relationship. There's still a residue of that today.

How to rehearse

GN: You have to find what is clear for the

orchestra. Sometimes it's an image or colour, sometimes players just want to know: do you want it louder, slower, faster? And the same goes for your gestures. Some orchestras really respond to the clarity when you show the subdivisions of a beat, and others will completely break down if you do that: they want a broader sweep. It's all about trying things out, and then seeing what response you get.

I might start the first rehearsal with a clear plan. But then, you know that everyone has their own experience and expression so, as you're listening, you have to make quick decisions about what will work within a unified interpretation. You need to make quick decisions about which tricky parts the players have already clocked and will fix themselves, which ones the players might appreciate doing again and which ones need just a verbal check to make sure we're all on the same page.

MW: What you don't want is for the performance to be simply a recreation of all the best bits of your rehearsal. You want it to be something beyond that. The ambition is to pace the journey – from that first read-through to the final performance – in such a way that everybody feels they are always moving forward. Some musicians want rigour in rehearsals to enable freedom in the concert. Others prefer to hold on to a musical discipline throughout. You can't please everybody all of the time, but trying to find that trajectory of constant creation is very rewarding.

The conductor's 'definitive' reading

MW: I don't think people are especially interested in the details of a conductor's interpretation. I think they're interested in the performance being unique. What audiences respond to is the feeling of something being created specifically with that orchestra, that conductor, in that hall. So what you're aiming for is an interpretation that lies within a triangular relationship between the composer, the players and yourself. It's at its best when you're conducting in a way that you might not have imagined when on your own, preparing the score at home.

I find that the more often I've done a piece, the wider I see the margin within which the players can express themselves while still maintaining my overall vision of it. When you do a piece for the first time, you tend to be quite stressed and intent on getting the interpretation that you've prepared. You'd think that the more often you do a piece, the more fixed your view is of it, but actually I've found the opposite.

GN: Yes, the first time you conduct a piece in concert, it has that high energy level and we're hoping to prove ourselves, in a way, but you want the subsequent performances to be just as special, and that only comes from being free and from directing the energy flow in the moment on the night.

Being a musical omnivore

GN: Here in Hamilton [Ontario], I like to theme each programme in a way that will satisfy experienced audience members and also be appealing to newcomers. To

66 The conductor must not only make his orchestra play; he must make them *want* to play ... It is not so much imposing his will on them like a dictator; it is more like projecting his feelings around him so that they reach the last man in the second violin section. And when this happens – when one hundred men share his feelings, exactly, simultaneously, responding as one to each rise and fall of the music, to each point of arrival and departure, to each little inner pulse – then there is a human identity of feeling that has no equal elsewhere. It is the closest thing I know to love itself.

Leonard Bernstein in his *Omnibus* TV episode on 'The Art of Conducting', 1955

❝ There's only one way to rehearse an orchestral piece … I play the whole thing through from beginning to end without a stop, the whole blessed thing. The orchestra makes a few mistakes, naturally. I play it through a second time; the orchestra makes no mistakes. I then just take a few little difficult parts. I pinpoint them, I emphasise them, I repeat those three or four times. I'm ready for performance!

Thomas Beecham – founder-conductor of the Beecham Symphony Orchestra, Beecham Opera Company, London Philharmonic Orchestra and Royal Philharmonic Orchestra – in a 1958 TV interview

do that, you need to present a wide variety of styles. So, if we have a contemporary piece – and that is absolutely something our audiences should feel they can relate to – we might include a special introduction and show the connections with the other works on the programme.

MW: You have to feel an emotional connection with a piece of music in order to do it justice. But you're not necessarily the best judge of that. I used to be more insecure about doing music that I wasn't sure I had that bond with. If I didn't feel I understood it, how could I persuade anybody else about it? Over the years, though, some of the most rewarding experiences have been when I've conducted a piece that I wouldn't have chosen off my own bat, but that someone else has suggested. I think I have quite a wide repertoire, but I'm in awe of the musicians themselves. I've probably conducted a hundred different symphonies, but most orchestral players will have probably performed nearer to a thousand. And they play music of all sorts of genres, including crossover and commercial music, as part of their orchestral life. The roundedness of that musicianship is something I admire hugely.

Musical red flags
GN: I avoided conducting Handel's *Messiah* for many years. There are so many ways in which one can approach it, and you need a well-marked set of parts to achieve a united and satisfying performance. Fortunately, the pandemic gave me the necessary time to make these parts, and now I'm happy to conduct it anytime.

MW: For me, there's a bridge between the Classical and Romantic periods where I'm not quite sure how the music sits, emotionally – how subjective or how abstract it is. Schumann is the most obvious example. I feel that, if I don't know where it lies within my own heartbeat, then perhaps I'm not going to do it very well. But sometimes the only way to find out is to try.

The Proms podium
GN: I feel like this is a very special occasion. I've been to one Prom before, on a quick visit to London as a student. I queued up for a Promming ticket and I got to stand in the front row. I was so excited and had the most magical time. So it feels really special to be coming back to conduct. I've watched a lot of Proms on TV and both of my parents are English, so it feels like part of my culture. Mark, you have a wealth of experience at the Proms – do you have any advice?

MW: Well, no – but it's interesting. Unlike you, being in England, I've grown up with the Proms and gone very often. I'm very proud to feel part of that connection to my own country. On the one hand, that's very comforting and, on the other, it creates its own pressures. I think what's encouraging for British musicians is that the Proms is about as mainstream as classical music gets in British culture, so it feels like the most culturally central performing that we do.

For you, Gemma, it might be the opposite. Not being part of that tradition reduces the pressure, in a way. But there's a different sort of pressure if something's new to you. The reality is that, once you've bowed to the audience and turned to face the orchestra, it is fundamentally the same as any other concert; because, as you said earlier, the most immediate relationship is with the players. You'll love it, you'll absolutely love it.

How to study the score

GN: Mark, I know it's a very personal process but I'd be interested to know how you go about studying a score?

MW: Yes, that doesn't get talked about much, does it? I think, ultimately, our job is structural, we're there to guide and pace the journey. So I spend a lot of time thinking about where the high point is, where the next high point is, where the middle point is, and where the lowest point is. And then … OK, how are we going to get from the bottom to the top? And I take a lot of time to study. But I also think you need to have a range of options in mind, and the more options you can envisage, the more embracing a musician and colleague you're going to be.

GN: I think you've hit it on the head. It takes many hours to figure out what's going on structurally, both on a macro and a micro level, and then to absorb all the details. And then, yes, there are all these grey areas where you have many options on how they could go.

MW: The conductors I admire the most are the ones who clearly know every detail of the score but are then able to sort of hover over them all and focus on

what really matters. I think you need to have time to study the score, but then you also need time to forget the score. So that you are only really controlling the most important aspects of it, and not micromanaging. That's something that took me a long time to discover.

Moments of glory

MW: There have been a few occasions when everything seemed to have worked out amazingly well, but I'm not despondent about how few there have been. If every performance was as perfect as we wanted it to be, we'd constantly be trying to recreate exactly the same thing. The audience has a huge role to play. The performances I remember the most are the ones in which the audiences have been the most engaged. We are responsible for their engagement, of course, but there are certain venues and certain occasions where their contribution is unforgettable.

GN: Yes. When, after a performance, you see the audience beaming and full of positive energy – and the musicians too – it feels so uplifting, and that makes you feel: that's why I do it. ●

Interview by Edward Bhesania. Mark Wigglesworth has written about the role of the conductor in *The Silent Musician: Why Conducting Matters* (Faber, 2018).

Mark Wigglesworth conducts the BBC Philharmonic
PROM 6 • 18 JULY

Gemma New conducts the BBC Scottish Symphony Orchestra
PROM 44 • 18 AUGUST

“ The orchestral sound is reflected in a conductor's physicality. It is no longer about how to make contact with an instrument, but how to make contact with the air, how to move silently through space. It needs to be controlled yet uninhibited. Even our facial expressions will be read, consciously or otherwise, by an orchestra. We are leaders, and like all good leaders, we are listening keenly and responding in the moment.

Alice Farnham in her book *In Good Hands: The Making of a Modern Conductor* (Faber), published this year

For all your tomorrows...

AURIENS

CHELSEA

THE GOLD STANDARD IN LATER LIVING
CALL 0204 549 8000 OR VISIT AURIENS.COM

DONATELLO
SCULPTING THE RENAISSANCE

Supported by

ROCCO FORTE HOTELS

V&A South Kensington
Until 11 June 2023
Members go free

DISCOVER DONATELLO'S
TALENT AND IMPACT
BROUGHT TO LIFE
THROUGH 120 OBJECTS

V&A

Santtu Matias Rouvali

Sheku Kanneh-Mason

Nicola Benedetti

Stephen Hough

Esther Yoo

Philharmonia

London season at the Royal Festival Hall

Santtu conducts Tchaikovsky & Shostakovich
With violinist Randall Goosby
Thursday 27 April

Stephen Hough plays Beethoven
Plus Nielsen's 'Inextinguishable' Symphony
Thursday 4 May

Yamada conducts Saint-Saëns's Organ Symphony
Plus Berg's Violin Concerto with Baiba Skride
Sunday 7 May

Scriabin's Prometheus & Rachmaninov's The Bells
With Scriabin's original lighting
Thursday 11 May

Santtu conducts Stravinsky I: The Firebird
Plus Prokofiev with pianist Behzod Abduraimov
Thursday 18 May

Santtu conducts Stravinsky II: Petrushka
Plus Prokofiev with violinist Esther Yoo
Sunday 21 May

The Bach Choir: The World Imagined
Boulanger, Debussy, Poulenc and Jackson
Thursday 25 May

Santtu conducts Beethoven & Strauss
Featuring Nicola Benedetti, Sheku Kanneh-Mason and Benjamin Grosvenor in Beethoven's Triple Concerto
Thursday 8 June

Tickets from £10
philharmonia.co.uk
0800 652 6717

SOUTHBANK CENTRE
RESIDENT

PEREGRINE'S PIANOS

Award-winning piano dealer

AUGUST FÖRSTER

SCHIMMEL PIANOS

Peregrine's Pianos is the exclusive dealer in London for two of the finest German piano manufacturers. We also offer concert piano hire, long-term domestic hire and fine rehearsal facilities that can accommodate up to fifty people.

www.peregrines-pianos.com

Peregrine's Pianos, 137A Grays Inn Road, London WC1X 8TU   Tel: 020 7242 9865

The Future of Music
ROYAL COLLEGE OF MUSIC London
Continue your musical experience at the Royal College of Music, opposite the Royal Albert Hall with concerts, café, courtyard and a beautiful museum.
rcm.ac.uk

The **Trojans**

Commissioned by Rome's first emperor, the *Aeneid* is a proud celebration of the founding of a nation. But, as **SARAH RUDEN** discovers, Virgil's epic, with its erotic, emotional and feminine takes on war, would prove much more than a work of unabashed nationalism, inspiring, among other works, Berlioz's grand opera *The Trojans*

erlioz's grand five-act opera *The Trojans* is the most ambitious work about the Trojan War and its aftermath since Virgil's *Aeneid*. The French composer (who also wrote the libretto) recalled in a letter how a passion for the great Roman epic had first seized him. As a young boy, he had been reading the 12th and final book in the original Latin under his father's direction. But 'construing', not 'reading', was how he put it; at that early age, he would have strained to puzzle out the intricate sentences. Even so, he was transported by its splendour and tragedy. He recalled how, while attending vespers one Sunday, the 'sad, persistent chant' of Psalm 114 – about the escape of the Israelites from Egypt – had the effect of plunging him back into a Virgilian daydream. He was struck by the heroic glory of the *Aeneid*'s characters, escaped from the fall of Troy – refugees on a quest for a secure realm in Italy. Significantly, Berlioz indicates that he found himself especially drawn to the women in the story, including the Italian princess Lavinia. (In Virgil's poem she does not speak a word but only sobs when her betrothal – hotly contested, because her dowry comprises her father's kingdom – ignites a catastrophic war.)

Upon leaving vespers, the young Berlioz wept for the rest of the day, powerless over his 'epic grief'. Such a response was not

a phenomenon unique to 19th-century French Romanticism. The boy was subject to an enchantment active since around the year 30 BCE, when the start of the *Aeneid*'s composition was little more than a rumour. Virgil had produced two beautiful but relatively short and personal poems, the *Eclogues* and the *Georgics*, under the sponsorship of the first Roman emperor Octavian (known after 27 BCE as Augustus); now his fellow poet Propertius announced that 'something greater than the *Iliad* is being born'.

Virgil's Latin reprise of Homeric epic celebrated Octavian's family as divinely descended and recounted his legendary ancestor Aeneas's quest to found the Roman nation as an indestructible replacement for devastated Troy. But it was the *Aeneid*'s erotic, emotional and feminine takes on war, religion and the state that won Roman readers' hearts. Schoolteachers favoured Book 1, with its ground-level and victim-oriented account of Troy's fall, and Book 4, the love story of the shipwrecked Aeneas and Dido, Queen of Carthage, which ends in her suicide when he leaves for his destined homeland in Italy. These parts of the *Aeneid*, elegies of human helplessness against the storm of history, marked young memories like a hissing brand, and within a few decades of the epic's publication quotations, allusions, parodies, graffiti, artwork and derivative performances testified that the *Aeneid* was the myth of myths, a powerful new way for Rome to think about itself, much as Virgil's exquisite versification had remade Latin poetry.

But that wasn't the effect the emperor had planned. True, there is plenty about the gods' will for Rome, and many examples of patriotic and patriarchal self-sacrifice decreed from on high. But altogether the exhortations and prophecies, toils and dangers, miracles, embassies and battles stand up poorly against a single figure: Dido. Her claims on the popular mind prevailed, even though she represents Rome's arch-enemy Carthage, which was devastated by a Roman army in the year 146 BCE; Virgil suggests that event by comparing the chaos caused by Dido's suicide to the city's sacking, which occurred a putative 1,000 years or so later.

Writing more than a century after Virgil's death, the Roman satirist Juvenal observes how tiresome Roman women could be at dinner parties when they got going in Dido's defence. But even Roman schoolboys could feel that the queen was special. In late antiquity, when the Empire began to wobble under barbarian invasions and the Christian Church was emerging as the regime that would outlast it, the schoolboy who was to become Saint Augustine of Hippo did not even think through the rights and wrongs of the heroine's situation, but merely 'wept for Dido'. Augustine was probably just one of many predecessors to Berlioz, sobbing deliciously over her proud pathos and doomed glory.

Hence the adult Berlioz's transformation of the *Aeneid* into the grandest of grand operas has far more behind it than the modern Romantic movement. He might have unwittingly privileged what I

◀ Italian soprano Anna Caterina Antonacci as Cassandra in a 2012 production of *The Trojans* at London's Royal Opera House

Dido welcomes Aeneas to her court (painting by Nathaniel Dance-Holland, 1735–1811); so enchanted was Berlioz by the Queen of Carthage that, in writing *The Trojans*, he dedicated three of its five acts to telling her story

believe was Virgil's own narrative nucleus, a 'little epic' about Dido in the affecting style of Greek Alexandrian literature and its imitators, the Roman Neoteric poets. Declaiming damsels in distress were not likely Augustus's preference for his nationalist epic, but time after time in his career Virgil got away with placing a proto-Romantic picture in a propagandistic frame.

In any event, Berlioz hurtled much further in the Romantic direction. In Virgil, Dido's story takes up part of Book 1 and all of Book 4; this is out of 12 books. At the start of Book 5, Aeneas is shaken to see the flames of Carthage as he sails away, but he is never shown thinking of Dido again, except briefly (in Book 6) when her angry ghost confronts him in the Underworld. By contrast, Berlioz nearly fills the final three acts of his five-act opera with Dido's story. This unfolds from her glorification by her subjects, builds to the climactic 'Royal Hunt and Storm' and the touching love duet that follows, and culminates in her spectacular suicide. Among all this, Aeneas's role is more like that of a subsidiary character than a leading man. If we knew the *Aeneid* story only through this opera, we would not suspect that he had ever been the protagonist.

But Dido is not the opera's only leading lady. The apotheosis of the feminine also informs the first two acts of *The Trojans* – perhaps even more strikingly by comparison. There are only three very brief mentions of Cassandra in the *Aeneid*'s story of the fall of Troy – and no

wonder. In the ancient world she was a byword for a victim, coming out of an affair with the god Apollo not with a half-divine child (as was usually the case when a god mated with a mortal) but with the curse of the world's deafness to her frantic prophecies. Mythology treats her ruthlessly: she is blighted in her chance for human love (her foreign suitors Chorebus and Othryoneus are besotted enough to come and fight for doomed Troy, but they are doomed as well), sacrilegiously raped during Troy's sacking, maddened with helpless grief, sexually enslaved, murdered.

But Berlioz's Cassandra is the real Trojan hero of the fall of Troy. Much unlike in the myths, she is not disregarded, as if she were babbling nonsense. She even manages to rally the Trojan women to choose death over the shame of rape and servitude. Freedom and dignity are embodied in her more than in any of her male compatriots; Aeneas's escape with Priam's treasure feels like a narrative afterthought in comparison to her lengthy eloquence.

Conditions for the expression of genius were very different in early Imperial Rome and in 19th-century France. At one point Augustus wrote a teasing letter to Virgil, trying to extract just a little of the epic that took more than decade to write, at the rate of two lines a day. In fact, the poet left it not quite complete at the time of his death, and demanded that it be destroyed as not perfect enough; it was instead reverently saved, to become an instant classic. Discounting later revisions, Berlioz finished his opera in only two years (despite the demands of journalism and many other enterprises), but he was the one utilising contacts at the court of Napoleon III, among untold other efforts, to wrangle a production. Yet he was unsuccessful and was left largely to the hazards of the commercial and semi-commercial music business in an age when audiences were jaded and mythological subjects were in disfavour. During Berlioz's lifetime, *The Trojans* was produced only once, and even then only including the Dido storyline, at the Théâtre Lyrique in Paris in 1863. It was not produced in full, with the original French libretto, until 1969, at Covent Garden.

But Berlioz was not entirely without fault. Like Cassandra and Dido, and like his boyhood self, he was exploding with heroic grandeur and did not acknowledge practical limitations. The work demanded a cast on a military scale and technology with precariously moving parts. He scorned consideration of (for example) what a sluice of diverted Seine water might do to an ordinary stage. Perhaps the 21st century, humble in its experience of real-life cataclysm, yet with a head-spinning range of production choices, is a propitious time to revisit this brilliant yet daunting work. ●

Sarah Ruden is a scholar, translator of ancient literature and visiting researcher at the University of Pennsylvania. Her latest books are an extensively revised second edition of her 2008 translation of the *Aeneid* (Yale UP, 2021) and a new English version of the Gospels (Modern Library, 2021).

The Trojans
PROM 64 • 3 SEPTEMBER

View from the Podium

Sir John Eliot Gardiner, who brings *The Trojans* to the Proms this season with his Orchestre Révolutionnaire et Romantique, reveals what he finds so inspiring about the opera

There is a deep poignancy about Berlioz, the greatest of French Romantic composers, insofar as his most important opera, *The Trojans*, never saw the light of day in his own lifetime, except in the most mutilated, truncated form. Bear in mind that he had been planning to compose this opera probably from the moment he decided to become a composer, against his father's wishes – but curiously inspired by his father's readings of Virgil to him in his early adolescence. Later in life he came to know Virgil – and Shakespeare as well – as though they were intimate friends; and, in the process of writing the libretto of *The Trojans*, he had both of these heroic figures breathing down his neck.

In the daunting task of writing both the libretto and the music for *The Trojans*, Berlioz confessed to Princess Carolyne Sayn-Wittgenstein, 'It will be hard. May all Virgil's gods come to my aid or I am lost. What is immensely difficult about it is to find the musical form, that form without which music does not exist or is no more than the downtrodden slave of the word. That is Wagner's crime; he wants to dethrone it, to reduce it to "expressive accents" … [whereas] I am on the side of music that you yourself call free. Yes, free and proud and sovereign and all-conquering: I want it to take everything, to assimilate everything, so that neither Alps nor Pyrenees bar its way.'

It is the sheer ambition and courage of Berlioz's vision for his great opera that I find deeply impressive and so touching. It was present in my mind during every second of every performance of the first run I conducted, on the occasion of Berlioz's bicentenary at the Théâtre du Châtelet in Paris in 2003. Incredibly, that was the first time the opera had been performed in Paris in a single evening, as originally planned by the composer, with no scenes omitted. Beyond the seductive idea that we were all engaged in an act of restitution aimed at wiping the board of past neglect and injustices, there was an infectious air of excitement about the whole enterprise. It affected the cast, the chorus and the orchestra, augmented by the exotic contingent of nine saxhorns. Perhaps the biggest surprise of all was the ecstatic response of the Parisian audience – historically sceptical and egged on by an uncomprehending, mostly hostile press – in recognition of their homegrown musical genius: Hector Berlioz.

Twenty years on, it is the timeless beauty of his music, the daring and imaginative scope of *The Trojans*, that I find so stirring. On every page of his score Berlioz shows himself to be a far-sighted observer of people and of the human condition. He reveals his mastery of vocal and orchestral timbres and his knack of bringing out the individual colour of each instrument perfectly adjusted to each dramatic moment. From start to finish, *The Trojans* contains music that is heart-rendingly truthful and ageless in its epic sweep. Be prepared to be moved!

Countess *and Composer*

Born at the height of Austro-German Romanticism, but away from its geographical epicentre, Dora Pejačević broke out of her comfortable aristocratic life to forge her own path as a composer. A hunderd years after her death, **JESSICA DUCHEN** celebrates the first female Croatian composer of note, whose passion and devotion to music and culture flourished powerfully but all too briefly in her tragically short life

ora Pejačević is a national treasure in Croatia. She is feted by the country's musicians as its first full-blown symphonist: a prolific composer whose works also included songs, chamber music, piano pieces and the first piano concerto by anyone of her nationality, before her untimely death in 1923, aged only 37. Elsewhere, however, it is only now, 100 years later, that she is gaining widespread recognition. This year the Proms is marking her centenary with its first performance of her Symphony in F sharp minor; and the season is studded with other gems from her output.

Her Cello Sonata adds a major recital item to the repertoire of that genre; pianists can have a field day exploring her extensive catalogue for their instrument; her violin sonatas, too, prove irresistible. Listening to her Symphony, a work overflowing with late-Romantic passion, I'd challenge anybody not to wonder why it has taken so long for her to reach the international limelight.

During her short life, Dora Pejačević – full name Countess Maria Theodora Paulina Pejačević – established a personal and powerful musical voice. Photographs show her as a strong-featured, characterful woman with blazing dark eyes and a no-nonsense air. She was born into the privileged world of an aristocracy that

she grew to loathe. Undaunted by the challenges she faced as a composer on the one hand and a human being on the other, she seems to have admitted no impediment to living her life to the full.

Pejačević was born in Budapest on 10 September 1885 (she was three years younger than Igor Stravinsky and Karol Szymanowski, four years younger than Bela Bartók and less than a year older than Rebecca Clarke). Her father, Count Teodor Pejačević, was a lawyer and politician, serving as the 'ban' (viceroy) of Croatia-Slavonia (1903–7) and later as Minister for Croatia, Slavonia and Dalmatia in the Hungarian government (1913–16). Her mother, Lilla Vay de Vaya, a Hungarian countess, was a gifted amateur musician and artist who became her daughter's first piano teacher. An English governess meanwhile provided Dora's schooling until she was about 10.

She grew up highly cultured, well versed in literature, art and acting as well as music. She cherished a passion for poetry and eagerly devoured writings in several languages, from Shakespeare and Goethe to the founder of the Dada movement, Hugo Ball. Her affinity for poetry and the flow of its words makes her songs particularly rewarding. She began composing at the age of 12; her parents encouraged her by arranging lessons with professors from the Croatian Music Institute in Zagreb.

The young Pejačević was blessed, however, with an enquiring mind and a driven, ambitious spirit that appears

to have been further-reaching than those charged with educating her, and she largely taught herself when it came to understanding counterpoint, orchestration and post-Wagnerian harmony. Later, with the privileges of money and leisure-time enabling her to travel extensively around Germany, Austria, Hungary, Bohemia and Moravia, she made connections and friendships in their substantial cultural circles, especially in Vienna, which became her home from home.

Besides numerous songs, throughout her compositional life Pejačević wrote extensively for the piano, her solo works including two sonatas as well as many sets of miniatures. Highlights include *Blumenleben* ('Flower Life', 1904–5), in which different flowers symbolise various stages of human experience, and the Sonata No. 2 in A flat (1921), a substantial one-movement fantasia. The piano also features prominently in her chamber music; try her lavishly beautiful Piano Quartet in D minor, Op. 25.

Aged 28, Pejačević wrote her first orchestral work: a big-boned, highly demanding piano concerto. Her life, however, was about to change. The outbreak of the First World War began an era that had a profound impact upon her.

During the war years, she enjoyed a crucial friendship with the Austrian poet Rainer Maria Rilke, whose far-left stance (he was in favour of the Russian Revolution in 1917) strongly appealed to the rebellious young countess. She met

◄ Dora Pejačević in 1905, aged 20 (colourised photo)

Teodor Pejačević, Dora Pejačević's father, who followed in a long line of aristocratic, high-ranking politicians; Dora rejected a comfortable lifestyle of leisure, instead working with determination to develop her musical skills (portait by Vlaho Bukovac, 1855–1922)

him in 1916 in Vienna, where Rilke, after being called up, was having to undergo military training. The two considered writing an opera together, but this remained only a tantalising might-have-been. Pejačević made several settings of his poetry, including a song-cycle, *Mädchengestalten*, and *Liebeslied* with orchestral accompaniment, which has something of the fervid atmosphere of Strauss or early Berg.

When the war's wounded began to arrive in the village of Našice, close to the Pejačević family's home, the composer was horrified by what she saw and duly volunteered as a nurse. The contrast between the appalling suffering of the soldiers and the self-centred laissez-faire she observed amid her own class led her to despise the latter: 'I simply cannot understand how people can live without work,' she wrote.

The experience fed her appetite for composition, too – perhaps to escape, or perhaps as an outlet for the turbulent emotions sparked within her (by contrast, Rilke was silenced for several years by his brief yet traumatic military experience). Her Symphony in F sharp minor dates from 1916–17, the height of the hostilities, and throughout its generous 45-minute span she often seems to mine a rich seam of raw anguish. She revised the work in 1920 and it was premiered that same year in Dresden.

Reviewing a recent recording of it by the BBC Symphony Orchestra under Sakari Oramo, the *Financial Times* offered high praise: 'the lyrical themes start to flow and Pejačević always seems to have another one up her sleeve … The cinematic sweep of the music and, above all, its super-Romantic idiom are hard to resist.' Oramo himself – who conducts this year's Proms performance of the work, also with the BBC SO – is clearly a convert. 'I feel at home with this music,' he has said. 'Very, very seldom does one encounter a composer that one has not heard about before, whose music just immediately talks to you. It is a magnificently colourful piece.'

Far from rejecting worldly life and love in favour of art, in 1921 Pejačević married a military officer of noble birth, Ottomar von Lumbe, with whom she settled in Munich. Tragically she died in 1923 one month after their son, Theo, was born. Some sources blame complications from childbirth, others a kidney infection. She instructed that she should not be buried in the family tomb, but instead with a simple tombstone inscribed only 'Dora' and 'Rest now'.

What has delayed the widespread recognition of Pejačević's work? Any answer can only be partial and messy. First, Pejačević died in the early 1920s after writing in a rich, late-Romantic style that was already being elbowed out to the perimeters of the musical world and that after the Second World War was banished from critical approval. It is always hard for a composer's output to survive for long in the years after their death without staunch championing, but even more so when the musical language is perceived as outdated (despite holding more direct, communicative audience appeal than certain mid-century modernists; in this era, even Rachmaninov was denigrated for decades for being too popular *(see pages 14–18)*. Some of Pejačević's approximate contemporaries, such as Szymanowski, Bartók and Stravinsky, continually reinvented their styles in response to the galloping changes of aesthetic around them. She, dying young, never had the chance to try.

Other factors, too, played roles in her neglect. Croatia and its neighbours were heavily affected by the two World Wars, before finding themselves behind the 'Iron Curtain', even if a relatively porous one, under the Yugoslav communist regime. Throughout the 1990s many countries of the former Yugoslavia then suffered a succession of appalling turf wars. Recovery has taken time. Meanwhile, the Serbo-Croatian language may have been a barrier for foreign researchers. We can, however, thank the Croatian Music Information Centre for its efforts to publish, record and disseminate Pejačević's work. It is getting through, and not a minute too soon.

Finally, the fact remains that for years – decades – centuries – performances of music by women were all too rare. Exceptions exist, but they tend to prove the rule. The hangover from 19th-century attitudes that assumed women incapable of fine artistic work, or that regarded such efforts as unseemly or unladylike, took a long time to dissipate. In some quarters, sad to say, these views still exist.

It is only in the past 10 years or so that a proper spotlight has been shone upon this heinous situation; much redressing of balance is still needed. During her 37 years, Pejačević left 106 compositions in 58 opus numbers and created the first modern symphony and piano concerto by a Croatian composer. Yet the *New Grove Dictionary of Music and Musicians* edition of 1980, a fine source of information about innumerable obscure male musicians, failed to grant her even a brief entry. Such discrimination is both historic and real.

If we are to assess any composer simply on merit, we must have a chance to hear the music. I hope you will enjoy Pejačević's as much as I have. With her extraordinary personality, her gift for melodiousness and the unshakeable passion that underpins her writing, she should – hopefully – be here to stay. ●

Jessica Duchen is a music critic, author and librettist. Her output includes seven novels, biographies of Fauré and Korngold, and the librettos for Roxanna Panufnik's operas *Silver Birch* and *Dalia* (commissioned by Garsington Opera). Her journalism appears in *The Sunday Times*, the *i* and *BBC Music Magazine*.

Cello Sonata
PROMS AT DEWSBURY • 6 AUGUST
(see pages 140–141)

Overture
PROM 32 • 8 AUGUST

Zwei Schmetterlingslieder; Verwandlung; Liebeslied
PROM 33 • 9 AUGUST

Symphony in F sharp minor
PROM 40 • 14 AUGUST

> " Art and music were an important part of the education of young aristocrats at the time, but girls and women especially were not supposed to build a proper career of their own. So Dora was definitely an exception. She was also exceptional in choosing to learn the violin. Women were mostly supposed to play the piano: playing the violin was not considered appropriate for an aristocratic girl.

Professor Iskra Iveljić of the University of Zagreb discussing Dora Pejačević's early inclination to go her own way with Donald Macleod in BBC Radio 3's *Composer of the Week* in May 2020

Taylor–Made
Sounds

Pianist and scholar **SAMANTHA EGE** surveys
the legacy of Samuel Coleridge-Taylor, whose
wide-ranging musical style drew on both his
English and Sierra Leonean heritage

Within the archives of the Associated Press lies rare footage of an outdoor rehearsal of *Hiawatha's Wedding Feast*, the first in a trilogy of cantatas by Samuel Coleridge-Taylor. The footage, taken in June 1931, shows Malcolm Sargent – an ardent *Hiawatha* champion – rehearsing his Royal Choral Society singers at Kensington Gardens. In preparation for their upcoming performance at the Royal Albert Hall, the chorus members sport Native American attire – or at least their appropriations of it. Feathered head-dresses and long tunics abound. They congregate around Sargent, who wears a suit typical of an English gentleman from the 1930s. They then re-enact (or, more accurately, parody) a powwow, with dancing and celebratory cries.

The footage grants unique insight into English classical performance culture during the interwar years. Of course, the parodic powwow and the donning of Native American 'fancy dress' seem jarring in the context of our modern-day sensibilities. But at the time it wasn't considered problematic. In fact, the commonplace nature of these displays echoed the Western trends during the late-19th and early 20th centuries of exoticism and fascination with the foreign 'other'.

The *Hiawatha* trilogy had received its first performance, at the Royal Albert Hall, in 1900, but in 1924 began the first in an annual series of extravagant stagings at the Hall, incorporating Coleridge-Taylor's separate ballet music. The venue was transformed with a set that included wigwams, pine trees and mountains. The performers comprised over 100 dancers, the 700-strong Royal Choral Society and the Royal Philharmonic Orchestra. Complete with costumes, the performance was truly a spectacle. It was so popular that repeat performances were given for the next 15 years – nearly three decades after Coleridge-Taylor's death.

Hiawatha's cherished place in the early-20th-century choral repertoire affirmed Coleridge-Taylor's posthumous position as an internationally celebrated composer. He did not live or die in obscurity. He worked at the heart of English classical music and his legacy resounded on the world stage. The 21st-century revival of his music indicates a renewed interest in his vast catalogue and represents a homecoming for this great composer.

Coleridge-Taylor was born in Holborn, London, in 1875. His mother, Alice Hare Martin, was a White Englishwoman. His father, Daniel Peter Hughes Taylor, was a Sierra Leonean man descended from formerly enslaved Africans who had repatriated from the Americas, establishing themselves in Sierra Leone's capital, Freetown. Taylor studied medicine there before travelling to London, where he met Martin. They never married, and Taylor returned to West Africa before Samuel was born. It was Samuel's mother who decided that her child's name would echo that of English poet Samuel Taylor Coleridge. (The hyphen would come later, supposedly the result of a clerical error.)

Coleridge-Taylor was raised largely in Croydon. As a mixed-race composer growing up in Victorian England, he had to contend with pervasive racism, his darker skin attracting taunts from peers. People of African descent were far more common in the UK at the time than is usually understood. With the expansion of the British Empire and the movement (or forcible displacement) of diverse populations, many came to live across the globe. The African diaspora transformed England's cultural landscape and Coleridge-Taylor, as a composer, violinist and conductor, would also make his mark.

In 1890, aged just 15, he entered London's Royal College of Music as a violin student. He soon shifted focus towards composition, studying under Stanford and counting Holst and Vaughan Williams among his classmates. After seven years at the RCM, securing Elgar's admiration along the way, he arrived at a mature compositional voice featuring resonances of Brahms, Grieg and Dvořák, particularly through his use of pensive lyricism, rich harmonies and lush orchestral colours. The American press regularly praised him as an 'African Mahler', no doubt due to his powerful command of orchestral forces and large compositional forms. But Coleridge-Taylor's voice was unmistakably his own: a blend of all that shaped him, from the European Romantics to the bucolic lyricism that characterised English music, and embracing the folk songs of the African continent and

A photographic portrait of Samuel Coleridge-Taylor taken *c*1905

Howard Fry and Avril Coleridge-Taylor (the composer's daughter) pose in Native American-style dress ahead of a *c*1930 performance of *Hiawatha's Wedding Feast*

diaspora that were, by way of his father, a key part of his heritage too.

Orchestral works such as the *Ballade* in A minor (1898), *Solemn Prelude* (1899) and Violin Concerto (published 1912) evince Coleridge-Taylor the Romanticist. Impassioned, virtuosic and brimming with thematic development, they exhibit his flair for orchestral genres and deep understanding of classical conventions. But in other works Coleridge-Taylor expanded his palette further, drawing influence from African and African American folk songs. This proved hugely inspirational for Black composers in the USA in the age of Jim Crow segregation: here was a prominent English composer honouring music that White Americans disparaged daily with displays of Black-face minstrelsy and other propaganda.

In 1905 Coleridge-Taylor composed an extended suite for solo piano called *24 Negro Melodies*. Here was a series of evocative, highly lyrical works based on spirituals – sacred folk songs of the enslaved, once sung on plantations in the American South – and other folk songs from Africa and the Caribbean. While the word 'Negro' is now generally understood as derogatory and archaic, Coleridge-Taylor used it with pride. And that sense of pride resonated with Black music-lovers in the USA. 'Deep River' is the best-known arrangement from this suite and one of his most-performed works.

Music schools named after Coleridge-Taylor proliferated in Black American communities around the turn of the

century. Chicago-born composer-pianist Margaret Bonds (1913–72) attended the Samuel Coleridge-Taylor School of Music, located on the city's predominantly Black South Side. Coleridge-Taylor spent much time with these communities during his US tours and, in turn, supported visiting African American concert artists, such as the violinist and composer Clarence Cameron White. A sense of pan-African solidarity remained throughout his life.

Coleridge-Taylor's death from pneumonia aged just 37 sent shockwaves through the communities his music touched. Despite his popularity, a lack of business acumen meant that lucrative royalties from works such as *Hiawatha* eluded him. His demise may have evoked the archetypal penniless artist, but his life – and the afterlife of his music – shattered all stereotypes and inspired music-lovers worldwide. ●

Samantha Ege is a musicologist, pianist and research fellow at the University of Southampton. Her first book is the forthcoming *South Side Impresarios: Race Women in the Realm of Music*. She is also co-author of a forthcoming biography of Florence Price and co-editor of *The Cambridge Companion to Florence B. Price*.

Ballade
PROM 5 • 17 JULY

Violin Concerto
PROM 7 • 19 JULY

Three Impromptus
PROM 54 • 26 AUGUST

Nonet
PROMS AT TRURO • 27 AUGUST
(see pages 140–141)

Four Novelletten
PROM 61 • 1 SEPTEMBER

Deep River (orch. S. Parkin)
PROM 71 • 9 SEPTEMBER

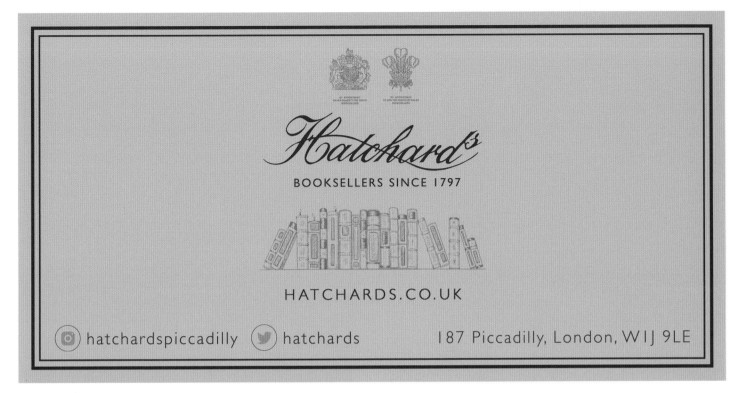

Hatchards

BOOKSELLERS SINCE 1797

HATCHARDS.CO.UK

hatchardspiccadilly   hatchards   187 Piccadilly, London, W1J 9LE

Your luxury boat awaits...

**London's Top Private Luxury
Sightseeing Charter Boat**

*02 Boat Transfers, Private River Tours,
Special Occasions, Evening Cruises*

thameslimo.co.uk
+44 (0) 770 458 2000
booking@thameslimo.co.uk

Thames Limo

JOHN WILSON
AND HIS
SINFONIA OF LONDON

LIVE IN CONCERT!   **70 PIECE ALL-STAR ORCHESTRA!**

HOLLYWOOD'S GREATEST HITS

★★★★★★★ PLUS SPECIAL GUESTS ★★★★★★★

Featuring hit songs **Singin' In The Rain
Over The Rainbow, 'S Wonderful, High Society
They Can't Take That Away From Me
That's Entertainment** *and many more...*

★★★★★ NOVEMBER 2023 ★★★★★

4	BASINGSTOKE	THE ANVIL	11	GATESHEAD	SAGE GATESHEAD
5	BRIGHTON	DOME	12	LIVERPOOL	PHILHARMONIC HALL
6	LONDON	ROYAL ALBERT HALL	13	GLASGOW	ROYAL CONCERT HALL
7	CARDIFF	ST. DAVID'S HALL	14	NOTTINGHAM	ROYAL CONCERT HALL
9	BIRMINGHAM	SYMPHONY HALL	15	MANCHESTER	BRIDGEWATER HALL

TICKETLINE.CO.UK   TICKETMASTER.CO.UK   OR VENUE BOX OFFICE

SINFONIA OF LONDON   SINFONIAOFLONDON.COM   A KENNEDY STREET PRESENTATION

A Twist *of Fate*

Two centuries after fado first emerged from the taverns and brothels of Lisbon's trading districts, **SIMON BROUGHTON** charts the difficult history of one of Portugal's most enduring musical exports

Her body beats to a trawler's engine.
She sells dreams and sea-spray;
Storms cry out her name

The imagery of the song's lyrics is all maritime – seabirds, seaweed, fishing boats and warships. The music ebbs and flows like waves against the shore, as the Portuguese guitar nimbly dances out the melody. The song is an affectionate portrait of Lisbon, personified as a fish wife.

Her first name is Maria, her surname Lisboa.

'Maria Lisboa' is one of the most popular songs in the Portuguese fado repertoire, a felicitous marriage of music and poetry. Performing it on stage, Mariza moves one way, then the other, as if driven by the continuous swell of the ocean. The song is iconic for two reasons. Firstly it's a portrait of the city where fado was born, secondly it was written for fado's most celebrated performer, Amália Rodrigues (1920–99). Usually known simply as 'Amália', she was the first person to bring fado to the international stage. 'For us, Amália is still very alive in our memory,' says Mariza, Portugal's leading contemporary fado singer, whose 2020 album *Mariza Canta Amália* ('Mariza Sings Amália') was a tribute to Amália in her centenary year. Mariza appears at the Proms this year as the fadista who has most closely followed in Amália's

◀ Playing with fate: *O Fado*, 1910, by the Portuguese painter José Malhoa (1855–1933)

footsteps in bringing Portugal's most distinctive music to the world.

In Portuguese 'fado' literally means 'fate' and, as a largely wistful, minor-key music, it's often described as the Portuguese blues. It's a description Mariza isn't unhappy with. 'Like the blues, fado has that melancholy feeling,' she says. 'Fado is not sad, it's a sweetly melancholic music. The beautiful thing in fado – again, like the blues – is that we sing the emotions of life. No matter what the culture or language or where you come from, everybody can understand it. Even if you don't literally understand the words, you can feel the emotion. That's why it works internationally.'

Fado isn't folk music, but rather music by known composers and lyricists, although there are some 'traditional' tunes to which 'improvised' lyrics can be attached. While there are cheerful and playful fados, it's melancholy they are famed for, although it's a sadness that consoles, in the way Tchaikovsky's *Romeo and Juliet* or 'Pathétique' Symphony can do. 'Fado português' ('Portuguese Fado'), written for Amália with lyrics by José Régio, says:

Fado was born one day,
When the wind had all but died away
And the sky stretched out the sea
Along the gunwale of a sailing boat,
In a sailor's aching throat,
As he turned his sadness into melancholy,
As he turned his sadness into melancholy.
[Translation by Philip Jenkins]

Although born in Lisbon, fado is multi-ethnic in origin. After Portugal was

invaded by French troops in 1807 during the Napoleonic Wars, the Portuguese royal family transferred the capital to Rio de Janeiro, while the British, allied to Portugal, fought what's known as the Peninsular War. Napoleon was defeated in 1814, and the royal family returned seven years later with a whole retinue of Brazilians and Afro-Brazilians to establish Lisbon's *assimilado* population. It was in the working-class fishing, trading and port districts of the city, where many of the *assimilado* population lived, notably Alfama and Mouraria, that fado took root.

Fado (also the name of an Afro-Brazilian dance) was first heard in the city's taverns and brothels. Its earliest star was a young prostitute called Maria Severa (1820–46), whose mother ran a tavern in Mouraria where she sang and played the Portuguese guitar. She had an affair with the Count of Vimioso, an aristocratic bullfighter, and introduced fado to high society, but died of tuberculosis aged just 26. This tragic early death inspired a book, *A Severa*, which became a play and eventually the first Portuguese sound film in 1931. The fado house where Amália Rodrigues first started performing in the late 1930s was Retiro da Severa, also named in memory of the singer.

As a form of working-class music associated with prostitutes and taverns, fado wasn't favoured by the military dictatorship which took power in a *coup d'état* in 1926 and the subsequent *Estado Novo* (New State) led by authoritarian

Graffiti in Lisbon depicting Portuguese fadista Amália Rodrigues, the first person to bring fado to the international stage

dictator António de Oliveira Salazar. In 1927 laws were introduced subjecting all lyrics to censorship. Songs that had not been approved could not be sung in public. In 1936 the regime ran a series of radio broadcasts entitled 'Fado, the Song of the Defeated' in an attempt to consign the genre to history.

But, despite the disapproval of the regime, fado didn't go away and, after the Second World War, the authorities radically shifted their approach and promoted it as Portugal's national music, emphasising its traditional and family values. 'The Three Fs' – Football, Fatima (referring to the popular Catholic shrine of the Virgin Mary) and Fado – were said to be the pillars of the regime. Amália Rodrigues's rise to fame coincided with this, but her views on the regime are still debated. She made her first recordings in Brazil in 1945 and performed frequently in Spain, France, Brazil and the USA.

Although Amália was promoted by the regime, many of the songs composed for her by Alain Oulman (1928–90) in the 1960s were celebrations of Lisbon and ordinary, working-class people. After nearly 50 years and continuing colonial wars, Portugal's military dictatorship was finally overthrown in the Carnation Revolution of 1974, and fado, tainted by its connections to the old regime, spent a decade or more in the shadows. Still, when Amália died in 1999, there were three days of national mourning – and the renaissance of fado had already begun. That was when Mariza started recording.

It was the world music boom of the 1990s, and a new generation of singers – Mísia, Mariza, Ana Moura and others – that started the serious revival. Mariza's debut album, *Fado em mim*, was released in 2001 and since then she's followed a path between traditional, experimental and crossover. So what to expect at this year's Proms?

'I'm soon releasing a new album, which I'm creating with a group of young Portuguese composers, producers and musicians. So it will be the first hearing of that in the UK, and I'll be revisiting songs from over my 20-year career, including some favourites from the *Amália* album. They will all be in arrangements done specially for this concert.'

In Lisbon, the fado revival is a real phenomenon. There's an excellent Fado Museum in the Alfama district, which opened in 1998; the music was put on the UNESCO Intangible Cultural Heritage list in 2011 (and Mariza was actively involved in the campaign); and, most important, there are many fado houses and a devoted audience. 'In Portugal it's unbelievable that 12-year-olds come to my concerts and really love it,' smiles Mariza. 'In the 1980s nobody took care of fado: no young people were interested. But now it's become really big again.' ●

Simon Broughton is Founding Editor of the world music magazine *Songlines*, and directed the documentary *Mariza and the Story of Fado* (BBC/RTP).

Mariza Sings Fado

PROM 9 • 21 JULY

WEXFORD
FESTIVAL OPERA

WOMEN WAR

24 OCTOBER | 5 NOVEMBER 2023

Donizetti
ZORAIDA DI GRANATA

Erlanger
L'AUBE ROUGE

Tutino
LA CIOCIARA
(Two Women)

WEXFORDOPERA.COM

KINDLY SUPPORTED BY

the arts council chomhairle ealaíon | funding opera artscouncil.ie

Wexford County Council

Fáilte Ireland

IRELAND'S ANCIENT EAST
Wonder Through Time

the **shop** at
BOOSEY.COM

The widest range of classical, educational and choral music available online

- Full scores, study scores and sheet music from all publishers
- Worldwide shipping
- Bulk discounts on choral music
- Digital sheet music
- Exam materials

ANNA CLYNE
MASQUERADE
for Orchestra

rachmaninoff
Piano Concerto No. 2, Op. 18

◀ **Scan for your special offer** | **www.boosey.com/shop**

BOOSEY & HAWKES
A CONCORD COMPANY

Oakham
SCHOOL

Experience.
An Oakham
Education.

We are a high-achieving,
co-educational boarding and day school,
where pupils aged 10-18 learn, grow and thrive
in the heart of rural Rutland.

**Scan to discover more about
our vibrant Music Department and
its national reputation for excellence.**

oakham.rutland.sch.uk

🐦 @OakhamSch   📷 @oakhamschool

f @OakhamSchool   in @Oakham School

Calling exceptional musicians

As one of the leading schools for music
in the country, King's offers generous
awards to outstanding applicants at
13+ and 16+, including full bursaries.
Contact music@kings-school.co.uk

The King's School
Canterbury

www.kings-school.co.uk

Imagine

WIMBLEDON
HIGH SCHOOL
EX HUMILIBUS EXCELSA

GDST
GIRLS' DAY SCHOOL TRUST

**Music Scholarships
at 11+ and 16+**

IMAGINE

This is where you light **your fire** find **your magic** learn to love **your mind**

Bryanston is a leading co-educational boarding and day school in Dorset for pupils aged between 3 and 18.

bryanston.co.uk/yourplace

Realise
your potential

With over 700 instrumental lessons a week and a bespoke music scholarship programme, every Wellington pupil has the opportunity to realise their musical potential.

wellingtoncollege.org.uk/music

QUEEN ETHELBURGA'S
COLLEGIATE

THE SUNDAY TIMES
SCHOOLS GUIDE 2023
INDEPENDENT SECONDARY SCHOOL OF THE YEAR IN THE NORTH FOR ACADEMIC PERFORMANCE

Outstanding academic results
Music and drama scholarships available
Extensive co-curricular programme

Excellent pastoral care for all
Minibus service across Yorkshire
Less than 2 hours from London

Thorpe Underwood Hall, Ouseburn, YO26 9SS | www.qe.org | admissions@qe.org | 01423 333330

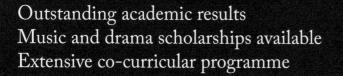

ACADEMY OF ANCIENT MUSIC

MOZART
PIANO CONCERTOS
Nos. 21 & 24

Robert Levin | Richard Egarr

AAM resumes a landmark project begun in 1993 to record Mozart's complete works for keyboard and orchestra.

This ninth volume is released after an extraordinary 20-year wait, and will be followed by the four final volumes later this year and in 2024.

"Levin lives Mozart throughout his entire body, and for every second of the score... he plays the music as if he's writing it himself – for the first time"
The Times

MOZART
PIANO CONCERTOS
K467 | K491
Academy of Ancient Music
Robert Levin | Richard Egarr

Pre-order all five volumes at **aam.co.uk**

Buy | Stream | Download

aam.co.uk

Music *for the* **Soul**

Radio 3's Researcher in Residence **SALLY MARLOW** summarises a range of recent research on how we react to music on an emotional level and, linked to the findings, curates a Proms playlist of works that can be heard this season

ou don't have to be a neuroscientist or a psychologist to believe that music, mental health and emotions are strongly related to each other. The acts of making and listening to music have long been documented as an integral part of the human experience: the Old Testament, for example, relates how King Saul – thought by some to have lived as long ago as 1,000 BCE – summoned David to play his lyre to provide relief from agitation and paranoia, recognising the power of music to help change how we feel. As medicine has progressed to take into account mind as well as body, music has become integrated into psychological therapies.

Much of modern psychiatric treatment was developed to treat the psychological scars of battle, and therapy as we know it today began in the mid-19th century, when musicians played for wounded soldiers in the Crimean War, and in the 1900s music was harnessed more formally into therapeutic treatment for soldiers returning from war with shell shock, or what might now be called Post-Traumatic Stress Disorder.

Today, the technological revolution in how we make and listen to music is being accompanied by a quieter revolution in examining the ways in which music affects mental health. Grass roots music-making and listening have been at the heart of many communities for centuries, but now there is also top-down recognition, spearheaded by an NHS initiative, the National Academy

for Social Prescribing. Social prescribing involves something other than pills or therapy – perhaps an art class, a gardening club or a singing group. As the name suggests, these 'prescriptions' are intensely social, bringing not only a new and meaningful activity into people's lives, but doing that in the context of a group, tackling isolation and bringing a sense of connectedness back to people – something known to be crucial for good mental health.

If social activities are to be prescribed by the NHS, particularly in times of scant resources, there must be evidence that they work. Researchers across the world are exploring how arts and culture might improve mental health outcomes. Data collected recently using scientific search engines identified almost 25,000 different research papers on music and well-being alone, with compelling scientific evidence that music is good for mental health.

So what does this mean for the Proms? There's the music itself – and we now know that different types of music may have different benefits (see following panels). There is also the 'social' part – the concerts themselves provide an opportunity to listen in the company of others (including the wider audience through radio and television), allowing for both an individual and a group experience, speaking to a connectedness in the listening experience. You don't need science to tell you that music can improve your mood or mental well-being but, increasingly, it is proving that these instincts are true.

Sad music can be uplifting

▶ MOZART: 'LACRIMOSA' FROM REQUIEM
Prom 69 • 7 September

Even those of us whose listening tastes tend towards the sunny and upbeat have a handful of sad tunes that we return to again and again. Many researchers have shown that music that by any objective measure should be described as sad can be experienced by listeners as both sad and uplifting. Melancholic music can make us feel that we are understood, that we are not alone and, although the experiences and intentions of the composer may be different to our own, there is something recognisable in the feelings the music conveys. Moreover, sorrowful music can provide a catharsis, a safe way of expressing extreme emotions and a justification for those emotions: someone else has experienced the same thing, so there can't be anything wrong in how we feel. Sad music might bring about physiological changes too: levels of the hormone prolactin increase when we are sad, and this is linked in turn to the production of tears – often shed during an emotional release.

Perhaps Mozart sensed this when he wrote the 'Lacrimosa' – part of the Latin Mass for the Dead, the words referring to the 'tearful' Day of Judgement – of his *Requiem*. But it is the music that expresses profound sorrow, paradoxically also experienced as heartbreakingly beautiful. Mozart returns again and again to the mournful opening motif associated with 'Lacrimosa', sharing his response to it, while we experience our own.

Film music can influence our mood

▶ RACHMANINOV: PIANO CONCERTO NO. 2

Prom 30 • 6 August

Music can make or break a film. Few of us think of *The Dam Busters* without hearing Eric Coates's 'The Dam Busters' March, or of Hitchock's *Psycho* without hearing the screeching strings of Bernard Herrmann's cue for 'The Murder'. These pieces stay with us not just because of their musical quality, but because they evoke strong emotions. 'The Dam Busters' March is hopeful and patriotic, whereas 'The Murder' is violent, unsettling and disturbing. But both have been identified as powerful examples in terms of creating mood states and emotional reactions. In a novel approach, musicologists and psychologists at the University of Oslo led by Dr Jonna Vuoskoski tested hundreds of clips of film music to explore their emotional qualities. They now use the resulting audio database to induce emotions in the psychology lab to test people's responses to stimuli while they are in different emotional states.

Even though it was composed almost half a century earlier, Rachmaninov's Piano Concerto No. 2 reflects the overwhelming, suppressed emotions in David Lean's 1945 film *Brief Encounter*, along with the bittersweet experience of the star-crossed lovers. As Vuoskoski's work in Norway has shown, it is music's ability to move us that gives it its heft: it somehow makes our emotions more accessible. In *Brief Encounter*, we are moved as much by Rachmaninov's music as we are by the story.

Music can unite people in hardship and give meaning to struggle

▶ SHOSTAKOVICH: SYMPHONY NO. 10

Prom 41 • 15 August

Music's capacity to forge connections between people can be particularly powerful in times of hardship. Protest songs such as Nina Simone's 'Ain't Got No, I Got Life' speak of how to preserve your spirit when your way of living is dictated by others; they can even unite listeners and call for action, for example Gil Scott-Heron's 'The Revolution Will Not Be Televised'. In protest songs, both music and lyrics can be equally hard-hitting.

However, music can be a form of protest even without words. Shostakovich's 10th Symphony is notable for the feelings of terror and violence it evokes, and for its underlying despair, yet there is triumph too. Exactly what meaning Shostakovich himself attached to this work has been hotly debated, but one widely accepted interpretation is that he wanted to convey the horror and fear of living in Stalin's Russia, and the triumph as well as the sense of a new beginning felt at Stalin's death. Shostakovich's music speaks to those beyond Stalin's Russia, to different hardships and struggles. Writer, composer and broadcaster Stephen Johnson explored the effect of Shostakovich's work on his own recovery from serious clinical depression in his Radio 3 documentary *A Journey into Light*, arguing that the music speaks to a deeper human spirit. It can soothe all who have suffered, not just those living under Stalin.

Communal singing boosts mental health

▶ MENDELSSOHN: ELIJAH

Prom 19 • 29 July

The recent explosion of television series documenting singing groups, pioneered by charismatic choir-masters such as Gareth Malone and brought to life by personal stories of transformation, is underpinned by strong scientific evidence that singing is good for mental health. Choirs reduce isolation and create a sense of achievement. Dr Daisy Fancourt of University College London is evaluating a singing intervention for women who are at risk of post-natal depression, using the gold standard in healthcare research, a large randomised controlled trial. The early findings of the singing scheme Breathe Melodies for Mums are so compelling that it has been commissioned by over 15 NHS Clinical Commissioning Groups across England. It's not only the mothers who are thought to benefit from these groups – their babies may be more engaged, and the mother/infant relationship may be strengthened too.

Recognising the pay-offs of belonging to a choir is not some 2020s fad. Amateur singing groups of all shapes and sizes have existed for centuries, regularly practising and performing together iconic pieces of music such as Handel's *Messiah* and Mendelssohn's *Elijah*, which were especially popular among Victorian choral societies. It's a safe bet that these groups didn't discuss the psychological benefits of singing together, but that doesn't mean there wasn't an underlying understanding of it.

Brain scans show that joyful music activates particular brain areas

▶ HELEN GRIME: MEDITATIONS ON JOY
Prom 12 • 23 July

Neuroscientists regularly use scanning techniques to explore how music affects the brain. While it might not be surprising that the auditory cortex is activated when listening to music, what's intriguing is that the pattern of activation is different when music is joyful, compared to when it is sad or neutral in mood. The amygdala brain region, central to our fear response, also reacts to joyful music but, again, differently to sad or neutral music. The hippocampus, often described as the seat of memory, is also activated, implying that joyful music is linked to memories, even if not conscious ones.

Composer Helen Grime wanted to capture the joyful in her *Meditations on Joy*: 'The act of composing, although often a huge challenge, can occasionally elicit the most intense feeling of joy, and that is something that I wanted to pervade the whole piece.' Moreover, perhaps neuroscience can help explain why Beethoven's exuberant 'Ode to Joy' from his 'Choral' Symphony has remained such a powerful musical statement through the ages.

Sally Marlow is Professor of Practice in the Public Understanding of Mental Health Research at King's College London, and BBC Radio 3's Researcher in Residence. Her work explores how art and science can combine to throw light on human issues such as mental health.

Relaxed Prom
PROM 25 • 3 AUGUST

Mindful Mix Prom
PROM 34 • 9 AUGUST

Revive, not Survive

Grace Meadows *(below)*, Programme Director of Music for Dementia, describes how music can alleviate the effects of this cruel brain condition

My first encounter with the use of music to help people with dementia happened almost 15 years ago, when I was beginning to explore music therapy. (The experience changed the direction of my life and reignited my relationship with music.) As I observed a music therapist working with a small group of older adults with dementia, I looked on in amazement as she brought the group to life. She was able to use the music to alleviate some of the symptoms of dementia – apathy, anxiety, agitation, depression – and provide the group with a channel through which they could communicate beyond the need for words. In that moment each person was empowered to be creative and contribute to a meaningful experience, enabling them to enjoy a different way of being. The full array of the benefits of music were being activated – cognitive, physiological, biological, neurological, emotional, social and psychological. Ultimately, it inspired me to train as a music therapist.

Music therapists and music practitioners across the country work with people with dementia every day, providing moments of connection, alleviation from symptoms and, most importantly, moments of joy. This was movingly brought to the country's attention in 2020 with Paul Harvey's improvisation 'Four Notes', later recorded by the BBC Philharmonic and released as a digital download in aid of dementia charities. Paul and his piece demonstrate how music provides a channel for people to be seen for who they are beyond their diagnosis.

Currently, not everyone living with dementia in the UK has access to music as part of their care, and not everyone providing care is aware of the power of music for those with dementia. Evidence demonstrates how music not only enhances the quality of life of those being cared for, but also supports the emotional and mental health of carers, improving morale and motivation.

We are inherently and innately musical beings. If we tapped further into this connection, we could be using music much more to address some of the many health and social care challenges we face today. Musical care isn't about being a concert pianist; it's about knowing small and meaningful ways to use music to make a difference to someone's everyday experience. In many cases, it's not about a cure, but about finding a way to live as well as possible with a long-term condition or diagnosis, such as dementia.

We have an opportunity right now to reimagine health and social care through music. We can build on the work of music therapists and music practitioners by equipping all those who use music as part of the care they provide, supporting our musicians who work therapeutically with music. Music can be a key public health tool. If, as a society, we can begin to value music as a necessity rather than a nicety when it comes to health and well-being, we will truly begin to feel and see the power of music in action for all.

Body *and* Spirit

The appearance of disabled performers onstage has become more common only in recent years. As two soloists who have transcended barriers appear at the Proms, **LLOYD COLEMAN** talks to them and looks at some of the work being done to fuel the change

It goes without saying that perhaps the most famous composer to have walked the earth was deaf. But beyond the towering figure of Beethoven, there are several other notable composers whose disabilities are less widely known about.

There's Handel, who was blind for the last years of his life because of a botched eye operation. Joaquín Rodrigo also became blind, aged 3, following a severe case of diphtheria. The contemporary Danish composer Hans Abrahamsen has spoken about living with cerebral palsy, and two prominent British composers, Michael Berkeley and Richard Ayres, have both dealt with the onset of hearing loss.

There has been a sprinkling of disabled performers too: superstar violinist Itzhak Perlman contracted polio as a child and has subsequently used mobility aids. German bass-baritone Thomas Quasthoff was born with shortened limbs as a result of thalidomide taken by his mother during pregnancy. Deaf percussionist Evelyn Glennie has forged a remarkable and unprecedented solo career.

Among the latest generation of disabled artists to join this lineage are two soloists making much-anticipated visits to the Proms this season. Japanese pianist Nobuyuki Tsujii and German horn player Felix Klieser, both yet to reach their mid-thirties, have already established enviable careers with loyal fanbases.

◀ James Rose conducting the Bournemouth Symphony Orchestra's disabled-led ensemble BSO Resound at the Relaxed Prom in 2018

For Nobuyuki Tsujii it's a second appearance, following his spellbinding performance of Rachmaninov's Second Piano Concerto in 2013. Speaking to me on a video call from his native Tokyo, he breaks into a broad smile and remembers it as a 'great honour' to play for the 'passionate and keen' audience.

His deep affinity for Rachmaninov is also clear – in 2009 he won the Van Cliburn International Piano Competition, playing the same work. It seems only natural Tsujii will play its successor, the mighty Third Concerto, for his Proms return this summer. Tsujii describes the Third as a 'challenging piece, but one that I very much love'.

Frenchman Louis Braille invented a universal system of music notation widely used by blind and vision-impaired musicians, but Tsujii explains how he favours learning scores by ear: 'I remember first encountering these Braille scores when I was in primary school. However, only a limited number are available and making new scores takes a long tme.' His piano teacher suggested that it would be faster if Tsujii learnt new pieces aurally, from recordings.

He goes on to describe the degree of trust he must build with the conductor in rehearsal: 'I particularly concentrate on their breathing and try to really feel that sense of breathing with them when playing.'

Aside from these different approaches Tsujii's playing technique is, of course, fundamentally the same as that of non-disabled pianists. By contrast, Felix Klieser's method of horn playing could not be more unorthodox. Born without arms, Klieser has by necessity forged his own path. His non-musical family fully supported his decision to become a professional horn player in his late teens, but there were fewer role models, disabled or otherwise. He found his way by resting the weight of the horn on a stand and using the toes of his left foot to operate the three valve keys.

'The technique of placing the right hand inside the bell is the biggest difference between a normal horn player and me,' he says. 'The hand contributes a lot to what we think of as the typical round, warm horn sound. When you have nothing in the bell, then the sound is completely different, more like a trumpet.'

He tells me about developing his unique technique while a student. 'Of course, there was no-one able to teach me in this specific situation, because no-one ever tried to play the French horn before without putting a hand in the bell. So it was something I worked on by myself. One of the most important things as a musician is to be able to listen to yourself – to listen to what you are doing, how you sound, and then to trust it.'

Trusting in that long process of self-discovery has paid off. Since completing his music studies in Hanover, Klieser has recorded all four Mozart horn concertos with the Camerata Salzburg, won the prestigious Leonard Bernstein Award and been appointed Artist-in-Residence with

Music without limits: Felix Klieser *(top)* and Nobuyuki Tsujii: two Proms artists who have overcome physical or sensory differences to achieve careers as international soloists

the Bournemouth Symphony Orchestra. His Proms debut this summer marks the culmination of his two-year residency with the Poole-based orchestra.

While it's undoubtedly a positive step seeing talents such as Klieser and Tsujii billed at festivals in this way, it was estimated by a 2019 Arts Council England study that just 2 per cent of the UK orchestra workforce identify as disabled. Set that against 19 per cent of the overall UK working-age population who are disabled and you can't miss the issue. As a dual sensory-impaired musician myself (having lived with hearing and vision loss all my life), I passionately believe the problem is not a shortage of talent, but that far too much of it is going to waste.

This is one of the many reasons I'm proud to work for Paraorchestra, a group based in Bristol and the only large-scale ensemble of its kind. Founded by conductor Charles Hazlewood in 2011, Paraorchestra aims to reimagine the concept of an orchestra in many ways, drawing from an integrated pool of brilliant disabled and non-disabled musicians for a project slate about as diverse as you can imagine – spanning music from Kraftwerk to Barry White, Beethoven to Pauline Oliveros, Steve Reich to Hannah Peel.

Our ambitious artistic and artist development programmes are proof that disabled talent exists; it simply needs the right conditions and support to flourish. I'd like to see an industry where more colleagues feel they don't

need to erase their disability, as some hearing-impaired musicians do for fear of being marginalised. Even in the year 2023, backstage facilities in many venues are inaccessible for wheelchair users. What hope do they have of sustaining a touring career if every other hall they go to has inadequate stage access? And the additional needs of performers with hidden disabilities such as chronic fatigue syndrome can make hectic touring schedules (with few days off) impossible for them.

Besides Paraorchestra, I'm relieved to see a small group of UK ensembles starting to address this challenge. BSO Resound – a subsidiary ensemble of the Bournemouth Symphony Orchestra comprising disabled musicians – debuted at the Proms in 2018 with a newly commissioned work by disabled composer Alexander Campkin. At Sage Gateshead, the Royal Northern Sinfonia has RNS Moves, forging new collaborations between its players and disabled talent.

If their experiences have been anything like ours at Paraorchestra, they will agree that a large part of the appeal of working with disabled musicians stems from the myriad new sonic possibilities of assistive technology. What composer wouldn't want to get their hands on a pair of Mi.Mu gloves, a wearable technology that allows the user to perform music in real-time through expressive movements of their hands? Or the Headspace, a headset invented for paraplegic musician (and founding Paraorchestra member)

Clarence Adoo, who can trigger and control a multitude of sampled sounds with small head movements and a blow tube?

There are dozens more examples, many of them supported by charities such as Drake Music, which removes barriers to music-making through the use of technology. And disabled musicians of the future are being greatly helped by OpenUp Music, which established the National Open Youth Orchestra as a training ground for promising young talent. Initiatives such as these simply didn't exist anywhere a few short decades ago.

Our orchestras and opera houses have been rightly challenged to diversify in order to better reflect society outside the concert hall. This of course also applies to rebalancing the number of women and people of colour that we see onstage. If the classical music world can continue to nurture and champion such fine musicians as Felix Klieser and Nobuyuki Tsujii, while addressing the root causes of the lack of disabled talent, then I remain hopeful disabled musicians have a brighter future ahead. ●

Composer, pianist and clarinettist Lloyd Coleman is Associate Music Director of Paraorchestra. He is Chair of the Classical Council for the Ivors Academy and is a member of the South West Area Council for Arts Council England.

Felix Klieser plays Mozart's Horn Concerto No. 4
PROMS 24 & 25 • 2 & 3 AUGUST

Nobuyuki Tsujii plays Rachmaninov's Piano Concerto No. 3
PROM 70 • 8 SEPTEMBER

Mind Over Mattter

BBC Symphony Orchestra Leader Stephen Bryant shares his journey of living and working with OCD

In 2006, just before the BBC Proms season started, I had a breakdown and was diagnosed with severe OCD (Obsessive Compulsive Disorder) and OCPD (Obsessive Compulsive Personality Disorder). At the time the psychiatrist said with a wry smile that this was not a great combination!

OCD is a mental health disorder that manifests itself in seemingly irrational, recurrent thoughts, images or compulsions that interfere with daily life. The compulsions result from an attempt to reduce the distress of the obsessive thoughts. OCPD is characterised by a lack of awareness of other people, rigidity or stubbornness, no coping mechanism for change and is ruled by perfectionism and obsessive attention to detail.

Looking back, the first signs of these conditions seem to have appeared when I was a child. I had a very strong obsession with perfectionism and with detail and got very angry and frustrated when I failed in these areas. At the time it was just put down to me being slightly different as a violinist.

I started playing professionally when I was 16 and from then on, through music college to the present day, I have found it extremely hard to deal with change – which is symptomatic of someone with OCPD.

It was when I was 24 and had been appointed to my first leading post, which I loved, that OCD symptoms began to appear. I started to have intrusive thoughts and distressing images in my head and I began to perform more and more rituals both mental and physical in an attempt to control them. I did not at the time realise what these were, which made it even more difficult to rationalise.

When I was 29, I was appointed leader of the BBC Symphony Orchestra and by then my coping mechanisms had become more extreme. OCD sufferers are usually aware and ashamed of the absurdity of their behaviour but have great difficulty controlling it. I was no different and, because I did not know the cause, I kept my rituals hidden.

During all these years, music (whether playing or listening) was my go-to activity to escape from the OCD, however briefly. When I had the breakdown in 2006 it was because that had finally stopped working.

Following the breakdown, I started seeing an experienced psychiatrist, who explained my condition and prescribed medication and cognitive behavioral therapy. The medication in particular was life-changing and has enabled me to cope with my condition and continue my playing career. I am immensely grateful that it worked for me – for many people it doesn't.

I recently made a conscious decision to talk about my condition – because there seems to be so little understanding of the disorder and so much misrepresentation of it in the media. I sincerely hope that, if more people with the condition talk about it and share their stories, in future years this will change.

Peak
Practice?

How have composers' ailments, afflictions and diseases been treated over time? Former surgeon **JONATHAN NOBLE** searches through the records to make his own diagnosis of how successfully (or otherwise) they were treated by medical professionals of the time

Beethoven triumphed over his health – what he called his 'Jealous Demon' – at a huge cost, and the world is a richer place for that. This leads us to wonder about the extent to which the productivity of composers has been overshadowed or overcome by illness. There is also the question of how accurate the diagnosis or treatment of many composers was in their time and, finally, how precisely posterity has reported this for us today.

Not until the 20th century – with the introduction of anaesthetics, X-rays and antibiotics – do we see appropriate treatment, and even then we can still encounter treatment falling short of the standard a patient was entitled to expect. In 1934 Elgar fell victim to a very late diagnosis. By the time he underwent an operation, bowel cancer had spread beyond any hope of surgical relief, although his symptoms had for many months beforehand suggested this diagnosis. Three years later Ravel died of brain-swelling and bleeding a few days after his head was opened surgically. The need for that operation is questionable, because he was clearly suffering from pre-senile dementia, not improvable by surgery. That same year Gershwin also died hours after neurosurgery for a malignant brain tumour. Pragmatically, both these deaths were probably a

kindness. Neither composer had any real hope of significant recovery; the outcome today would have been the same as that in 1937. Nevertheless, it is concerning to note that a reputable neurologist wrote of Gershwin's symptoms as pointing to the composer being 'probably hysterical', only weeks before he died. By contrast, Bartók's diagnosis of leukaemia was possibly a little late and his life might have been prolonged, like Finzi's a decade later with a similar condition.

But what about lost future works? With better treatment, Elgar might have completed his Third Symphony. Perhaps the most tortured cry on how disease affects composition came from Ravel, who said in 1936 that he still had so much music in his head that he was unable to commit to paper, to play or to sing. He was musically locked in. J. S. Bach and Handel were operated upon for cataracts by a charlatan ophthalmologist, known as the 'Chevalier', John Taylor. Dr Johnson said Taylor's career was 'an instance of how far impudence will carry ignorance'. For Bach and Handel, the legacy of Taylor's ministrations was infection, severe pain and subsequent complete blindness, so that both men composed very little thereafter.

Certain composers' deaths have evoked heated controversy. Tchaikovsky is often said to have committed suicide, on the instruction of a 'kangaroo court', allegedly because the Tsar had learnt of his homosexuality (although this was common within his own household). Alexander Poznansky's careful research

revealed that, within the known facts of Tchaikovsky's movements in his last few days, he couldn't have been at this court. Poznansky also discovered that the story of Tchaikovsky drinking cholera-infected water at Leiner's Restaurant was invented many years later by the composer's nephew, Yury, to prevent any stigma of homosexuality or suicide – both forbidden in Stalin's Soviet utopia – attaching to his uncle's reputation. One of medicine's great mantras is that common things are common, and nearly half a million people contracted cholera in St Petersburg at the time of Tchaikovsky's death, 45 per cent of whom died. The clinical features of Tchaikovsky's last illness were absolutely typical of cholera. When there was a brief improvement in his illness, he thanked his doctors for saving him, an unlikely response for someone who truly wanted to kill himself. Cholera it surely was, but how he contracted it, we will never know.

Another contentious case is that of Robert Schumann, who some believe died of syphilis, though the evidence is circumstantial. Many claim that the proof of his having had syphilis is that, in 1831, he reported a painful wound on his penis. Such lesions are common in sexually active, uncircumcised young men, such as Schumann, whereas syphilitic chancres (sores or ulcers) of the penis are painless. So the case for syphilis weakens. What we do know is that Dr Richarz's care of his patient was awful and sometimes inhumane. Schumann was subjected to cold baths

Under the skin: the muscles of the thorax and abdomen, as depicted by painter and anatomist Jacques Fabien Gautier d'Agoty (1716–85)

Composers' notes: Ravel *(top)* died following an operation to investigate a suspected brain tumour; Tchaikovsky's demise was likely from cholera; Stravinsky lived with a catalogue of ailments but eventually succumbed to heart failure

and straitjackets, and was not allowed visits from his wife Clara. The post-mortem revealed two key findings – first, little evidence of syphilis and, second, an enlarged flabby heart, very common in those who have died of starvation or anorexia. Suffering from bipolar disorder, Schumann died miserable and emaciated in an institution where self-starvation was well known.

There are stories of better treatment enabling composers to continue writing. Debussy's bowel cancer was well treated in late 1915, and he was an early colostomy patient. His last months were awful, but he did manage to complete the Violin Sonata in April 1917 and even dabbled with operatic settings of Shakespeare's *As You Like It* and Poe's *The Fall of the House of Usher*. Stravinsky's life was often extended by heroic medical care. Before 1920 he survived typhoid and Spanish flu. In 1937 he developed a peptic ulcer, then overcame tuberculosis, from which his first wife and daughter perished. In the 1940s he survived pneumonia and began a long-lasting problem with his arthritic neck. In the 1950s he developed colitis, and he recovered well from a stroke in 1956. Serious problems arose when he erroneously gargled with formalin, which, as a preservative of biological specimens, is generally of greater use to the dead than the living. But he was able to travel and fulfil engagements. In 1962 he was profoundly moved on returning, after almost half a century, to Russia. Two years later, he attended the premiere

of his *Abraham and Isaac* in Jerusalem. *Pulcinella* in Toronto in 1967 was the last time he conducted in public. Thereafter, he was treated for his bleeding ulcer, anaemia and gout, then he suffered both arterial and deep-vein thrombosis. The astute have noted that, while he was often regarded as a frail, rambling old man, when lawyers or finance people called, his mind was immediately restored to its famous sharp clarity. In 1971 Stravinsky was observed seated at the piano, still trying to compose. A month later, he was finally admitted to hospital with heart failure and passed away in his sleep. Stravinsky's case is a tribute to 20th-century medicine, and so we may ask how different would the medical outcomes have been for those composers from earlier centuries, had modern medicine been available?

George Pickering, Oxford Professor of Medicine for a dozen years from 1956, once said that the history of medicine is a monument to human folly, the best example being bleeding the patient, a practice that crept even into the 20th century. With modern medicine, Mozart's early death would probably have been averted. In my study of ill health and death in 70 composers, I concluded that half would today have lived much longer. One can fantasise about what further music we might have heard from Mozart, Schubert, Mendelssohn or Chopin, had they lived beyond their thirties.

Curiously, most of those dying young were still among the most prolific composers. Perhaps, if they had lived longer, they would just have retired early, like Rossini and Sibelius. The conductor Hans von Bülow once suggested that Mendelssohn, who died at 38, started as a genius and ended as a talent. Prolonged cases of compositional inactivity were not rare anyway, as we see with Elgar, Rimsky-Korsakov, Glazunov, Rachmaninov and others. Perhaps they, like the retirees, had little or nothing more to say, unlike Delius, who did die of late-stage syphilis. Nevertheless, he soldiered on with his amanuensis, Eric Fenby, his mind alert, despite blindness, shooting pains and paralysis.

We all go about our lives and work to some degree despite bad health, and composers are no different. Chopin, Schubert, Beethoven and Mahler all composed in spite of chronic illnesses. Mahler's demise is distinguished by his having a very early laboratory diagnosis of bacterial endocarditis (an inflammation of the heart lining) in 1910. It did little to prevent his death the following year. But in 1907 he had suffered the dreadful triple hammer blows of his forced departure from his post in Vienna, his little daughter's death and his doctors' discovery of heart murmurs. He was told to avoid strenuous exercise, despite his being very athletic. Although the murmurs betrayed damaged heart valves which led to his ultimate death, the imposition of severe restrictions was unkind and, until near his end, inappropriate – but

that is a modern view, and he would have died as he did until antibiotics became available more than 30 years later.

Finally, far too many composers have been assumed to have suffered from mental breakdown or alcoholism, although Schumann did have bipolar manic depression and Bruckner is likely to have lived with obsessive compulsive disorder. Malcolm Arnold certainly wrestled with alcoholism and psychosis. Sibelius sometimes drank excessively, but true alcoholics seldom lead bourgeois, ordered later lives with a loving family, ultimately dying at the age of 91, as he did. For a pattern of true alcoholism, one needs to look no further than kind, gentle and helpless Mussorgsky, but his case is rather exceptional.

And so countless authors have speculated as to the diseases and causes of death of eminent composers, offering, it is said, over 100 different diagnoses each in the cases of Mozart and Beethoven. The lists of those said to be syphilitic and/or alcoholic are often lengthened, with little or no foundation. Many great composers have left us a legacy of inestimable pleasure and joy, despite having suffered horribly. By looking with clear sight into past clinical judgements, we can do much to rehabilitate the reputations of many of our most popular composers. They deserve it. ●

Jonathan Noble is a retired orthopaedic surgeon who has treated musicians and dancers. A Fellow of the Royal College of Surgeons, he is the author of *That Jealous Demon, My Wretched Health* (Boydell, 2018), which examines the illnesses and deaths of many composers.

A French doctor administers a transfusion of his own blood to a woman dying of a haemorrhage in 1921; the first classification of blood types came only 20 years earlier, significantly improving the success rate of such a procedure

We're proud to champion bold and innovative work by unparalleled artists.

Let's make theatre happen.

Discover more at
concordtheatricals.co.uk

f ⊙ y ▶ ⑤ @concordUKshows

concord
theatricals

WHERE WILL YOUR

LOVE
of
MUSIC

TAKE YOU?

50 ROYAL NORTHERN COLLEGE of MUSIC

rncm.ac.uk

ALLEYN'S
1619

MUSIC IS AT THE HEART OF ALLEYN'S

Alleyn's offers co-educational excellence in a caring community for children aged 11-18. Scholarships and means-tested bursaries of up to 100% of fees are available, including the W.J. Smith Award for exceptional musical promise.

TATLER SCHOOLS GUIDE 2023 Alleyn's School

THE GOOD SCHOOLS GUIDE

@alleyns_music • www.alleyns.org.uk
020 8557 1500 • Townley Road, Dulwich, London, SE22 8SU

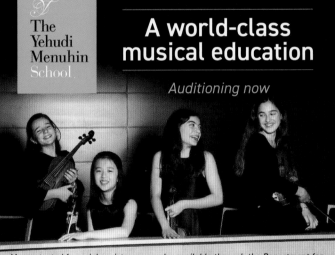

The Yehudi Menuhin School

A world-class musical education

Auditioning now

Means-tested financial assistance may be available through the Department for Education's Music and Dance Scheme or through the School's Bursary Fund.

To find out more, visit **www.menuhinschool.co.uk**
or email: **admin@menuhinschool.co.uk**

The Yehudi Menuhin School, Stoke D'Abernon, Surrey, KT11 3QQ
Registered Charity No. 312010

The Choir of
New College Oxford

director
Robert Quinney

An exciting environment for young singers to experience high-quality music making alongside a world-class education.

Explore opportunities for choral & organ scholars, lay clerks & choristers in concerts, tours & recordings
www.newcollegechoir.com

latest release with Linn Records:
New College Commissions & Premieres

New College

ROBERT QUINNEY CHOIR OF NEW COLLEGE OXFORD

HK Andrews, Paul Drayton, William Harris, Caitlin Harrison, Herbert Howells, Kenneth Leighton, Joanna Marsh, Deborah Pritchard, Toby Young

DULWICH COLLEGE
FOUNDED 1619

Music Scholarships and Bursaries

Dulwich College offers instrumental, organ and choral scholarships and bursaries for talented musicians.

Mr Richard Mayo, our Director of Music, is always pleased to meet prospective candidates and their parents to advise and discuss musical life at the College.

Telephone: 020 8299 9258   Email: music@dulwich.org.uk   www.dulwich.org.uk

THE STOLLER HALL

MANCHESTER'S NEWEST AND MOST UNIQUE CONCERT HALL

A YEAR-ROUND PROGRAMME OF **WORLD-CLASS ARTISTS** AND **ENSEMBLES**

STOLLERHALL.COM

Today's talent prepared for tomorrow's opera

Expert, tailored training to a small number of exceptional opera singers and repetiteurs for free, providing them with the skills they need to survive in a long, successful career in opera.

Get in touch to find out more about our training programmes or if you are interested in supporting our work: info@nationaloperastudio.org.uk
nationaloperastudio.org.uk
Registered charity No. 274755

In partnership with

ENO   GLYNDEBOURNE   opera north   ROYAL OPERA HOUSE   Scottish Opera   WNO WELSH NATIONAL OPERA CENEDLAETHOL CYMRU

NATIONAL OPERA STUDIO

GEORGE ENESCU
FESTIVAL

Generosity Through Music

Full programme on
festivalenescu.ro

27 August - 24 September 2023
Bucharest, Romania

ROMÂNIA
PREȘEDINTELE
ROMÂNIEI

Event held
under the
High Patronage
of the President
of Romania

Cultural Project financed by the
Romanian Government through the
Ministry of Culture

CO-PRODUCER

GUVERNUL
ROMÂNIEI
MINISTERUL CULTURII

ORGANIZER

artexim

Reeling in
the Years

40 °

20 °

This year two visiting Proms ensembles, the Budapest Festival Orchestra and Les Siècles, celebrate significant anniversaries. **RICHARD BRATBY** speaks to their respective founder-conductors and discovers how each is reinventing the role of an orchestra

There must have been hundreds of encores over the 128 years of the Proms. But, even so, no-one who witnessed the second of the Budapest Festival Orchestra's two appearances at the 2018 Proms is likely to forget what happened at the end of that night's concert. Half of the orchestra put down their instruments and – as their colleagues coiled and caressed their way around the opening bars of Brahms's *Hungarian Dance* No. 4 – they sang. Before a speechless Royal Albert Hall audience, Brahms's borrowed melody was returned to its folk-song roots by artists willing to lay aside the tools of their trade – all that hard-won virtuosity – and make music straight from the heart.

Unexpected? Yes. Captivating? Without question. And yet, to anyone who's followed the development of this orchestra over the four decades since its foundation in 1983, it was almost business as usual. If the spontaneity and verve of that evening's performance under Music Director Iván Fischer hadn't already been sufficient proof, that encore demonstrated – once again – that the BFO is not like other orchestras. But then, it was never meant to be.

'The Budapest Festival Orchestra is a kind of laboratory for the orchestra of the future,' says Fischer. The orchestra of the future! Oceans of ink have been spilt

◀ Podium poses: Iván Fischer *(left)* and François-Xavier Roth, founders respectively of the Budapest Festival Orchestra and Les Siècles

in recent years over that vexed but unavoidable subject: there's been talk of new concert formats, of a revised repertoire, of experiments in structure and governance. The BFO is one of a handful of international ensembles that have actually done something about it. 'We have always been a reform orchestra,' says Fischer. 'We're reforming this art form, fundamentally, because I don't think symphony orchestras will exist in the same way in centuries to come.'

'One aspect is the repertoire. We extend the repertoire – not only in terms of earlier or later music, but through specialised groups in the orchestra. We have a group playing Baroque music on period instruments. We have another group specialising in Hungarian instrumental folk music. We have a group specialising in improvisation, and we have jazz groups. The philosophy is that orchestral music is only a narrow segment of our musical heritage. So in our last subscription concert, for example, we started with *Scherzi musicali* ['Musical Jokes'] by Monteverdi, with half of the orchestra playing on period instruments and the other half singing. It's just one example, but we want to be much more open to experiments than other symphony orchestras.'

It's hard to overstate just how liberating those ideas can feel in an orchestral world that is still dominated by the cult of specialism – of excellence in a rich but necessarily circumscribed field. The idea of symphony orchestra players swapping their instruments and adjusting their

technique to play on period instruments would, until recently, have raised eyebrows (and lowered expectations). But a handful of visionary ensembles have been demonstrating that – with the right players and the right philosophy – excellence and experimentation needn't be mutually exclusive. Rather the opposite, in fact: in 2008 the BFO was named by *Gramophone* as one of the 20 greatest orchestras in the world.

> ❝ Les Siècles is an orchestra that aspires to travel between centuries as confidently – and as creatively – as the Budapest Festival Orchestra skips between genres. ❞

Meanwhile the French orchestra Les Siècles, which celebrates its 20th anniversary this year, made its name by playing repertoire – Mahler, Debussy, Stravinsky's scores for the Ballets Russes – in which other period-instrument ensembles feared to tread. Now it comes to the Proms playing on both modern and period instruments in the same concert: one set of instruments for Ligeti, another set for Mozart. For the group's founder-conductor François-Xavier Roth, that's certainly a challenge – but a challenge that gets to the heart of the orchestra's ambition since its inception. Les Siècles is an orchestra that aspires to travel between centuries as confidently – and as creatively – as the BFO skips between genres.

'We want to be much more open to experiments than other symphony orchestras': members of the BFO string section give a 'moving' performance on the streets of Budapest

'When I was a teenager in Paris, I used to listen to Pierre Boulez's concerts – when he'd do programmes with two different orchestras: the Ensemble intercontemporain alongside the Orchestre de Paris or Les Arts Florissants, all in the same concert. For me, it was absolutely gorgeous to experience. But I was already wondering if it could be done with the same players – so that both they and the audience would experience the journey from one style to another. When we first did it 18 years ago, it was a dream come true. I can tell you that it's not easy. It requires very precise rehearsal planning. But it's very, very exciting.'

Still, no amount of rehearsal will generate results like these (and the list of awards and awards nominations racked up by Les Siècles' 2022 recording of Debussy's *Pelléas et Mélisande* says it all) without musicians who are as committed as their conductors to thinking differently.

For Fischer too, the roundedness of his players is key, a feature sought out in the recruitment process. 'One thing which we don't do is auditions,' he says. 'We don't believe in auditions. We believe in inviting people and talking to them, testing them in all kinds of musical activities. We are not only interested in their playing. We are interested in the individual – in their creativity, in the human aspects.' Fischer has said that he feels little interest in being a conductor purely for its own sake. 'I absolutely think the conductor must lead. But what I really don't like is the jaded, bored attitude which usually comes because people

'It's not easy,' says Roth. 'It's what I call real virtuosity – our players change not only the instruments, but also the pitch at which they play. So it's not just the tools for the job that change, but the whole sound-envelope of the orchestra. It's an experience that is very rare – the same concert, with the same players, but with this complete change of sonic costume.' Like Fischer, Roth sees orchestral music as part of a larger cultural conversation – embracing the past, of course, but also the future and, in the process, living thrillingly in the moment.

have to follow instructions all their life. I want to encourage the musicians' creativity, so I give them a lot of freedom. I'm interested in a symphony orchestra that plays with the creativity, risk-taking and emotional impact of a chamber group. An orchestra should be like a magnified string quartet.'

Roth, too, tells a story of musicians who think beyond the routine. 'Part of the richness of Les Siècles is that we took this whole journey together. When I founded the group, it was a chamber orchestra – we rehearsed in my living room. We had no money. We had players coming from the period-instrument scene and others who'd had modern orchestral training, and we learnt from each other. Our first period-instrument project was Bizet's Symphony in C. And so we started to look for and restore the appropriate instruments. It was the same after that for Stravinsky and Debussy and Berlioz. The players and I became completely addicted to that process – we learnt together. Shared learning is part of the DNA of Les Siècles. It was like a drug. Some players had to move into bigger apartments because they'd collected so many historic tubas or bassoons!'

And, once a whole orchestra shares that readiness to experiment, all sorts of innovations become possible. For Roth, the joy of shared discovery is still very fresh – 'We're still babies: 20 years old is a baby age for an orchestra!' – though the ensemble's project-based pattern of working and decision to base itself in the northern French city of Tourcoing are the

marks of an orchestra whose thinking isn't limited by established routines or metropolitan assumptions.

The Budapest Festival Orchestra has a much longer history of experimentation, and the folk bands and the singing aren't the half of it. There have been major successes: 'Cocoa Concerts' for the 5–10 age group – 'I don't know if the children come to hear the music because of the cocoa,' says Fischer, 'or they drink the cocoa because of the music, but the concerts are hugely popular'; and midnight gigs aimed at a student crowd, in which the audience sits on beanbags among the musicians. 'It's a clear message to the younger generation that it's their concert – and they love it.'

There have been occasional misfires, too: the BFO's concert performances of operas – in which Fischer also acts as stage director – have sometimes drawn mixed reviews. That doesn't matter: experimentation, by its nature, implies the right to fail. What matters is that something new has been tried and that the art is moving forwards. It's hard to imagine many orchestras taking a gamble as daring as the BFO's Sunday-afternoon Prom on 13 August, in which the audience will vote on the pieces to be performed from a 'menu' of some 250 orchestral works. How can an orchestra – any orchestra – have 250 pieces up its sleeve, ready to play? The answer is that it can't. The BFO is going to wing it, and the players are not even slightly fazed at the prospect. 'This type of music-making – which is basically sight-reading in front

> **"** I think you need to plant the seed of classical music. The crucial age is between 5 and 10. If in those years you hear some classical music, it will stay with you, even if between 10 and 20 you only listen to pop music. If people are not exposed to classical music, for them it is scary. They don't believe they would understand it.
>
> Iván Fischer in a 2018 interview with *The Times*

François-Xavier Roth leads Les Siècles in Lully's overture to Molière's comedy *Le bourgeois gentilhomme* at the 2013 Proms; Lully famously died from gangrene after reputedly striking his own foot with a similar conducting staff

the musician takes the job as seriously as an actor plays a part in a play, then this wouldn't be a problem.'

So watch this space. And, in the meantime, experience the sound of the orchestra of the future. Or, equally, just enjoy the music in the knowledge that, whether it's Les Siècles or the BFO, whether they're playing Mozart, Ligeti or something entirely unexpected, there isn't a musician present who takes your reaction for granted.

'Absolutely,' agrees François-Xavier Roth. 'We are musicians: we try to celebrate the composer's dreams and everything that surrounded them in their time. But it's also to do with our time, nowadays, and I find it very refreshing that this very old institution, the symphony orchestra, is finding a way to renew itself. Repetition for its own sake is boring. A concert should be something so exciting and so new, and absolutely nothing to do with routine. That's really our goal.' ●

Richard Bratby writes on music and culture for *The Spectator*, *Gramophone*, *The Arts Desk* and the *Birmingham Post*. His book *Forward: 100 Years of the City of Birmingham Symphony Orchestra* was published in 2019.

of the audience – is one example of our innovations,' says Fischer, cool as you like.

And yet you just know that it's going to be amazing. That's one outcome of building an orchestra that consistently thinks and plays differently: doing the impossible comes as standard. Fischer's only regret, after four decades with the BFO, is that he hasn't gone far enough. 'I think, if I started again, I would be more radical. Playing from sheet music and playing seated are two conventions that unfortunately I wasn't radical enough to abolish. Sheet music is a compromise – if

BRISBANE, QUEENSLAND

THE RING CYCLE

WAGNER

OPERA AUSTRALIA

Escape to sunny Australia for this spectacular new production

1–21 December

Queensland Performing Arts Centre

Book now **opera.org.au**

STRATEGIC PARTNERS

   WAGNER 2020 — Generous Patrons Supporting New Productions

| UNIVERSITY PARTNER | PRESENTING PARTNER | ORCHESTRA PARTNER | PRESENTING GOVERNMENT PARTNER | PATRON-IN-CHIEF **DR HARUHISA HANDA** | OPERA AUSTRALIA GOVERNMENT PARTNER |

Book an Australian travel package

Mood Music

Commissioning new music has been central to the ethos of the Proms for many decades. Ahead of the 2023 season, three commissioned composers put their creative process under the microscope, arranging the themes and inspirations behind their music into a series of musical 'mood boards'

Helen Grime

Meditations on Joy
BBC co-commission: UK premiere
PROM 12 • 23 JULY

Scottish composer Helen Grime first came to prominence in 2003, when her Oboe Concerto won a British Composer Award. Twenty years later her third BBC commission, *Meditations on Joy*, receives its UK premiere at the Proms, performed by the BBC Scottish Symphony Orchestra. Grime describes the piece as 'an exploration of joy in its many different forms, from a personal perspective'. Its genesis can be traced back to her discovery of a collection of poems called *Joy*, edited by US poet Christian Wiman. Each of the new work's three movements takes its starting point from a different poem in the collection. Non-musical artworks often provide inspiration for Grime, although, as she points out, 'once the piece starts to take on a life of its own, it can go off in quite a different direction'.

Ancient Jewellery
Early music and a deep connection to human history are important to Grime. A keen collector of Scandinavian and Scottish jewellery, she draws inspiration from their intricate, ancient designs.

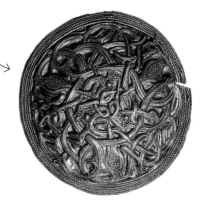

Undercurrent
Meditations was written after a difficult period in Grime's life and is partly about those 'tiny moments where I was starting to feel joy – in life generally, but also in composing'. Among other manifestations, this can be felt in her music as a 'constant, bubbling undercurrent' – a hot spring of feeling.

Creative Cocoon

When composing, Grime likes to create 'a kind of safe cocoon', surrounding herself with things that symbolise power, beauty and strength. In the case of *Meditations*, that included a painting by Paul Harraway and a collection of miniature horses. These suggested depth, layering and colour.

The Tod Head Lighthouse, Catterline

Visual artist Joan Eardley's dedication to her craft continues to be a huge inspiration to Grime, whose 2016 Proms commission (*Two Eardley Pictures*) was written as a direct response to the painter's work.

Elliott Carter

Grime's compositional process often involves building up strands of material into complex layers. It is 'painstaking, slow and linear work' – something she feels has resonances with the music of American modernist Elliott Carter.

Scottish Landscapes

Though she no longer lives in Scotland, Grime says its landscapes and culture are deeply rooted in her identity as a composer. Barren, open spaces in particular have left a lasting impression.

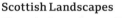

Samy Moussa

Symphony No. 2 *BBC co-commission: European premiere*
PROM 44 • 18 AUGUST

Although based in Germany, Montreal-born composer and conductor Samy Moussa maintains close ties to his North American roots. He is Artist-in-Residence with the Toronto Symphony Orchestra, which co-commissioned his Symphony No. 2 alongside the BBC. As with most of Moussa's work, this is 'absolute' music – not linked to any external narrative or idea – what he calls the 'purest form of composition'. The six images that make up this collage represent themes or 'ideals' that have been long-standing influences on him and his way of thinking. It is his hope that some of what makes these ideals powerful will also be present in his music.

Clarity

Still Life with Three Medlars and a Butterfly by Dutch Golden Age painter Adriaen Coorte is, for Moussa, a perfect example of clarity of expression. It is made, and its subject is presented, in such a way as Moussa would hope to apply in his own practice as an artist.

Austerity

Both 'austerity of content' and 'severity of expression' can be present in Moussa's music, but correspondence between both varies. The former can also suggest majesty: broad, dramatic structures – not unlike Utah's Bryce Canyon – that explore 'the magnitudes of grandness'.

Ontology

For Moussa, composition seeks to discover the fundamental principles of being. Russian artist Ivan Kliun's 1923 painting *Red Light: Spherical Composition* is part of a series focussed on astronomical phenomena and represents an attempt to understand the very nature of being.

The Globe

'It is all one to me where I begin, for I shall come back again there.' Moussa sees these words, from the Greek philosopher Parmenides, as a beautiful expression of circular, globe-like form – an important aspect of his thinking.

Mythological and Ancient Origins

Moussa's work is a contemporary expression of an ancient impulse. He points to a passage from Xenophon's war chronicle *Anabasis* (c400 BCE), with its account of carnyx-like horns, as an example of the power music can hold: 'At this stage entered musicians blowing upon horns such as they use for signal calls, and trumpeting on trumpets, made of raw oxhide, tunes and airs, like the music of the double-octave harp.'

Classicism

The Herodium, an ancient Jewish fortress located in what is now the Palestinian West Bank, is an architectural example of the order Moussa aspires to in his music, with its sharply defined shapes fuctioning as a coherent, monolithic whole.

Derrick Skye

Nova Plexus *BBC commission: world premiere*
PROM 21 • 31 JULY

Los Angeles-based composer Derrick Syke has written music for
ensembles across North America and Europe. His diverse ancestry
has led him to develop what he calls an 'American' musical aesthetic
that embraces a wide range of cultural influences. As such, *Nova
Plexus* combines West African, North African and Indian classical
rhythms and melodies with Eastern European ornamentations and
tonal systems found in Persian classical music; complementing the
full symphony orchestra are parts for various acoustic percussion
instruments, electric guitar and electric bass. Conceptually, however,
Nova Plexus draws inspiration 'from the elegance and power of the sun',
which 'treats all things equally and spreads over all things exposed
to it, causing spectacular effects and reflections depending on the
materials it encounters'.

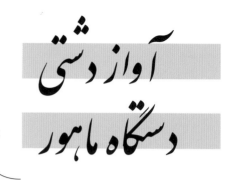

Imprints of Persia
Skye incorporates two Persian tonal
systems in his piece: Âvâz-e Dashti
and Dastgâh-e Mâhur.

Cultural Connections
Skye says he uses music 'as a bridge to
cross cultures and genres in the hope that
it will connect people to each other'. With
its wide range of cultural touchstones,
Nova Plexus fulfils that mission statement.

Tabla Drums
Rhythmic cycles from Indian classical
music feature throughout the piece.

Solar Power

'The sun is the source of life on earth, yet it is also violently destroying itself in the process': *Nova Plexus* takes conceptual inspiration from the sun and its immense capacity for both destruction and beauty.

Sole Music

Movement, momentum and rhythm are central tenets of Skye's music, and body percussion – music for feet and hands – features prominently in Skye's piece.

Patterns in Music

Nova Plexus contains polyrhythms derived from West African music and dance. These complex patterns come together to create 'a single design' reminiscent of the vibrant patterns found in West African textiles.

Kojo Baiden

This Ghanaian adinkra symbol, which translates literally as 'rays', refers symbolically to the cosmos, omnipresence and being-at-one with the universe – important themes in Skye's music.

Gentlemen of the Chappell.

Servants
of the Church and State

William Byrd and Thomas Weelkes, who both died 400 years ago, formed the first apex of the English choral tradition, composing both sacred and secular music. **KERRY MCCARTHY** outlines how, though rebellious in their own ways, they steered a course through the monarchical and religious upheavals of their time

Anyone who has heard English madrigals, or the singing of an English cathedral choir, has heard a sound that was forged by William Byrd and Thomas Weelkes. Both composers died 400 years ago in 1623: Byrd in his early eighties, celebrated as 'a Father of Musick'; Weelkes in his late forties, having been sacked from his cathedral post as a 'common drunkard'. They belonged to the first cohort of English musicians to enjoy the benefits of cheap, fast, accurate music printing, which has made their work splendidly accessible to us four centuries later. Theirs is the sound of the Elizabethan and Jacobean Renaissance in full flower.

As the elder of the two composers, Byrd grew up in a constantly changing world.

◄ The Gentlemen of the Chapel Royal at the funeral procession for Elizabeth I in 1603; the figure far right may be William Byrd, who by this time had been in the Queen's service for over 30 years

He may well have been the boy chorister 'Byrd' (no first name is given) who was in the choir at Windsor Castle in the late 1540s, when the Calvinist-inspired reforms of Edward VI turned musical life upside down from one day to the next: cutting the choir's busy routine down to a handful of minimal services in English and making obsolete every single piece they had ever sung. Byrd was already active as a composer during the brief and fervent Tudor Catholic revival of the 1550s. By his late teens, he was collaborating with older colleagues in London and crossing paths with the visiting court musicians of Queen Mary's husband, Philip II of Spain. Byrd's first long-term post was at Lincoln Cathedral in the 1560s, where the pendulum had already swung back to reformed severity, and where he found himself (like the young Bach in Arnstadt 140 years later) in trouble for excessively ornate organ playing.

By the time Weelkes was born in 1576, Byrd had found a more or less stable position as a member of the Chapel Royal, the monarch's private body of priests and singers. He had also just obtained a 17-year monopoly, shared with his Chapel colleague Thomas Tallis, on the production and sale of printed music. Monopolies and licences of this sort were often handed out as royal favours to lucky clients. Similar privileges were granted for the trade in textiles, gunpowder, starch and the various other substances that held Elizabethan society together. Byrd and Tallis celebrated the occasion with a big collection of motets, the former's first published work ever. His opening piece, *Emendemus in melius*, captures the intense, direct, uncompromising voice of a composer who would have a lot to say in the next 50 years.

Weelkes first appeared on the music scene near the end of the 16th century as a young man with a very new (his own self-deprecating term was 'unripe') book of madrigals. This more or less

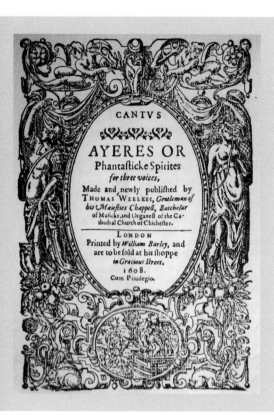

The title-page to Weelkes's *Ayeres or Phantasticke Spirites*, the collection of three-part songs published in 1608

immediately established him as one of the great secular composers of the Renaissance. Weelkes had an unfailing ear for poetry and an almost endless flow of musical inspiration. His subject matter ranges from bawdy fa-la-las to courtly songs with layers of metaphor and exotic imagery. He dips into fashionable Italian texts and Italianate chromatic sounds. Byrd set one Italian poem to music, and his tune is lovely, but his setting is awkward: he comes across as a middle-aged tourist clumsily sounding out the syllables from his travel-guide phrasebook. Weelkes never falters, not once.

Around 1602 Weelkes was appointed by Chichester Cathedral to the triple post of organist, choirmaster and lay clerk, a job that would have been exhausting even under the slimmed-down post-Reformation regime but that gave him the comfortable salary and social status he needed to go on pursuing his own work as a composer. It was during his cathedral years that he produced his last and most modern collection of madrigals, a book of three-voice songs with the delightful name *Ayeres or Phantasticke Spirites*. He also composed some first-rate sacred music, such as the lament *When David heard* and the irresistibly singable *Hosanna to the Son of David*. He himself did not live to enjoy its success. He had wrecked his musical career by 45 and did not survive to see 50.

Byrd's career took an unexpected turn during the same years. After two decades of relative tolerance, Elizabeth I began in the 1580s to crack down hard on Catholics, their religious practices and their daily lives. Byrd, as a Catholic himself, was soon involved in all of this on a quite visceral level. His house was searched, his mail was read, his family members were arrested, and one colleague was interrogated until he admitted that he had been singing 'songs of Mr Byrd and Mr Tallis, and no other unlawful song'. Many of Byrd's 'songs' from these years could easily have been perceived as 'unlawful'. He had been composing Latin motets with anguished political messages about the captivity and exile of his fellow Catholics. Then he began to write and publish a series of Latin Masses, one each for three, four and five voices. The celebration of a Catholic Mass was just about the most illegal activity that could take place in Elizabethan England. Byrd's three Masses contain music of unforgettable beauty, especially in their settings of the Agnus Dei; he quietly had them printed, as small pamphlets, with no dedication or title-page. He also composed some fine pieces for the Church of England in his later years, although he had left his active duties as a court musician and retired to rural Essex to live a less hazardous life. Some of those English-texted works have become classics of the cathedral repertoire, including his anthem *Sing joyfully* (sung at the christening of King James I's baby daughter in 1605) and his sonorous double-choir 'Great Service'.

Both Byrd and Weelkes have attracted their share of legends and exaggerations, even in their own lifetime. An English Jesuit who gave a first-hand account of

Byrd's clandestine Catholic music-making (he noted that there were both men and women singers) also claimed of Byrd that 'for his religion he sacrificed everything, both his office and the court, and all those hopes which are nurtured by such persons'. This was not entirely true. In fact some of Byrd's most uncompromisingly Catholic publications were approved by Church of England censors, who seem to have been happy to overlook the nonconformity of a brilliant musician. He also kept his official status at court and was paid every penny of his salary until the day he died.

Weelkes seems to have been exaggerating in the other direction when he declared on the title-page of his *Ayeres or Phantasticke Spirites* that he was a 'Gentleman of his Maiesties Chappell', a claim that may have helped him sell books but for which there is absolutely no evidence. The appalling and hilarious story of a drunken Weelkes urinating on the Dean of Chichester from the organ loft is also not found in any historical source or any document before the 20th century. It seems to be nothing more than modern musicians' lore.

Unlike many of their English musical contemporaries, neither Byrd nor Weelkes ever chose to travel abroad. That did not stop Weelkes from achieving one of Renaissance England's great feats of imaginative exploration, his madrigal *Thule, the period of cosmography*, which takes the listener on a tour of the world and its wonders. Several members of Byrd's own family were involved in international commerce – most notably

his elder brother John, who had been a chorister at St Paul's Cathedral but who traded in his music books for a fleet of ships that he sent to four of the seven continents, exporting, importing and sometimes engaging in armed privateering. Byrd himself had many interests other than music. He liked to indulge in amateur lawyering, with mixed results. He was an avid reader of political books (usually of an anti-Catholic bent) and he inscribed his own name on their title-pages. He was known to be 'excellent in the Mathematicks'. Although Weelkes had a talent for marketing and a finger on the pulse of English Renaissance poetry, he (unlike Byrd) did not spend time on the pursuits of the gentleman amateur. In the preface to his monumental *Madrigals of Five and Six Parts*, he wrote: 'I confess my conscience is untouched with any other arts.' He followed that with a striking statement that will still ring true to many ears: 'Many of us musicians think it as much praise to be somewhat more than musicians, as it is for gold to be somewhat more than gold.' •

Kerry McCarthy is known for her work on the English Renaissance. Her publications include biographies of Thomas Tallis (OUP, 2020) and William Byrd (OUP, 2013). She is also active as a professional singer, and her next book is a wide-ranging study of the lives of singers in Tudor England.

Byrd sacred and secular choral music
PROMS AT LONDONDERRY • 15 JULY
(see pages 140–141)

Weelkes secular madrigals
PROMS AT ABERYSTWYTH • 30 JULY
(see pages 140–141)

Byrd Diliges Dominum
PROM 34 • 9 AUGUST

> 66 The exercise of singing is delightful to Nature, and good to preserve the health of man.
>
> The better the voice is, the meeter it is to honour and serve God therewith; and the voice of man is chiefly to be employed to that end.

Two of William Byrd's eight 'reasons briefly set down … to persuade everyone to learn to sing', from the preface to his 1588 collection *Psalms, Sonnets and Songs of Sadness and Piety*

**Berliner
Philharmoniker**

\ Digital
Concert Hall

Stream our concerts live and on demand

- Over 700 concerts and many playlists in a unique archive

- A look behind the scenes with portraits, interviews and films

- In the best picture and sound quality available

Start your 7-day trial today
digitalconcerthall.com

IIJ Internet Initiative Japan Streaming Partner of the
Digital Concert Hall

The Proms on *Radio, TV and Online*

" I will never forget balancing the small [radio] on the iron bar to which my chains were secured and tuning in for the first time. It was the First Night of the Proms and Elgar was being played. That music ... was the first I had heard for years and it meant so much to me.

Humanitarian and author Terry Waite, who was held in captivity in Beirut for over four years, recalls hearing the Proms broadcast on the BBC World Service

The BBC has been broadcasting Proms since 1927, so fulfilling its remit to 'inform, educate and entertain' while at the same time honouring the festival's goal as outlined by founder-conductor Henry Wood: to bring the best in orchestral music to the widest possible audience. Today, with Proms broadcasts available across radio, TV and online, Wood's vision remains at the core of the festival.

On Radio

Hear every Prom live on BBC Radio 3 and on BBC Sounds, where you can listen on demand for a full year afterwards and also access all of BBC music, radio and podcasts. Proms artists will also feature on Radio 3's *In Tune* every weekday evening throughout the season, with live performances and conversation, while *Summer Record Review* will highlight a Proms composer in its weekly 'Building a Library' feature.

On TV

Suzy Klein, Head of Arts and Classical Music TV, says: 'The Proms remains the greatest classical music festival in the world, not only for the quality of the music but also for its extensive broadcast coverage. I'm delighted we're once again bringing the best of this season's concerts to your screens, whether you're watching on a TV, laptop, smartphone or tablet, and wherever you are in the UK. Audiences on BBC One, BBC Two, BBC Four and iPlayer can enjoy breathtaking musicianship from the First Night anticipation of a thrilling season ahead to the fun and tradition of the Last Night, and much in between!'

Online

Make sure you visit bbc.co.uk/proms for everything you need to know about the Proms, including what's on, how to buy tickets, an A–Z of past performances and full details on how to watch and listen. ●

🐦 @bbcproms   ⓕ @theproms   ⊙ @bbc_proms   #bbcproms

SOUNDS   **iPLAYER**

SCAN ME

Welcome to Knightsbridge School

Discover a vibrant community and bold education for pupils aged 3-16 years located in the heart of central London.

Tours available each week by appointment
Please scan the QR code above to book a school tour today.

www.knightsbridgeschool.com

PLEYEL
Depuis 1807 à Paris

WHEN THE CONCERT IS OVER, LET THE MUSIC CONTINUE

GRAND PASSION
PIANOS
distinction restored

The only piano company in the UK
solely offering grand pianos
www.grandpassionpianos.co.uk
info@grandpassionpianos.co.uk
0800 233 5213
020 7323 9529

1896 Pleyel Modèle D grand piano

2007 Steinway Model B grand piano
Grand Passion Pianos offers instruments from Steinway & Sons as a wholly independent dealer

KINGS PLACE
SOUND UNWRAPPED

A deep dive into spatialised listening
experiences and immersive sonic events

Fri 22 Sep
Aurora Orchestra
Music by Anna Meredith &
UK premiere by Caroline Shaw

Sat 24 Jun
London Sinfonietta
Sound Unwrapped: Turning Points

Sun 16 Jul
Genesis Sixteen & Friends
Spem In Allium

Fri 29 Sep
I Fagiolini
Monteverdi 1610 Vespers

Sun 1 Oct
Éliane Radigue
Exploring
Occam
Rhodri Davies
& friends

Thu 12 Oct
Gesualdo Six
& Matilda
Lloyd
Radiant Dawn

Thu 16 Nov
Voces8
Secret Chorales

Sat 25 Nov
Aurora Orchestra
In the Light of Air

Sat 2 Dec
Sean Shibe & Shiva Feshareki
Seismic Orchestra Wave

Book tickets at kingsplace.co.uk
90 York Way, King's Cross, London N1
The cultural pulse of King's Cross

DECCA

> "SPELLBINDING"
> — NEW YORK TIMES

BENJAMIN GROSVENOR

> "A PIONEERING MUSICIAN"
> — LE MONDE

LISTEN TO BENJAMIN GROSVENOR'S AWARD-WINNING PIANO RECORDINGS

---

arcola theatre

OPERA FESTIVAL GRIMEBORN
12.07.23 - 23.09.23

Grimeborn Opera Festival is back for its 16th year! Join us at the Arcola Theatre in the heart of East London for a festival of opera, contemporary music and theatrical innovation.

Grimeborn not only makes opera as accessible as possible, by providing some of the lowest ticket prices across the UK, but also challenges the perception of opera, staging distinctly radical, thought-provoking productions from artists and companies who are revered worldwide.

Supported using public funding by
ARTS COUNCIL ENGLAND

020 7503 1646
www.arcolatheatre.com

Arcola Theatre
24 Ashwin Street
E8 3DL

LAKE DISTRICT SUMMER MUSIC FESTIVAL
28 JULY - 6 AUGUST 2023

BOOK YOUR ESCAPE TO THE LAKE DISTRICT

www.ldsm.org.uk | 01539 266200

Last year we helped to save over 200 churches

NATIONAL CHURCHES TRUST

Yours for good.

(C) Marylebone Music Festival: photographer Sam Gregg

Music needs churches.
Please help keep them open for the future.

From Evensong to Elgar, Rock to Requiems the UK's churches are the perfect home for concerts and choirs as well as being vital venues for rehearsals and recordings.

Churches have also nurtured musicians such as Tasmin Little and Ed Sheeran.

But time takes its toll on all of us and churches are no exception.

Many are threatened with leaking roofs, crumbling stonework and the lasting effects of closure during the pandemic.

Last year, we helped fund urgent repairs and new community facilities at over 200 churches, helping keep them open and the music playing today, and tomorrow.

A legacy from you can help save even more.

To find out how you can help keep the UK's churches alive, please call Claire Walker on **020 7222 0605,** email: **legacy@nationalchurchestrust.org,** visit: **nationalchurchestrust.org/legacy** or complete the coupon below.

☐ Please send me details about leaving a legacy to the National Churches Trust. (Please affix a stamp.)

Forename _____ Surname _____

Address _____

Postcode _____ Email _____

Return to Claire Walker, National Churches Trust, 7 Tufton Street London SW1P 3QB.

Your information will be treated as private and kept securely, we will never make public, swap or sell your details: www.nationalchurchestrust.org/privacy-policy. We will write to you around four times a year with newsletters, our Annual Review and invitations to events. If you would rather NOT hear from us by post please tick this box ☐

PG - 23

◎ SCAN ME

Registered charity number 1119845

(FR) Registered with FUNDRAISING REGULATOR

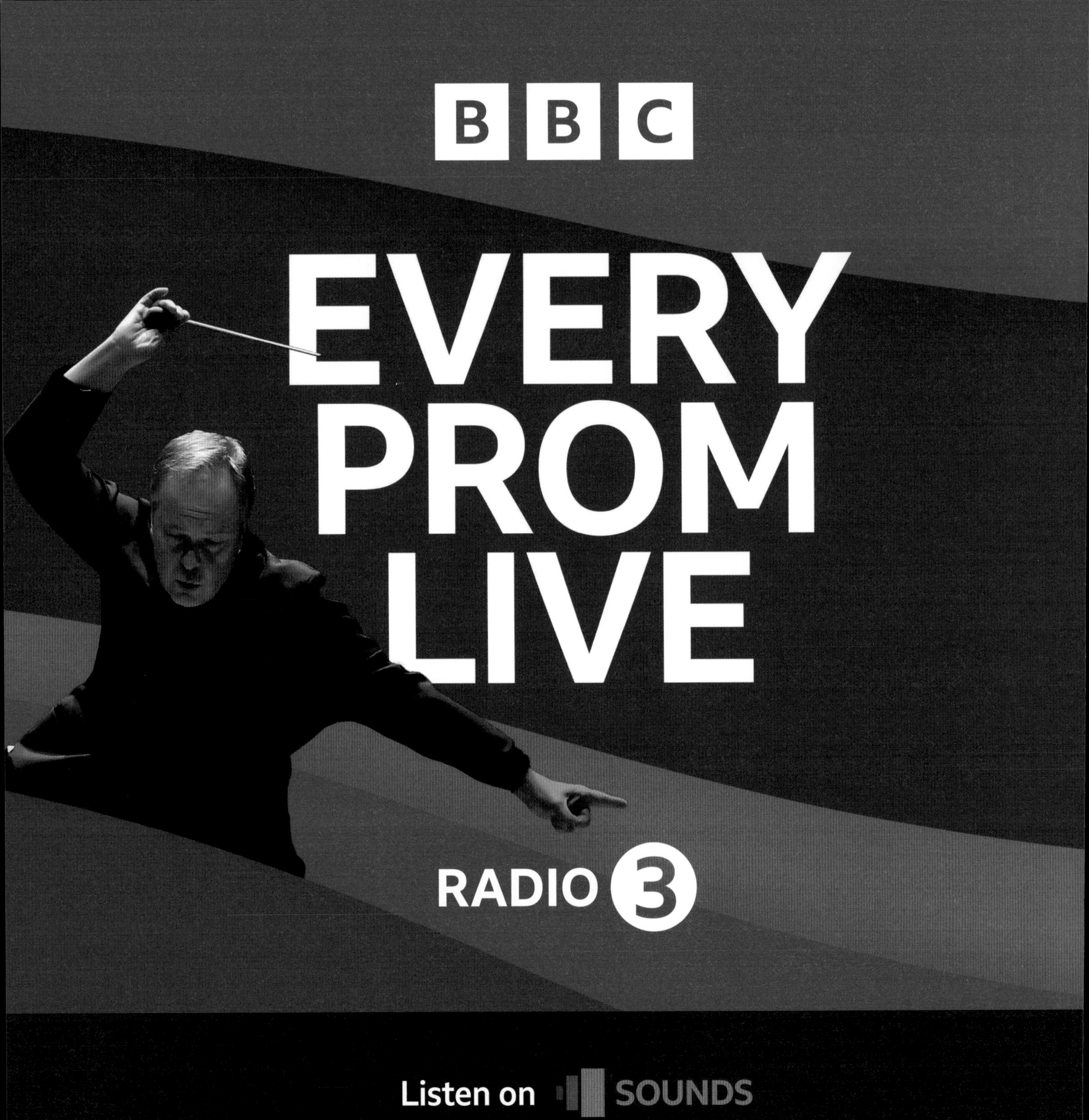
BBC
EVERY
PROM
LIVE
RADIO 3
Listen on SOUNDS

Concert Listings

Full details of all the 2023 BBC Proms concerts – 71 Proms at the Royal Albert Hall, plus five 'Proms at' Chamber Concerts around the country, the first weekend festival of Proms at Sage Gateshead and a BBC Concert Orchestra performance in Great Yarmouth – are listed in these pages, as well as Spotlight interviews with 25 artists.

For an at-a-glance calendar of the whole season, see inside front cover.

Please note: concert start-times vary – check before you book.

We hope you enjoy a summer of world-class music-making.

On Radio, TV and Online

BBC RADIO 3 — **Every Prom is broadcast live on BBC Radio 3 and available on BBC Sounds.**

Many Proms are also broadcast on BBC TV and available on BBC iPlayer.

Booking

Online
bbc.co.uk/promstickets
or royalalberthall.com

By phone
on 020 7070 4441*

General booking
opens at 9.00am on Saturday 13 May.
For booking, venue and access information, see pages 145–153.

PROGRAMME CHANGES
Concert details were correct at the time of going to press. Please check the BBC Proms website for the latest information. The BBC reserves the right to alter artists or programmes as necessary.

*CALL COSTS
Standard geographic charges from landlines and mobiles apply. All calls may be recorded and monitored for training and quality-control purposes.

Spotlight on ...

Paul Lewis • Prom 1

'I've no idea when I first got to know the Grieg Piano Concerto. I must have been 8 or so.' Pianist Paul Lewis is reflecting on his long relationship with one of the best-known and most-loved piano concertos in the repertoire, which he performs at this year's First Night of the Proms on 14 July. 'I played it a lot in my twenties ... But then I left it for about 15 years, and coming back was like meeting an old friend. I used to think it was a beautiful piece. Now I think it's a great and a wonderfully written one.'

That's 'wonderfully written', however, with certain reservations. 'The piano writing can be quite awkward: it's exposed in ways you might not expect, and it doesn't lie under the hands in a particularly grateful way.' But those challenges, he continues, are just part of the concerto's charm. 'It's the job of the performer to make it sound in the most naturally lyrical way possible, because that's the character of the music.'

Lewis performed the concerto last year, closing the annual festival in Grieg's home town, Bergen. 'That was quite a big deal – it's not somewhere where you want to play it badly. But then neither is the First Night of the Proms!' Lewis has been a regular Proms visitor for many years but, he says, it never loses its magic. 'It could never become commonplace. The huge Arena is challenging for a pianist, but it's really a case of not overthinking how you play in that space, not being afraid to play softly and draw the audience in.'

Friday 14 July

PROM 1
7.00pm–c9.00pm • Royal Albert Hall

● £14–£62 *(plus booking fee')*

DALIA STASEVSKA

First Night of the Proms 2023

Sibelius Finlandia	8'
Bohdana Frolyak new work	c5'
BBC commission: world premiere	
Grieg Piano Concerto in A minor	30'
INTERVAL	
Sibelius Snöfrid	14'
Britten The Young Person's Guide to the Orchestra	18'

Paul Lewis *piano*

BBC Symphony Chorus
BBC Symphony Orchestra
Dalia Stasevska *conductor*

The BBC Proms kicks off with a musical introduction to the orchestra from the BBC Symphony Orchestra, Chorus and Principal Guest Conductor Dalia Stasevska. Get to know every section from strings to timps in Benjamin Britten's much-loved *Young Person's Guide to the Orchestra* – a witty showcase for each instrument, culminating in an exuberant fugue. There's a Nordic flavour to a first half that includes Grieg's passionate Piano Concerto, steeped in the sounds of Norway, and Sibelius's powerful statement of national identity, *Finlandia*, as well as a world premiere from Ukrainian composer Bohdana Frolyak.

🖵 *Broadcast on BBC TV*

Saturday 15 July

PROM 2
8.00pm–c9.30pm • Royal Albert Hall

● £14–£62 *(plus booking fee')*

NORTHERN SOUL

Keep the Faith: Northern Soul

BBC Concert Orchestra
Edwin Outwater *conductor*

There will be no interval

Writer and broadcaster Stuart Maconie curates a stomping celebration of the underground British club phenomenon of the 1960s and 1970s that took English towns across the industrial North and Midlands by storm: Northern Soul. What began as a celebration of forgotten American soul B-sides, combining impassioned lyrics with an upbeat rock tempo, became a euphoric release at all-night dances for a young generation working in the industrial North and living for the weekends. Tracks including 'There's a Ghost in My House', 'Turnin' My Heartbeat Up', 'Tainted Love' and 'Out on the Floor' are given the symphonic edge by the BBC Concert Orchestra under Edwin Outwater. Experience the non-stop beats that drew people from across the country to clubs such as Manchester's Twisted Wheel, Wigan's Casino and Blackpool's Mecca.

🖵 *Broadcast on BBC TV*

Every Prom live on BBC Radio 3 and available on BBC Sounds

Sunday 16 July

PROM 3
11.00am–c12.30pm • Royal Albert Hall ☀

● £10–£52 *(plus booking fee')*

BENJAMIN GROSVENOR

Liszt Réminiscences de Norma   17'
Debussy, arr. Borwick Prélude
à l'après-midi d'un faune   10'
Ravel
Le tombeau de Couperin   26'
La valse   12'

Benjamin Grosvenor *piano*

There will be no interval

Former BBC Young Musician of the Year
Benjamin Grosvenor has been a regular since
his Proms debut over a decade ago. This season
the 'intelligent' and 'dazzling' pianist presents
a solo recital with a French accent. A pair of
transcriptions and arrangements bring new
textures and colours to works better known
in other guises. The sensuality of Debussy's
Prélude à l'après-midi d'un faune melts into
Ravel's tender *Le tombeau de Couperin* suite and
his heady, war-scarred *La valse*, while a passing
visit to the Italian opera comes courtesy of
Liszt's virtuosic reimagining of Bellini's *Norma*,
a bel canto tale of warring Druids and Romans,
set in ancient Gaul. *See 'Peak Practice?',*
pages 76–79.

Sunday 16 July

PROM 4
7.30pm–c9.40pm • Royal Albert Hall

● £14–£62 *(plus booking fee')*

PEKKA KUUSISTO

Andrea Tarrodi Birds of Paradise   8'
Beethoven Symphony No. 1
in C major   26'

INTERVAL

Vivaldi The Four Seasons   55'

interspersed with folk music improvisations

Ale Carr *cittern*

Deutsche Kammerphilharmonie Bremen
Pekka Kuusisto *violin/conductor*

Birdsong and barking dogs, trickling streams
and chilly winter winds come to musical life
in a concert inspired by the natural world.
A BBC documentary was the starting point
for Swedish composer Andrea Tarrodi's *Birds
of Paradise*, whose iridescent colours and
sharp textural contrasts capture the 'strange
and beautiful' exotic birds. Closer to home, a
cuckoo calls out in Vivaldi's *The Four Seasons
(see Prom 68)*, whose pastoral scenes are heard
as never before here – interspersed with folk
music improvisations by dynamic soloist Pekka
Kuusisto and citternist Ale Carr. One of the
most distinctive and exciting musicians of
his generation, Kuusisto also conducts one
of Europe's leading chamber orchestras –
the Deutsche Kammerphilharmonie Bremen.

📺 *Broadcast on BBC TV*

Monday 17 July

PROM 5
7.30pm–c9.35pm • Royal Albert Hall

● £9–£42 *(plus booking fee')*

ANJA BIHLMAIER

Coleridge-Taylor Ballade   11'
Bruch Violin Concerto No. 1
in G minor   25'

INTERVAL

Brahms Hungarian Dances –
Nos. 1, 3 & 10   7'
Bartók Concerto for Orchestra   36'

Bomsori *violin*

BBC Philharmonic
Anja Bihlmaier *conductor*

South Korean star violinist Bomsori
makes her Proms debut with Bruch's much-
loved First Violin Concerto – the 'richest'
and 'most seductive' of all the concertos for
the instrument, according to 19th-century
virtuoso Joseph Joachim. The folk music that
runs through the Bruch also pulses through
Brahms's lively *Hungarian Dances*, transformed
in turn by Bartók into new sophistication and
brilliance in his *Concerto for Orchestra* – a
musical tour de force that takes listeners from
'sternness' to 'life-assertion'. This season's
focus on the music of Samuel Coleridge-Taylor
begins with the composer's lyrical, Elgar-
inspired *Ballade*. Anja Bihlmaier conducts the
BBC Philharmonic, also making her Proms
debut. *See 'Taylor-Made Sounds', pages 56–58.*

📺 *Broadcast on BBC TV*

Spotlight on ...

Elena Urioste • Prom 7

Connecticut-born, London-based violinist Elena Urioste has found herself something of a champion of Coleridge-Taylor's often overlooked Violin Concerto, through several performances and a recording with the Chineke! Orchestra. 'It's one of the most emotionally direct, sumptuous, romantic works I've ever had the pleasure of playing. It absolutely belongs in the same league as the Bruch or Mendelssohn concertos: it's accessible for players and listeners, and it takes everyone on an emotionally fulfilling journey.' She's looking forward to her performance of the concerto with the BBC NOW and Tadaaki Otaka on 19 July, following her Proms debut last year: 'Walking out onto the stage of the Royal Albert Hall was one of the greatest thrills of my career so far.'

Coleridge-Taylor was himself a violinist. How does Urioste find his writing for her instrument? 'It works beautifully: he knew all the virtuoso "tricks" and how to write them so as not to scare off the performer.' Urioste also feels it's crucial for us to gain a fuller appreciation of the breadth of music that's been created, but perhaps unfairly disregarded. 'I'd rather perform a great work that's in need of a bit of advocacy than an old war-horse. It enables me to treat the performance with an "allow me to tell you a story" mindset, which is infinitely more liberating than fretting that an audience will be comparing me with the last person they heard play a famous concerto.'

Tuesday 18 July

PROM 6
7.30pm–c9.40pm • Royal Albert Hall

● £10–£52 *(plus booking fee')*

SIR STEPHEN HOUGH

Grace-Evangeline Mason
new work   c5'
BBC commission: world premiere

Rachmaninov Piano Concerto No. 1
in F sharp minor   27'

INTERVAL

Mahler Symphony No. 1
in D major   53'

Sir Stephen Hough *piano*

BBC Philharmonic
Mark Wigglesworth *conductor*

In the 50th-anniversary year of the Royal Northern College of Music, the BBC Philharmonic alongside players from the college, under Mark Wigglesworth, perform a concert of early-career works. RNCM alumnus Sir Stephen Hough is the soloist in Rachmaninov's First Piano Concerto – a work full of Romantic passion and 'youthful freshness', written while the composer was still a teenage student. Mahler's First Symphony began life as a tone-poem, and vivid echoes still remain in the birdsong, fanfares, storm and funeral march of the spirited final work. The concert opens with a new commission from rising-star composer and RNCM graduate Grace-Evangeline Mason. *See 'Welcome Back, Mr Rachmaninov', pages 14–18; 'Agony and Ecstasy', pages 38–43.*

Wednesday 19 July

PROM 7
7.00pm–c9.10pm • Royal Albert Hall

● £9–£42 *(plus booking fee')*

TADAAKI OTAKA

Rachmaninov, orch. Respighi
Five Études-tableaux   25'

Coleridge-Taylor Violin Concerto
in G minor   33'

INTERVAL

Beethoven Symphony No. 5
in C minor   31'

Elena Urioste *violin*

BBC National Orchestra of Wales
Tadaaki Otaka *conductor*

Just four notes – a thunderclap? Fate's heavy knock? – are the kernel of Beethoven's most famous symphony, while Rachmaninov's *Études-tableaux*, richly orchestrated by Respighi, teem with stories and images: the sea, a bustling fairground, Little Red Riding Hood. For Samuel Coleridge-Taylor, inspiration took human form. American violinist Maud Powell – a fellow musical pioneer, battling gender discrimination even as the composer himself faced racial discrimination – prompted a rhapsodic, 'Taylor-made' Violin Concerto, with echoes of Dvořák and Elgar and a ravishing slow movement. Violinist Elena Urioste, a former BBC Radio 3 New Generation Artist, joins the BBC National Orchestra of Wales and Conductor Laureate Tadaaki Otaka. *See 'Welcome Back, Mr Rachmaninov', pages 14–18; 'Taylor-Made Sounds', pages 56–58.*

💻 *Broadcast on BBC TV*

Thursday 20 July

PROM 8
7.30pm–c9.30pm • Royal Albert Hall

🔵 £9–£42 *(plus booking fee*)*

MARÍA DUEÑAS

Falla La vida breve – Interlude and Dance   8'
Lalo Symphonie espagnole   33'

INTERVAL

Debussy Images – Ibéria   20'
Ravel Boléro   13'

María Dueñas *violin*

BBC Symphony Orchestra
Josep Pons *conductor*

Josep Pons and the BBC Symphony Orchestra mark the 200th anniversary of French Romantic composer Édouard Lalo's birth with his most famous work, the vivacious *Symphonie espagnole* – a fiesta in sound. 'Dazzling' young Spanish violinist María Dueñas – a BBC Radio 3 New Generation Artist and winner of the 2021 Yehudi Menuhin International Violin Competition – is the soloist. Debussy and Ravel paint Spain in their own distinctive colours: Ravel with the raw heat and insistent thrum of his *Boléro* and Debussy in the vivid musical vignettes of *Ibéria* – people dancing in the streets, a perfumed garden at night, and a bustling feast-day celebration. The concert opens in Andalusia, with music from Falla's tragic opera *La vida breve*, set in sun-soaked Granada. *See 'Peak Practice?', pages 76–79.*

Friday 21 July

PROM 9
8.00pm–c9.30pm • Royal Albert Hall

🔵 £9–£42 *(plus booking fee*)*

MARIZA

Mariza Sings Fado

Mariza

Luís Guerreiro *Portuguese guitar*
Phelipe Ferreira *guitar*
João Frade *accordion*
Dinga *bass guitar*
João Freitas *percussion*

There will be no interval

The 'musical soul' of Portugal, its keening melodies charged with passion, longing and despair, fado comes to the Proms for the first time in this performance by one of its greatest living exponents. Award-winning singer Mariza makes her Proms debut, bringing her own distinctive style to the music that put fado on the international map. She is joined by fado instrumentalists and an ensemble of strings for a Prom that includes favourite songs from her 20-year career and a glimpse of her forthcoming album. *See 'A Twist of Fate', pages 60–62.*

📻
Every Prom live on BBC Radio 3 and available on BBC Sounds

Spotlight on …

Josep Pons • Prom 8

Catalan-born conductor Josep Pons brings a Spanish-themed programme to the Proms on 20 July. But it's a Spain mostly conjured through the musical imaginations of three Frenchmen: Lalo, Debussy and Ravel. 'There was a fascination with all things "Spanish" in the second half of the 19th century in Paris. Really, though, this was a gaze towards the unknown – an "imaginary paradise". Everything was imagined, with little travel involved! But it produced some beautiful music.' Pons points to some immediately identifiable Spanish elements in these pieces. 'Using the orchestra to imitate a guitar – that's found repeatedly in the Lalo and Debussy. Also percussion instruments – castanets and tambourines – and Spanish rhythms. More importantly, though, each composer captured the spirit – "el duende", which is the essence of Spanish music – in their own way.'

He's joined by Granada-born violinist María Dueñas for Lalo's *Symphonie espagnole*. Do Spanish performers bring a particular authenticity to this music? Pons isn't so sure. 'I don't believe in the exclusivity of genres according to geographical origin. I believe in talent, sensitivity and study. Being Spanish is no guarantee for doing Spanish music well, just as being German doesn't mean you'll necessarily do Brahms or Wagner well. If Debussy and Ravel can capture the most intimate essence of Spanish music with absolute precision, performers from other countries can too.'

Saturday 22 July

PROMS 10 & 11 ☀
2.00pm–c4.00pm & 6.00pm–c8.00pm
Royal Albert Hall

● £9–£25 *(plus booking fee')*

HORRIBLE HISTORIES

Horrible Histories: 'Orrible Opera

The English National Opera Chorus
The English National Opera Orchestra
Keri-Lynn Wilson conductor

BSL *British Sign Language-interpreted by Angie Newman (both performances)*

There will be one interval

From dying divas and spellbinding sorceresses to ghosts, Gypsies and generals, join us for a high-decibel dive into the Horrible History of Opera. Experience the very best of music's biggest, bloodiest and most dramatic genre, and discover the stories behind some of opera's best-loved tunes in the company of your favourite *Horrible Histories* characters, joining the English National Opera Chorus and Orchestra for this specially devised concert experience. *See 'My First Prom', pages 30–33.*

Prom 11 is a relaxed performance. BBC Proms relaxed performances are designed to suit individuals or groups who feel more comfortable attending concerts in a relaxed environment. There is a relaxed attitude to noise and audience members are free to leave and re-enter the auditorium at any point. There will be chill-out areas, where spaces are made for anyone needing a bit of quiet time before or during the performance. For full details, visit bbc.co.uk/proms.

📻 *Prom 10 broadcast live on BBC Radio 3*

🖥 *Broadcast on BBC TV*

Sunday 23 July

PROM 12
7.30pm–c9.25pm • Royal Albert Hall

● £14–£62 *(plus booking fee')*

RYAN WIGGLESWORTH

Helen Grime Meditations on Joy   15'
BBC co-commission: UK premiere

INTERVAL

Beethoven Symphony No. 9
in D minor, 'Choral'   65'

Eleanor Dennis *soprano*
Karen Cargill *mezzo-soprano*
Nicky Spence *tenor*
Michael Mofidian *bass-baritone*

BBC Symphony Chorus
BBC Scottish Symphony Orchestra
Ryan Wigglesworth *conductor*

For the first of their two Proms together this season *(see Prom 43)*, the BBC Scottish Symphony Orchestra and new Chief Conductor Ryan Wigglesworth are joined by an all-Scottish team of soloists for Beethoven's mighty 'Choral' Symphony. At the heart of this monumental, revolutionary musical statement – seizing hope and happiness from doubt and struggle – is the famous 'Ode to Joy', a vision of a future shaped by brotherhood. This idea is picked up in Helen Grime's Proms co-commission *Meditations on Joy*, whose three movements are each inspired by a different poem and facet of joy. There's melancholy here as well as ecstasy, dance as well as a peaceful lullaby. *See 'Music for the Soul', pages 68–71; 'Mood Music', pages 90–95.*

🖥 *Broadcast on BBC TV*

Monday 24 July

PROM 13
7.30pm–c9.25pm • Royal Albert Hall

● £9–£42 *(plus booking fee')*

ILAN VOLKOV

Catherine Lamb
Portions Transparent/Opaque   c36'
BBC commission: world premiere (Portions 2 & 3)

INTERVAL

Tchaikovsky Symphony No. 6
in B minor, 'Pathétique'   46'

BBC Scottish Symphony Orchestra
Ilan Volkov *conductor*

Ilan Volkov and the BBC Scottish Symphony Orchestra draw together the intensely personal with the abstract, pairing a classic 19th-century symphony with the world premiere of a newly completed orchestral triptych. Premiered just days before the composer's sudden death, Tchaikovsky's 'Pathétique' Symphony, with its evocative subtitle, is entangled with its author's own struggles and emotions. Its passionate outpourings meet the intricate play of proportion, density and energy in American composer Catherine Lamb's mesmerising *Portions Transparent/Opaque* – a trio of movements inspired by colour theory that move gradually from sonic expansion to collapse. *See 'Peak Practice?', pages 76–79.*

Tuesday 25 July

PROM 14
7.00pm–c8.40pm • Royal Albert Hall

● £9–£42 *(plus booking fee*)*

ELIM CHAN

Noriko Koide Swaddling Silk
and Gossamer Rain   12'
BBC commission: European premiere

Beethoven Piano Concerto No. 3
in C minor   34'

Elgar 'Enigma' Variations   31'

Jan Lisiecki *piano*

BBC Symphony Orchestra
Elim Chan *conductor*

There will be no interval

'The Enigma I will not explain – its "dark saying"
must be left unguessed ...' So wrote Edward
Elgar, establishing the mystery at the heart
of his career-making 'Enigma' Variations.
What's not in question, however, is the tender
playfulness of orchestral variations inspired by
the composer's friends and family, including
the serenity and nobility of the much-loved
'Nimrod'. Pianist Jan Lisiecki joins Elim Chan
and the BBC SO for Beethoven's Piano
Concerto No. 3 – a Romantic tussle between
conflict and lyricism. The concert opens with
the European premiere of Noriko Koide's
silkworm-inspired *Swaddling Silk and Gossamer
Rain*, commissioned for last year's BBC Proms
Japan. *See 'Peak Practice?', pages 76–79.*

Tuesday 25 July

PROM 15 • LATE NIGHT ☾
10.15pm–c11.30pm • Royal Albert Hall

● £10–£35 *(plus booking fee*)*

ANNA LAPWOOD

Moon and Stars

Hans Zimmer, arr. Lapwood
Interstellar Suite – excerpts   15'

Philip Glass Mad Rush   7'

Kristina Arakelyan Dreamland;
Star Fantasy   11'

Debussy, arr. Guilmant
String Quartet in G minor – 3rd mvt   8'

Debussy, arr. Lapwood
Suite bergamasque – Clair de lune   5'

Ludovico Einaudi, arr. Lapwood
Experience   6'

Ghislaine Reece-Trapp
In Paradisum   5'

Anna Lapwood *organ*

There will be no interval

Royal Albert Hall Associate Artist and TikTok
organ phenomenon Anna Lapwood makes
her Proms solo recital debut with an evocative
late-night event. Stars shine and moonlight
gleams in music by Debussy, Glass, Einaudi and
others, spinning further out into the universe
with excerpts from Hans Zimmer's *Interstellar
Suite*. The concert also showcases works by
two of the 12 contemporary women composers
recently commissioned by Lapwood to compose
new chant-based organ pieces for her 2022
collection *Gregoriana*. *See 'Peak Practice?',
pages 76–79.*

Spotlight on ...
Anna Lapwood • Prom 15

Organist, conductor and TV and radio
presenter Anna Lapwood knows the Royal
Albert Hall's immense Henry Willis organ
well. 'I'm lucky enough to be one of the
Hall's Associate Artists. The team has been
amazing at getting me practice time on the
organ, about once a month, and the only
time that can happen is the middle of the
night. I tend to practise from midnight till
6.00am. It's the most wonderful place to
be at that time – it's like the building comes
to life in its own way. The cleaning crew
come and say 'Hi', the stage crew shout
up requests and the security guys make
me tea. It's one of the friendliest spaces
ever. So I'm really excited about bringing
people into that world, particularly
as I'm doing a Late Night Prom.'

The darkness of the evening sky has also
inspired Lapwood's choice of music for her
Prom, which has a definite space theme
to it. 'It's all linked to a new album, *Moon
and Stars*, that will be out around the same
time,' she explains. Running through her
programme is music by Hans Zimmer from
a recent movie contemplating the vastness
of time and the cosmos. 'Transcriptions
for organ are one of the main things I've
been doing in my practice time at the
Royal Albert Hall, and the big piece I've
been working on is a new suite based
on the *Interstellar* soundtrack. It's music
I so associate with the Hall, because I've
been playing it there in the middle of the
night, with the crew whistling along.'

Spotlight on …
Sir Mark Elder • Prom 16

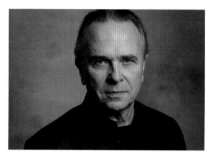

Sir Mark Elder has been conducting at the Proms for almost half a century, with concerts virtually every year since 1975. 'I had my first experience of going to live orchestral concerts at the Proms, when I was a teenager in the 1960s,' he recalls. 'My sister and I would meet friends in the queue, and I heard a lot of pieces for the first time there.' He has a similarly long relationship as Music Director with the Hallé, the orchestra he's bringing on 26 July. 'We've been together nearly 24 years. And, of course, I feel very close to the players – the majority of them I've actually appointed in the course of that period! They play with such commitment and intensity – I know when I can push them, but of course they know what to expect from me too.'

He describes this year's Prom as 'a contrast between two great Russian giants'. Rachmaninov's *The Bells* is effectively a choral symphony: 'It's a wonderful piece for the Royal Albert Hall, with its vast variety of contrast and drama,' Elder explains. Shostakovich's Fifth Symphony is a notoriously enigmatic work, supposedly a response to Soviet state censure, but it is so much more than that. How does Elder approach it? 'What's absolutely clear to me is that this is a completely autobiographical work. It's not in any way political. It's full of Shostakovich's own feelings. The sadness and stillness in the slow movement are very introverted, but it's full of defiance, and a determination not to be dictated to.'

Wednesday 26 July

PROM 16
7.30pm–c9.30pm • Royal Albert Hall

⬤ **£10–£52** *(plus booking fee¹)*

MANÉ GALOYAN

Rachmaninov The Bells   35'

INTERVAL

Shostakovich Symphony No. 5 in D minor   50'

Mané Galoyan *soprano*
Dmytro Popov *tenor*
Rodion Pogossov *baritone*

BBC Symphony Chorus
Hallé Choir
Hallé
Sir Mark Elder *conductor*

'I heard the bell voices, and tried to set down on paper their lovely tones that seemed to express the varying shades of human experience.' So wrote Rachmaninov of his choral symphony *The Bells*, which opens an all-Russian programme from Sir Mark Elder and the Hallé. Based on an Edgar Allan Poe poem, *The Bells* blends gothic drama with mystical intensity, haunted by the tolling of the *Dies irae* chant. Fear of death also lurks beneath the triumphant fanfares and jollity of Shostakovich's Symphony No. 5 – the composer's attempt to satisfy Stalin and the Soviet regime after his career-riskingly provocative opera *The Lady Macbeth of the Mtsensk District*. See 'Welcome Back, Mr Rachmaninov', pages 14–18.

Thursday 27 July

PROM 17
7.30pm–c9.30pm • Royal Albert Hall

⬤ **£10–£52** *(plus booking fee¹)*

KAZUKI YAMADA

Stravinsky Symphony of Psalms   21'

INTERVAL

Orff Carmina burana   65'

Mari Eriksmoen *soprano*
Levy Sekgapane *tenor*
Germán Olvera *baritone*

CBSO Youth Chorus
CBSO Chorus
University of Birmingham Voices
City of Birmingham Symphony Orchestra
Kazuki Yamada *conductor*

Psalms meet drinking songs and penitent prayers give way to raucous shouts as sacred and secular collide. The City of Birmingham Symphony Orchestra and Chief Conductor Kazuki Yamada bring together two choral classics: ritual austerity and radiance from Stravinsky's *Symphony of Psalms* – music steeped in Classical tradition, but seen from a fresh perspective – and riotous debauchery from Carl Orff's *Carmina burana* – an extravagant musical celebration of the pleasures of springtime, youth, wine and sex. The soloists are Norwegian soprano Mari Eriksmoen, South African tenor Levy Sekgapane and Mexican baritone Germán Olvera. See 'Peak Practice?', pages 76–79.

Friday 28 July

PROM 18
7.30pm–c9.30pm • Royal Albert Hall

● £14–£62 *(plus booking fee*)*

LATA MANGESHKAR

Lata Mangeshkar: Bollywood Legend

City of Birmingham Symphony Orchestra
Michael Seal *conductor*

There will be one interval

The Proms pays tribute to the 'Nightingale of India' and 'Queen of Melody', Lata Mangeshkar – the legendary Bollywood playback singer whose songs supplied the soundtrack for generations of cinema-goers, and who died last year aged 92. The City of Birmingham Symphony Orchestra – no stranger to Bollywood shows in its home city – is joined by guest vocalists to celebrate the immense career and catalogue of an extraordinary, era-defining artist. *See 'The Nightingale of India', pages 34–36.*

📻 *Broadcast live on BBC Radio 3 and Asian Network*

📺 *Broadcast on BBC TV*

Every Prom live on BBC Radio 3 and available on BBC Sounds

Saturday 29 July

PROM 19
6.30pm–c9.20pm • Royal Albert Hall

● £10–£52 *(plus booking fee*)*

RODERICK WILLIAMS

Mendelssohn Elijah   131'
(sung in English)

Carolyn Sampson *soprano*
Helen Charlston *mezzo-soprano*
Andrew Staples *tenor*
Roderick Williams *baritone*

Scottish Chamber Orchestra Chorus
Scottish Chamber Orchestra
Maxim Emelyanychev *conductor*

There will be one interval

Once second only to Handel's *Messiah* as the most popular work in the British choral repertoire, Mendelssohn's *Elijah* is an intensely dramatic oratorio, full of earthquakes and hurricanes, fiery chariots, wicked queens and holy visions. This powerful choral masterpiece is brought to life by the Scottish Chamber Orchestra and its exciting young Music Director Maxim Emelyanychev. Roderick Williams sings the biblical 'Prophet of Fire', alongside soprano Carolyn Sampson and an outstanding team of other soloists. *See 'Music for the Soul', pages 68–71.*

Sunday 30 July

PROM 20
7.30pm–c9.30pm • Royal Albert Hall

● £10–£52 *(plus booking fee*)*

DANIIL TRIFONOV

Herrmann Vertigo – Suite   12'
Mason Bates Piano Concerto   27'
UK premiere

INTERVAL

Prokofiev Symphony No. 3
in C minor   34'

Daniil Trifonov *piano*

BBC Symphony Orchestra
Gustavo Gimeno *conductor*

Cinematic drama stalks through a concert that opens with the ominous tension of Bernard Herrmann's suite from his score for Alfred Hitchcock's *Vertigo*. Prokofiev's demonic opera *The Fiery Angel* provides the material for the composer's intensely vivid Third Symphony, heavy with bells, cymbals, sinister dances and flashes of bright musical moonlight. Praised for his 'staggering dexterity', piano superstar Daniil Trifonov is the soloist in the first UK performance of Grammy Award-winner Mason Bates's Piano Concerto, which he premiered in Philadelphia last year. A musical journey through time, the mercurial work opens with Renaissance clarity of texture, moving through a richly Romantic slow movement to a sleek finale where jazz meets Minimalism.

Spotlight on …
Dee Dee Bridgewater
Prom 23

Memphis-born Dee Dee Bridgewater has sung with some of the greatest figures in jazz throughout her five-decade career, as well as winning two Grammy Awards and numerous international accolades. But it's quite a different group of musicians she'll be collaborating with at her Proms debut on 1 August: Carnegie Hall's NYO Jazz, which brings together the cream of the USA's young jazz players under seasoned band director Sean Jones. 'It's so exciting to work with these young musicians,' she says, 'especially as they've got such a passion for jazz. I always find it interesting to have a fresh outlook on music, and on life in general. I've got two teenage grandkids myself, and I like looking at the world through their lens. It's also good to be able to give suggestions and share the knowledge that I have accumulated.'

Having lived for several years in Paris, where she established something of a parallel career to her US activities, Bridgewater says that returning to Europe 'feels like coming home'. She's bringing a typically eclectic collection of songs to the concert, with which she has enjoyed a long association. How does she feel returning to these songs after such a long history with them? 'Well, in a big-band setting, it all depends on the band and the kind of energy I get, whether I meld with them or kind of lead them myself. But I know there are some amazing players here – I'm just going in to have fun!'

Monday 31 July
PROM 21
7.00pm–c8.55pm • Royal Albert Hall

● **£9–£42** (plus booking fee*)

RYAN BANCROFT

Derrick Skye Nova Plexus   *c18'*
BBC commission: world premiere

Copland Clarinet Concerto   *18'*

INTERVAL

John Adams Harmonium   *33'*

Annelien Van Wauwe *clarinet*
BBC National Chorus of Wales
Crouch End Festival Chorus
BBC National Orchestra of Wales
Ryan Bancroft *conductor*

Two poems by Emily Dickinson provide the starting point for one of American Post-Minimalist John Adams's most powerful works for chorus and orchestra – an all-encompassing sonic experience. Propulsive, motoric urgency gives way briefly to blissful waves of sound, before a blazing conclusion. Jazz runs through the veins of Copland's Clarinet Concerto, commissioned by 'King of Swing' Benny Goodman. The concert opens with a world premiere from Los Angeles-based composer Derrick Skye, whose music has been described as 'deliciously head-spinning'. In the first of two consecutive concerts this week, the BBC National Orchestra of Wales is conducted by its RPS Award-winning Principal Conductor Ryan Bancroft. *See 'Mood Music', pages 90–95.*

Tuesday 1 August
PROM 22
7.00pm–c8.40pm • Royal Albert Hall

● **£10–£52** (plus booking fee*)

ISATA KANNEH-MASON

Prokofiev Piano Concerto No. 3 in C major   *27'*

Tchaikovsky Symphony No. 5 in E minor   *44'*

Isata Kanneh-Mason *piano*

BBC National Orchestra of Wales
Ryan Bancroft *conductor*

There will be no interval

The BBC National Orchestra of Wales and Principal Conductor Ryan Bancroft return, joined by exciting young soloist Isata Kanneh-Mason. Having made her Proms debut alongside her cellist brother Sheku in 2020 and returned in 2021 to perform alongside her siblings and other musicians, she now makes her solo Proms debut with Prokofiev's Piano Concerto No. 3, in which heady, rhapsodic melody meets restless rhythmic exuberance. Tchaikovsky's Symphony No. 5 wrestles with its ominous 'fate' motif, overpowering it first with a rapturous love theme, before finally turning darkness to light in the powerful closing movement. *See 'Peak Practice?', pages 76–79.*

▢ *Broadcast on BBC TV*

Tuesday 1 August

PROM 23 • LATE NIGHT 🌙

10.15pm–c11.30pm • Royal Albert Hall

● £9–£26 (plus booking fee*)

DEE DEE BRIDGEWATER

NYO Jazz and Dee Dee Bridgewater

Dee Dee Bridgewater

NYO Jazz – Carnegie Hall's National Youth Jazz Orchestra
Sean Jones *trumpet/director*

There will be no interval

The 'electrifying' NYO Jazz, recently praised for its 'jaw-dropping virtuosity', brings together the best teenage performers from across the USA. For its Proms debut, Carnegie Hall's National Youth Jazz Orchestra performs jazz standards and big-band classics alongside contemporary works exploring jazz's influence on hip-hop, R&B and pop music. This late-night performance also features Grammy Award-winning singer-songwriter Dee Dee Bridgewater, who performs a collection of jazz standards.

🖥 *Broadcast on BBC TV*

Every Prom live on BBC Radio 3 and available on BBC Sounds

Wednesday 2 August

PROM 24

7.30pm–c9.45pm • Royal Albert Hall

● £10–£52 (plus booking fee*)

FELIX KLIESER

I. Karabits Concerto for Orchestra No. 1, 'A Musical Gift to Kyiv'   *13'*
UK premiere

Mozart Horn Concerto No. 4 in E flat major   *16'*

INTERVAL

Rachmaninov Symphony No. 2 in E minor   *60'*

Felix Klieser *horn*

Bournemouth Symphony Orchestra
Kirill Karabits *conductor*

A defiant musical riposte to his critics, a passionate, unashamedly emotional score from a man who once declared himself 'completely under the spell of Tchaikovsky', Rachmaninov's Symphony No. 2 is paired here with a kaleidoscopic tour of the orchestra by the Ukrainian composer Ivan Karabits, father of the Bournemouth Symphony Orchestra's long-standing Chief Conductor, Kirill Karabits. His *Concerto for Orchestra* No. 1 was written to celebrate the 1,500th anniversary in 1982 of the founding of Kyiv, with chiming bells, fanfares and marches: a sonic snapshot of a city in happier days. Horn virtuoso Felix Kleiser makes his Proms debut with Mozart's sunny Concerto No. 4. *See 'Welcome Back, Mr Rachmaninov', pages 14–18; 'Body and Spirit', pages 72–75.*

🖥 *Broadcast on BBC TV*

Spotlight on …

Kirill Karabits
Proms 24 & 25

'I spent my childhood observing my father composing … It's difficult to express the excitement and joy I feel to be able to perform his music at the Proms.' Kyiv-born Kirill Karabits is talking about his father Ivan Karabits, and it's with his First *Concerto for Orchestra* – named 'A Musical Gift to Kyiv' – that Kirill opens his Proms performance on 2 August. It's clearly a crucial time to appreciate and celebrate Ukrainian music and wider culture, something that Karabits has made it his personal mission to do in recent months. And his father's piece has a special meaning for him. 'It paints a picture of the great and ancient city of Kyiv – it's a celebration of Kyiv's glory and beauty. When I hear or conduct this music, it gives me the feeling of belonging to a certain place and land … It will be so special to share the music of my native city with the orchestra and the Proms audience in such a positive way, especially at a time when Ukraine reports sad news every single day.'

He lines up his father's glittering, colourful music alongside Mozart and Rachmaninov in his performance with the Bournemouth Symphony Orchestra, where he's made a decisive impact in his 14 years as Chief Conductor. And he returns to some of the concert's music the following afternoon in a relaxed performance: 'It will be my first experience of a Relaxed Prom, and I'm looking forward to seeing a broader audience, in a freer atmosphere.'

Thursday 3 August

PROM 25 ☀
11.30am–c12.30pm • Royal Albert Hall

● £9–£25 *(plus booking fee')*

KIRILL KARABITS

Relaxed Prom

Walton Coronation March 'Orb and
Sceptre'   6'

Mozart Horn Concerto No. 4
in E flat major   16'

Skoryk The High Pass – Melody   4'

Rachmaninov Symphony No. 2
in E minor – Allegro vivace (4th mvt) 15'

Felix Klieser *horn*

Bournemouth Symphony Orchestra
Kirill Karabits *conductor*

BSL *British Sign Language-interpreted performance*
There will be no interval

Highlights from last night's Prom with the
Bournemouth Symphony Orchestra – plus
pieces by Walton and Ukrainian composer
Myroslav Skoryk – in a short, relaxed
performance with British Sign Language
interpretation and onstage presentation.
*See 'Welcome Back, Mr Rachmaninov', pages
14–18; 'Body and Spirit', pages 72–75.*

*BBC Proms relaxed performances are designed to
suit individuals or groups who feel more comfortable
attending concerts in a relaxed environment. There
is a relaxed attitude to noise and audience members
are free to leave and re-enter the auditorium at any
point. There will be chill-out areas, where spaces are
made for anyone needing a bit of quiet time before
or during the performance. For full details, visit
bbc.co.uk/proms.*

Thursday 3 August

PROM 26
7.30pm–c9.35pm • Royal Albert Hall

● £9–£42 *(plus booking fee')*

JAMES EHNES

Gerald Barry Kafka's Earplugs   *c12'*
BBC commission: world premiere

Walton Violin Concerto   31'

INTERVAL

Sibelius Symphony No. 1
in E minor   38'

James Ehnes *violin*

BBC Philharmonic
John Storgårds *conductor*

With its surging first movement, Sibelius's
Symphony No. 1 is a thrilling glimpse of a
composer emerging from the shadow of
Tchaikovsky and his fellow Romantics – passion
allied to musical form that emerges with tidal
or tectonic force. Canadian violinist James
Ehnes is the soloist in Walton's fiercely direct
Violin Concerto – a work full of song, dance
and drama. The concert opens with a world
premiere from heartily irreverent Irish composer
Gerald Barry, focusing on Franz Kafka's
obsession with wearing earplugs to silence the
noise around him. 'In the music,' Barry says,
'you are Kafka, hearing the world's sounds
as he heard them. You are inside his head.'

Friday 4 August

PROM 27
7.30pm–c9.30pm • Royal Albert Hall

● £18–£72 *(plus booking fee')*

YUJA WANG

Jimmy López Bellido
Perú negro   16'
UK premiere

Rachmaninov Rhapsody on a
Theme of Paganini   22'

INTERVAL

Walton Belshazzar's Feast   36'

Yuja Wang *piano*
Thomas Hampson *baritone*

BBC Symphony Chorus
BBC Symphony Orchestra
Klaus Mäkelä *conductor*

After an 'extraordinary' Proms debut last
season, rising-star conductor Klaus Mäkelä
is reunited with sensational pianist Yuja Wang
for Rachmaninov's glittering *Rhapsody on a
Theme of Paganini* – its mercurial moods and
technical demands a tour de force for any
soloist. Celebrated American baritone Thomas
Hampson is the soloist in Walton's biblical
blockbuster *Belshazzar's Feast* – a choral
symphony by any other name, whose cinematic
scope and oversize orchestra give the Old
Testament epic its impact. Orchestral colour is
also on display in Jimmy López Bellido's *Perú
negro* – a vibrant homage to the songs, dances
and traditions of Afro-Peruvian music. *See
'Welcome Back, Mr Rachmaninov', pages 14–18.*

🖵 *Broadcast on BBC TV*

Saturday 5 August

PROM 28
7.30pm–c9.45pm • Royal Albert Hall

● £9–£42 *(plus booking fee')*

MASABANE CECILIA RANGWANASHA

Hindemith Symphonic Metamorphosis of Themes by Carl Maria von Weber   *21'*

R. Strauss Four Last Songs   *24'*

INTERVAL

Copland Symphony No. 3   *43'*

Masabane Cecilia Rangwanasha *soprano*

National Youth Orchestra of Great Britain
Carlos Miguel Prieto *conductor*

After a 'stunning' debut at 2022's First Night of the Proms, South African soprano Masabane Cecilia Rangwanasha, winner of the Song Prize at the 2021 Cardiff Singer of the World, returns to perform in Richard Strauss's *Four Last Songs* – luminous musical farewells to life, love and a changing world. Drawn from the UK's finest teenage musicians, the National Youth Orchestra of Great Britain also performs Hindemith's jovial reworking of themes by Weber, before crossing the Atlantic for Copland's lyrical Symphony No. 3 – '*very symphonic* and *very* jazzy', according to Leonard Bernstein – which incorporates his much-loved *Fanfare for the Common Man* as a springboard for its final movement.

🖥 *Broadcast on BBC TV*

Sunday 6 August

PROM 29
11.00am–c12.55pm • Royal Albert Hall   ☀

● £14–£62 *(plus booking fee')*

NARDUS WILLIAMS

J. S. Bach
Sinfonia in D major, BWV 1045   *6'*
Singet dem Herrn ein neues Lied, BWV 225   *15'*

C. P. E. Bach
Heilig ist Gott   *7'*

INTERVAL

Mozart, compl. C. Kemme
Mass in C minor, K427   *50'*

Lucy Crowe *soprano*
Nardus Williams *soprano*
Benjamin Hulett *tenor*
Robert Davies *baritone*

Dunedin Consort
John Butt *harpsichord/conductor*

'Now she will listen to nothing but fugues, and particularly the works of Handel and Bach.' So wrote Mozart of his new wife Constanze, and her passion soon became his – one that flowered in his Mass in C minor. Begun to celebrate their marriage, but unaccountably left unfinished, it's a magnificent musical torso whose roots can clearly be traced back to the choral writing of Bach and his son heard earlier in the concert. Period-performance specialist John Butt and the award-winning Dunedin Consort unpack the Mass's musical genealogy, with the help of soloists including Lucy Crowe and Nardus Williams.

🖥 *Broadcast on BBC TV*

Spotlight on …

Thomas Hampson • Prom 27

Walton's choral showpiece *Belshazzar's Feast* is a work that US baritone Thomas Hampson knows well, from performances across his decades-long career, as well as a recording. 'It's a wonderful cantata, one I first sang several years ago in my home town of Spokane, Washington,' he recalls. 'I've loved coming back to it. Walton's vocal writing is accessible, dramatic and a beautiful setting of the English text. The mixture of lyrical melody and declamation makes it very interesting – and challenging.'

Rather than singing Belshazzar himself, however, Hampson's role is as narrator of events at a fateful gathering in the biblical Book of Daniel: 'Of course it's impressive on musical and biblical levels, but what I enjoy is being this priest figure who tells the tragic story of what Belshazzar's last night was all about. There's great impetus given by these declarations as that figure in the piece, and I enjoy that enormously.'

Hampson also enjoys the relatively recent musical relationship he's established with young Finnish conductor Klaus Mäkelä, who conducts the BBC Symphony Orchestra at the performance on 4 August. 'I met Klaus around four years ago in Finland. We were doing a concert of Mahler songs and found an immediate musical friendship, and then a personal one too. He's truly one of the more remarkable young musicians I've worked with – there's nothing I wouldn't enjoy singing on stage in collaboration with him.'

Spotlight on …
Golda Schultz • Prom 31

Cape Town-born soprano Golda Schultz has mixed memories of her most recent Proms performance, at the 2020 Last Night in the midst of the Covid-19 pandemic. 'I remember very clearly walking into the space that usually holds so many friendly faces, and being greeted by empty seats and camera equipment. The moment that had the greatest impact on me was singing 'You'll Never Walk Alone': it spoke so specifically to what each of us was feeling.'

Schultz returns this year to a live audience in a concert performance of Poulenc's *Dialogues of the Carmelites*. It's a work she was first involved in as a student at New York's Juilliard School. 'I love this opera – it became a favourite when I did it at school in 2010. I was only a chorus nun, but to be in a room every day with other women and make music together was so special. I love that it's one of the few operas that passes the Bechdel Test, and that the women are so fully constructed, complex and self-aware. As a Catholic, I've always been drawn to the themes within the opera. The notion of what one is willing to do for the profession of one's faith is so inspiring.' How would she describe Madame Lidoine, the role she's singing? 'She is a country woman with humble beginnings, and it's this humility that makes her such a profound leader. She's everything I wish I was, and that I hope to be one day – a person who can carry the pain of others when it becomes too much for them.'

Sunday 6 August

PROM 30
7.30pm–*c*9.35pm • Royal Albert Hall

● £14–£62 *(plus booking fee*)*

JOHN WILSON

L. Boulanger D'un matin de printemps   5'

Rachmaninov Piano Concerto No. 2 in C minor   34'

INTERVAL

Walton Symphony No. 1 in B flat minor   43'

Benjamin Grosvenor *piano*

Sinfonia of London
John Wilson *conductor*

Following their debut concert at the Proms in 2021 and their return last summer, John Wilson and his orchestral supergroup the Sinfonia of London return with a musical snapshot of the early 20th century. Few symphonies seize hold of an audience quite like Walton's arresting First. A young man's musical manifesto, composed between the two World Wars, it's a white-hot outpouring of personal conflict that resolves (or does it?) into a glowing ceremonial finale. Trauma also lurks behind the lyrical outpourings of Rachmaninov's Second Piano Concerto, performed here by popular British pianist Benjamin Grosvenor, as well as Lili Boulanger's mercurial tone-poem *D'un matin de printemps*, composed shortly before her tragically early death at the age of only 24. *See 'Welcome Back, Mr Rachmaninov', pages 14–18; 'Music for the Soul', pages 68–71.*

🖥 Broadcast on BBC TV

Monday 7 August

PROM 31
7.00pm–*c*10.05pm • Royal Albert Hall

● £14–£62 *(plus booking fee*)*

SALLY MATTHEWS

Poulenc
Dialogues of the Carmelites   151'
(semi-staged; sung in French, with English surtitles)

Sally Matthews *Blanche de la Force*
Katarina Dalayman *Madame de Croissy (Old Prioress)*
Golda Schultz *Madame Lidoine (New Prioress)*
Karen Cargill *Mother Marie of the Incarnation*
Florie Valiquette *Sister Constance of St Denis*
Fiona Kimm *Mother Jeanne of the Child Jesus*
Paul Gay *Marquis de la Force*
Valentin Thill *Chevalier de la Force*
Vincent Ordonneau *Father Confessor*
Theodore Platt *Jailer*

Glyndebourne Festival Opera
London Philharmonic Orchestra
Robin Ticciati *conductor*

There will be one interval

At the outbreak of the French Revolution, Blanche de la Force flees the violence on Paris's streets and enters a Carmelite convent. But horror pursues her, and she is forced to confront her fears. Can she find the courage to live – or die? A 20th-century masterpiece, Francis Poulenc's opera is a devastatingly powerful portrait of human courage, faith and community. The radiant score is shot through with plainchant, cinematic drama unfolding in a great sweep of melody. Robin Ticciati conducts an all-star cast including Sally Matthews and Golda Schultz in this concert staging fresh from the Glyndebourne Festival.

Tuesday 8 August

PROM 32
7.30pm–c9.05pm • Royal Albert Hall

● £10–£52 (plus booking fee')

GENEVA LEWIS

Pejačević Overture · 6'
G. Williams Violin Concerto · 25'

INTERVAL

Holst The Planets · 51'

Geneva Lewis *violin*

London Symphony Chorus
BBC National Orchestra of Wales
Jaime Martín *conductor*

Written in the shadow of war, Holst's colourful character portraits of our Solar System's seven planets (excluding Earth) is by turns powerfully visceral and captivatingly luminous, opening with the battle-hungry 'Mars' and concluding with 'Neptune', whose alluring sounds float off into the ether. Welsh composer Grace Williams was a fellow student with Holst's daughter Imogen, at the Royal College of Music. Her elegiac concerto, which she suppressed following its first performance in 1950, is an intensely lyrical work whose bittersweet opening gives way to an ecstatic slow movement – based on a Welsh hymn tune – and a joyful finale. It is performed by BBC Radio 3 New Generation Artist Geneva Lewis, making her Proms debut. The concert opens with centenary composer Dora Pejačević's surging Overture, whose sumptuous textures are married to bold, thrusting energy. *See 'Countess and Composer', pages 52–55.*

Wednesday 9 August

PROM 33
7.00pm–c8.35pm • Royal Albert Hall

● £9–£42 (plus booking fee')

JOHN STORGÅRDS

Weber Oberon – overture · 10'
Pejačević
Zwei Schmetterlingslieder, Op. 52 · 4'
Verwandlung, Op. 37b · 6'
Liebeslied, Op. 39 · 6'
Mahler-Werfel,
orch. C. & D. Matthews
'Die stille Stadt'; 'Licht in der Nacht';
'Bei dir ist es traut' · 9'
Rachmaninov Symphony No. 1
in D minor · 42'

Dame Sarah Connolly *mezzo-soprano*

BBC Philharmonic
John Storgårds *conductor*

There will be no interval

If the audience was hostile to the 23-year-old Rachmaninov's first symphonic venture, history has been far kinder, embracing its ability to reimagine Russian musical tradition. John Storgårds and the BBC Philharmonic are joined by mezzo-soprano Dame Sarah Connolly for turn-of-the-century songs by Alma Mahler-Werfel and Croatia's Dora Pejačević, and the curtain rises with the overture to Weber's 'Grand Romantic and Fairy Opera', written for London's Covent Garden. *See 'Welcome Back, Mr Rachmaninov', pages 14–18; 'Countess and Composer', pages 52–55.*

Spotlight on …
Dame Sarah Connolly
Prom 33

Dora Pejačević was a respected composer in the first years of the 20th century, but she's also one of the many female musicians we're only now beginning to appreciate again after years of disregard. For Dame Sarah Connolly, who sings four Pejačević songs on 9 August, she's a major figure. 'I've been particularly impressed by her sumptuous Symphony *(see Prom 40).* Her harmonic style has shades of Strauss, Bruckner, Rachmaninov or Gounod, but there's an energy and voice all her own … It's a great pity she died at 37. I would say her gorgeous writing has verve and conviction, and is fresh, melodic and confident – almost filmic at times.'

Connolly also performs works by Alma Mahler-Werfel. 'Alma was discouraged from composing by her husband Gustav's refusal to allow her to write, but these few songs written at various times in her life are really special. The two sets – Pejačević's and Alma Mahler's – will be contrasting and fascinatingly comparable. Both composers wrote very well for the voice and understood how to engage a beautiful legato line. Both were highly educated and deeply interested in cultural and political life – they were both working slap bang in the middle of the highly cultural melting pot of Europe. Both strongly own their own styles, and have a unique harmonic language ahead of its time. It's very exciting to champion the music of these strong, trailblazing women.'

Spotlight on ...
Edward Gardner • Prom 36

'Stanley Kubrick knew his music: I can't think of another film director who did so much for 20th-century classical music.' Conductor Edward Gardner is highlighting one thread linking together the pieces that he performs with the London Philharmonic Orchestra on 11 August. The director was especially fond of Ligeti's other-worldly, throbbing clouds of sound: music from the composer's *Requiem* accompanies *2001: A Space Odyssey*'s enigmatic alien monolith, for example. 'Ligeti is a composer of the most utter genius and individuality that I wanted to celebrate in his centenary year,' Gardner explains. 'The *Requiem* has such a range of textures, and the Royal Albert Hall really suits those pieces that you want to feel more mystical or expansive. It still gives you total brain-ache to rehearse, though – it's so multi-layered.'

The unforgettable sunrise opening of Strauss's *Also sprach Zarathustra* is what gave *2001* its iconic beginning. But it only forms the first few moments of Strauss's epic musical contemplation of Nietzschean superhuman self-fulfilment. 'It's such a journey of a piece. I haven't conducted it for about three years now, but coming back to it fresh has been beautiful. You don't have to read tomes on philosophy to understand Strauss's journey of aspiration, away from the earthbound qualities of humanity towards something greater. The piece itself has this amazing sense of reaching out and opening out.'

Wednesday 9 August
PROM 34 • LATE NIGHT 🌙
10.15pm–c11.30pm • Royal Albert Hall

● £9–£26 *(plus booking fee*)*

VOCES8

Mindful Mix Prom
Programme to include:

Ola Gjeilo Still; Serenity *8'*

Radiohead, arr. G. Lawson
Pyramid Song *5'*

Philip Glass String Quartet No. 3, 'Mishima' – Mishima/Closing *3'*

Roxanna Panufnik Floral Tribute *c5'*
BBC co-commission: world premiere

Caroline Shaw and the swallow *4'*

Eric Whitacre All Seems Beautiful to Me *5'*

Ken Burton A Prayer *5'*

Byrd Diliges Dominum *4'*

Ola Gjeilo *piano*

Carducci String Quartet
VOCES8

There will be no interval

Let go of your pressures and stresses, and step into this live experience of the popular BBC Sounds Mindful Mix – a late-night, immersive musical meditation with the sounds of piano, strings and voices, spanning centuries of music. Night, stillness and prayer are the themes that recur across works by composers including Ola Gjeilo, Philip Glass, Radiohead and Caroline Shaw. *See 'Servants of the Church and State', pages 96–99. Music for the Soul', pages 68–71.*

Thursday 10 August
PROM 35
7.30pm–c9.50pm • Royal Albert Hall

● £9–£42 *(plus booking fee*)*

SIR ANDREW DAVIS

Berg Violin Concerto *22'*
INTERVAL

Mahler, compl. D. Cooke
Symphony No. 10 in F sharp major *72'*

Leila Josefowicz *violin*

BBC Symphony Orchestra
Sir Andrew Davis *conductor*

Grief and loss haunt an emotionally charged programme from Sir Andrew Davis and the BBC Symphony Orchestra pairing two 20th-century masterpieces, each premiered after their composers' deaths. Berg's Violin Concerto was dedicated 'To the memory of an angel', referring to Alma Mahler-Werfel's daughter Manon Gropius, who died aged just 18 from polio. It weaves quotations from Bach into music contrasting expressive Romanticism with cooler serial techniques. Heard here in Deryck Cooke's performing version, Mahler's Symphony No. 10 is another deeply personal work, charged with anguished love for an unfaithful wife *(see Prom 33)*, and written on the brink of the composer's own final illness.

Every Prom live on BBC Radio 3 and available on BBC Sounds

Friday 11 August

PROM 36
7.30pm–c9.20pm • Royal Albert Hall

● £9–£42 *(plus booking fee*)*

JENNIFER FRANCE

Ligeti Requiem 29'

INTERVAL

Lux aeterna 9'

R. Strauss Also sprach
Zarathustra 34'

Jennifer France *soprano*
Clare Presland *mezzo-soprano*

Edvard Grieg Kor
London Philharmonic Choir
Royal Northern College of Music
  Chamber Choir
London Philharmonic Orchestra
Edward Gardner *conductor*

This year marks 100 years since the birth of
György Ligeti – one of the boldest voices of
the 20th century, whose ear-bending sounds
brought wit as well as invention to the concert
hall. His sounds seeped into popular culture
thanks to Stanley Kubrick's films, and it's the
music from the director's 1968 sci-fi epic *2001:
A Space Odyssey* that has inspired Edward
Gardner and his large forces here. They reunite
the shimmering choral miasma of *Lux aeterna*
and the teeming, terrifying vastness of the
Requiem with Richard Strauss's tone-poem
Also sprach Zarathustra, with its dazzling
opening sunrise. *See 'Hungary's Caterpillar',
pages 20–23.*

Saturday 12 August

PROM 37
7.30pm–c9.35pm • Royal Albert Hall

● £14–£62 *(plus booking fee*)*

SIR ANDRÁS SCHIFF

Weber Der Freischütz – overture 10'

Schumann Piano Concerto
in A minor 31'

INTERVAL

Mendelssohn Symphony No. 3
in A minor, 'Scottish' 40'

Sir András Schiff *piano*

Budapest Festival Orchestra
Iván Fischer *conductor*

In the first of its three Proms this weekend,
the Budapest Festival Orchestra and founder-
conductor Iván Fischer are joined by piano giant
Sir András Schiff for one of the great Romantic
piano concertos – Schumann's generous, poetic
bravura piece that renegotiates the relationship
between soloist and orchestra. Weber's
overture to *Der Freischütz* sees Romanticism
take a supernatural turn when a huntsman
makes a deal with the Devil. Darkness and
light also meet in Mendelssohn's atmospheric
'Scottish' Symphony, inspired by a twilight
visit to the Palace of Holyrood, haunted by
memories of Mary, Queen of Scots. *See 'Peak
Practice?', pages 76–79; 'Reeling in the Years',
pages 84–88.*

🖵 Broadcast on BBC TV

Spotlight on ...
Sir András Schiff
Proms 37 & 39

'Both concertos are very, very beautiful –
but please don't ask me why!' Sir András
Schiff is thinking about the two very
different piano concertos he performs at
the Proms this year: Schumann's lyrical
masterpiece on 12 August, and Bartók's far
more forceful Third the following evening.
'Schumann wanted to be a concert pianist
but, having injured his hands, couldn't fulfil
his dream. Bartók, on the other hand, was
a fantastic pianist, as we can hear on his
recordings. Both concertos are very close
to my heart, and they've both been with
me for more than 50 years. I actually made
my debuts in Vienna and Chicago with
Bartók's Third about half a century ago.'

It's a similarly long relationship that
Schiff has enjoyed with the two concerts'
conductor, Iván Fischer. 'He's a close
friend – we grew up together in Budapest,
and our backgrounds are similar. Many of
the Budapest Festival Orchestra musicians
are also friends of mine, although my
contemporaries have now retired. As a
pianist I'm allowed to play on for a while!'

Schiff's Proms connection dates back to
1977, when he made his debut in Mozart's
Concerto for Two Pianos alongside George
Malcolm. 'I simply adore the Proms,'
he says. 'It's just unique. Under normal
circumstances, the Royal Albert Hall would
hardly qualify as an ideal concert hall, but
with the Prommers we get an unbelievable
atmosphere. We no longer notice the size
of the venue. It can even feel intimate.'

Spotlight on …
Anna-Lena Elbert • Prom 39

'I was still a student when a young conductor drew my attention to the piece. I was immediately hooked!' György Ligeti's madcap *Mysteries of the Macabre* calls for what Munich-born soprano Anna-Lena Elbert describes as 'fast, complicated rhythms, demanding leaps, long, high trills, a mad text, meaningless sounds, even animal noises'. It's a virtuoso showpiece that displays a singer's vocal prowess, as well as their insights into a rather curious character. 'The piece is actually an arrangement of three arias from Ligeti's opera *Le Grand Macabre*, all performed by the head of the secret police, who, in a complete panic, predicts the end of the world caused by a comet! But, when I prepare a piece from an opera, it's always an important part of the process to look closely at the character and the story too.'

It's a piece she's performed several times in recent years. How has she grown into it over that time? 'It becomes more natural with every performance, and I can enjoy it more: I feel the crazy moments with greater intensity and I feel more pleasure throwing myself into this world of unusual sounds and language.' Joining Elbert will be the Budapest Festival Orchestra and conductor Iván Fischer. 'They're so wonderful,' Elbert says. 'There's a great family atmosphere, and I've always felt so carried by Iván and the players. You can feel how well everyone knows each other, and how well they're aligned with each other.'

Sunday 13 August
PROM 38
2.00pm–*c*3.15pm • Royal Albert Hall

● £10–£52 *(plus booking fee*)*

IVÁN FISCHER

Audience Choice

Budapest Festival Orchestra
Iván Fischer *conductor*

There will be no interval

They play the music, but you decide the programme. No-one puts on a show quite like Iván Fischer and the Budapest Festival Orchestra and, after an 'irresistible' outing in 2011, full of 'sheer blinding energy', they finally bring their showstopping Audience Choice concert back to the Proms. Choose and vote live for your favourites from a list of 250 dances, overtures, marches and symphonic movements by all the great classical composers. It's a spectacle unlike any other, all woven together by members of the orchestra bringing a bit of extra Hungarian flair to proceedings. *See 'Reeling in the Years', pages 84–88.*

For details of how to vote in advance for a piece of music to be played, visit bbc.co.uk/proms nearer the time of the concert.

Every Prom live on BBC Radio 3 and available on BBC Sounds

Sunday 13 August
PROM 39
7.30pm–*c*9.35pm • Royal Albert Hall

● £14–£62 *(plus booking fee*)*

ANNA-LENA ELBERT

Ligeti Mysteries of the Macabre   *9'*
Bartók Piano Concerto No. 3   *23'*
INTERVAL
Beethoven Symphony No. 3 in E flat major, 'Eroica'   *47'*

Anna-Lena Elbert *soprano*
Sir András Schiff *piano*

Budapest Festival Orchestra
Iván Fischer *conductor*

Iván Fischer and his Budapest Festival Orchestra mark the 100th anniversary of one of the 20th century's great originals with *Mysteries of the Macabre* – three arias from Ligeti's opera *Le Grand Macabre* that explode in a cartoonish riot of irony and bravura technique. The contrast with Bartók's Third Piano Concerto – composed in his final days – is striking. Sir András Schiff is the soloist in this exquisite, elegiac musical farewell. Beethoven's 'Eroica' Symphony marks both an ending and a new beginning: a passionate, provocative statement of musical and human possibility. *See 'Hungary's Caterpillar', pages 20–23; 'Reeling in the Years', pages 84–88.*

Monday 14 August

PROM 40
7.30pm–c9.45pm • Royal Albert Hall

● £9–£42 *(plus booking fee')*

MARTIN HELMCHEN

Brahms Piano Concerto No. 2
in B flat major   *46'*

INTERVAL

Pejačević Symphony
in F sharp minor   *48'*

Martin Helmchen *piano*
BBC Symphony Orchestra
Sakari Oramo *conductor*

Brahms may have described it as 'a very small piano concerto, with a very small and pretty scherzo', but the Second Piano Concerto is a vast work full of mercurial mood swings and technical demands. Award-winning German pianist Martin Helmchen makes his Proms debut as soloist. The concerto's late-Romantic spirit and generous scope find an echo in Dora Pejačević's Symphony in F sharp minor. Following a critically acclaimed recording, Sakari Oramo and the BBC Symphony Orchestra give this work – the first major Croatian symphony – its Proms premiere. Composed during the First World War, when Pejačević worked as a nurse, the richly scored symphony, resplendent with brass, is charged with urgent emotion: yearning, playful delight and ferocity. *See 'Countess and Composer', pages 52–55.*

Tuesday 15 August

PROM 41
7.30pm–c9.55pm • Royal Albert Hall

● £10–£52 *(plus booking fee')*

VASILY PETRENKO

Ligeti Lontano   *10'*
Beethoven Piano Concerto No. 4
in G major   *37'*

INTERVAL

Shostakovich Symphony No. 10
in E minor   *57'*

Alexandre Kantorow *piano*
Royal Philharmonic Orchestra
Vasily Petrenko *conductor*

Tchaikovsky Competition-winner Alexandre Kantorow has been hailed as 'Liszt reincarnated' and a 'fire-breathing virtuoso'. Still in his twenties, this exceptional young pianist makes a much-anticipated Proms debut, joining Vasily Petrenko and the Royal Philharmonic Orchestra as soloist in Beethoven's poetic Piano Concerto No. 4. Music of terror and despair, frenzied horror and – eventually – a flicker of triumph supply a musical portrait of Stalin in Shostakovich's impassioned Symphony No. 10, while more abstract orchestral soundscapes come courtesy of anniversary composer Ligeti's *Lontano*. See 'Hungary's Caterpillar', pages 20–23; 'Music for the Soul', pages 68–71.

Wednesday 16 August

PROM 42
7.30pm–c10.05pm • Royal Albert Hall

● £10–£52 *(plus booking fee')*

SANTTU-MATIAS ROUVALI

Elgar In the South (Alassio)   *20'*
Chopin Piano Concerto No. 1
in E minor   *43'*

INTERVAL

R. Strauss Aus Italien   *47'*

Seong-Jin Cho *piano*
Philharmonia Orchestra
Santtu-Matias Rouvali *conductor*

International Chopin Piano Competition-winner Seong-Jin Cho is one of the world's most exciting young pianists, praised for his 'remarkable technique' and the elegance of his interpretations. Who better to perform Chopin's Piano Concerto No. 1 – a heady combination of brilliance and poetry, its slow movement a vision of 'a beloved landscape on a moonlit spring night'. Could that landscape perhaps be Italian? Italy's warmth and summer sunshine suffuse both Elgar's bucolic *In the South* overture and Strauss's tone-poem *Aus Italien*, each inspired by a visit to the country. The Philharmonia Orchestra is conducted by its Finnish-born Principal Conductor Santtu-Matias Rouvali. *See 'Peak Practice?', pages 76–79.*

Spotlight on ...
Hilary Summers • Prom 43

'Kurtág makes what, in Beckett's original play, is essentially a fairly underwhelming 10-minute episode for Nell into a ravishing 25-minute scene of tenderness, fun, memory and heartache and irritable, crabby old people who still love each other, even though they have no legs and live in dustbins. It's such wonderful music and orchestration. He really is a genius.'

Contralto Hilary Summers is talking about her favourite section of *Endgame*, György Kurtág's operatic adaptation of Samuel Beckett's enigmatic tragicomedy, originally published as *Fin de partie*. She sings a role quite unlike any other: Nell has no legs and lives in a dustbin alongside her husband Nagg. They are parents to the blind, wheelchair-bound Hamm, the work's central character. How does Summers feel about embodying such an unconventional figure? 'I love the role of Nell, mainly for its beauty and fun, and because it's challenging but brings such great rewards. The vocal challenges are about keeping it contained – never to overblow.'

Endgame has, Summers says, 'been a massive part of my life since 2015': she took part in its 2018 premiere at La Scala, Milan, following months of jetting to Budapest for close work with Kurtág himself on the part. 'They were gruelling but very bonding sessions, but by the time we worked on the actual production, we were so close and we had such a clear understanding of Kurtág's style that it was a joy to get it on stage.'

Thursday 17 August
PROM 43
7.30pm–*c*9.15pm • Royal Albert Hall

● £9–£42 *(plus booking fee')*

FRODE OLSEN

György Kurtág Endgame   125'
(semi-staged; sung in French, with English surtitles)
UK premiere

Frode Olsen *Hamm*
Morgan Moody *Clov*
Hilary Summers *Nell*
Leonardo Cortellazzi *Nagg*

BBC Scottish Symphony Orchestra
Ryan Wigglesworth *conductor*

There will be no interval

'Beckett has been waiting for Kurtág all this time,' wrote *The New Yorker* after the triumphant La Scala premiere of György Kurtág's *Endgame* ('*Fin de partie*') in 2018. Subsequently named one of the greatest operas of the century by *The Guardian*, Kurtág's 'unforgettable' adaption of Samuel Beckett's absurdist play finally has its UK premiere.

Every Prom live on BBC Radio 3 and available on BBC Sounds

Friday 18 August
PROM 44
7.30pm–*c*9.40pm • Royal Albert Hall

● £10–£52 *(plus booking fee')*

GEMMA NEW

Samy Moussa Symphony No. 2   20'
BBC co-commission: European premiere

Shostakovich Piano Concerto No. 2 in F major   20'

INTERVAL

Stravinsky The Firebird   45'

Pavel Kolesnikov *piano*

BBC Scottish Symphony Orchestra
Gemma New *conductor*

'Terrifically gifted' New Zealand-born conductor Gemma New makes her Proms debut with a colourful programme of 20th- and 21st-century orchestral masterworks. The graceful charm of Shostakovich's Piano Concerto No. 2 – a birthday gift for the composer's talented teenage son – meets the dazzling dances and acerbic brilliance of Stravinsky's ballet *The Firebird*. We move into the present with the European premiere of Canadian composer Samy Moussa's Symphony No. 2, reflecting an array of themes, including mythological and ancient origins, clarity and austerity. Prize-winning pianist Pavel Kolesnikov joins the BBC Scottish Symphony Orchestra. *See 'Agony and Ecstasy', pages 38–43; 'Peak Practice?', pages 76–79; 'Mood Music', pages 90–95.*

Saturday 19 August

PROM 45
7.00pm–c8.45pm • Royal Albert Hall

⬤ **£10–£52** *(plus booking fee')*

SAKARI ORAMO

Mahler Symphony No. 3
in D minor   95'

Jenny Carlstedt *mezzo-soprano*

BBC Symphony Chorus
Trinity Boys Choir
BBC Symphony Orchestra
Sakari Oramo *conductor*

There will be no interval

'The symphony must be like the world. It must embrace everything.' Nowhere is Mahler's philosophy more magnificently fulfilled than in his Symphony No. 3. The vast work might start with menacing brass fanfares, but threat and oppressive summer heat soon clear to reveal one of the composer's most radiant and expansive works – a vision of man and nature, earth and heaven that wrestles with death and transcendence before coming to a conclusion in which 'words are stilled' – a slow movement of solemn and transformative grace. Sakari Oramo conducts the BBC Symphony Orchestra and Chorus, joined by Trinity Boys Choir and Finnish-Swedish mezzo-soprano Jenny Carlstedt in the climactic setting of Nietzsche's 'Midnight Song' from *Also sprach Zarathustra*.

Saturday 19 August

PROM 46 • LATE NIGHT 🌙
10.15pm–c11.30pm • Royal Albert Hall

⬤ **£9–£26** *(plus booking fee')*

RAKHI SINGH

Manchester Collective: Neon
Hannah Peel Neon   11'
Ben Nobuto SERENITY 2.0   13'
Oliver Leith A different 'Fantasie
from Suite No. 5 in G minor'   5'
David Lang Mystery Sonata No. 7,
'Glory'   8'
Steve Reich Double Sextet   23'

Manchester Collective
Rakhi Singh *violin/director*

There will be no interval

The restless energy of crowded streets and sleepless nights runs through this concert by the Manchester Collective. Here is an urban musical world: bright with neon light, tense with uncertainty. Steve Reich's Pulitzer Prize-winning *Double Sextet* with its motoric rhythms and thick web of counterpoint sits alongside Hannah Peel's *Neon* – a fusion of electronic and acoustic elements with the sounds of Tokyo's Shinjuku Station – and Ben Nobuto's euphoric sound-collage *SERENITY 2.0*. The musical prayer of David Lang's *Mystery Sonata* No. 7 and Oliver Leith's 'slippy arrangement' of a 17th-century original help slow the pulse again.

Spotlight on …
Pavel Kolesnikov • Prom 44

Shostakovich composed his Second Piano Concerto as a 19th-birthday present to his son Maxim. Pianist Pavel Kolesnikov, who performs the work on 18 August, was even younger when he first got to know it. 'I was about 10 or 11, and I learnt it for one of my exams at my music school. I loved it, but only performed it once and never went back to it until now.' Kolesnikov was born in Siberia but is now based in London. Does a performer's birthplace provide a particular affinity for that country's music? 'There may be some truth in that, but I prefer not to generalise. Every case is unique. I have a strong predilection for French music, for instance.' Nonetheless, he feels a closeness to Shostakovich. 'He's one of the composers I revere the most. Every note has an almost physical effect on me – I'm mesmerised by his double, even triple meanings. Does it have to do with where I grew up? Perhaps, on a very primitive level. But true art transcends such basic limits.'

Though only 34, Kolesnikov is amassing quite a history of Proms performances, including a 2021 solo outing with Bach's 'Goldberg' Variations. That same year, the bright orange trainers he wore for Rachmaninov's *Paganini Rhapsody* drew quite a lot of comment. 'I was amazed by the discussions. For me it's simple: I wear what I consider suits the performance. I recently started collaborating with the designer Yohji Yamamoto … He'll be helping me find the right look for 2023!'

Spotlight on …
Lucy Crowe • Proms 26 & 49

It's an unconventional and – until recently – rather overlooked work by Schumann that Staffordshire-born soprano Lucy Crowe sings on 22 August. '*Das Paradies und die Peri* is unique. Schumann himself described it as "not an opera – I believe it's a new genre for the concert hall". Musically he blends elements from oratorio, opera and song, so you really feel like you're getting a bit of everything from the composer at the top of his game.' And Crowe is firmly in the spotlight, singing the work's central role. 'I am the Peri, a fairy-like spirit from Persian mythology who's been cast out of heaven. My only way back is to find "the gift that is most dear to heaven" … The main challenge comes right at the end, when Schumann gives the Peri a long-held top C to ride above the orchestra and chorus – and, boy, does it feel long! But it's an incredible climax to a beautiful, soul-searching work, one that will hopefully leave the audience skipping their way home.'

She sings Schumann's vivid musical drama alongside the London Symphony Orchestra and Sir Simon Rattle ('a dream come true' in Crowe's words), and also joins the Dunedin Consort under John Butt in Mozart on 6 August. 'It's really important for me to maintain a breadth of repertoire to keep my job exciting and challenging – variety is the key to being fulfilled. We even have a karaoke machine at home readily available for when I feel the need to release my inner pop diva!'

Sunday 20 August

PROM 47
7.30pm–c9.50pm • Royal Albert Hall

● £10–£52 *(plus booking fee')*

ISABELLE FAUST

Ligeti
Concert Românesc   *12'*
Violin Concerto   *27'*

INTERVAL

Mozart
Piano Concerto No. 23 in A major   *25'*
Symphony No. 41 in C major,
'Jupiter'   *31'*

Isabelle Faust *violin*
Alexander Melnikov *piano*

Les Siècles
François-Xavier Roth *conductor*

Celebrating its 20th anniversary this year, François-Xavier Roth's award-winning orchestra Les Siècles presents a typically eclectic programme. Music from sonic pioneer György Ligeti meets two late works by Mozart – pieces separated by two centuries, but united by the spirit of revolution. Unperformed until 1971, Ligeti's vibrant *Concert Românesc* ('Romanian Concerto') is a light-footed celebration of Romanian folk music – real and invented. His Violin Concerto – a 'wild collage of atmosphere and colours' – is one of the most original of any age, while Mozart's final symphony, the 'Jupiter', with its astonishing finale, is the last word on the genre from a master innovator. *See 'Hungary's Caterpillar', pages 20–23; 'Reeling in the Years', pages 84–88.*

Monday 21 August

PROM 48
8.00pm–c9.30pm • Royal Albert Hall

● £9–£42 *(plus booking fee')*

JULES BUCKLEY

Jules Buckley Orchestra

Jules Buckley Orchestra
Jules Buckley *conductor*

Following last year's spectacular debut at the Proms with a tribute to Aretha Franklin, the Jules Buckley Orchestra returns with its Grammy Award-winning conductor and special guests. *See bbc.co.uk/proms for further details.*

Every Prom live on BBC Radio 3 and available on BBC Sounds

Tuesday 22 August

PROM 49

7.30pm–c9.45pm • Royal Albert Hall

● £14–£62 (plus booking fee')

MAGDALENA KOŽENÁ

Schumann Das Paradies
und die Peri

99'

(sung in German, with English surtitles)

Lucy Crowe *soprano*
Jeanine De Bique *soprano*
Magdalena Kožená *mezzo-soprano*
Andrew Staples *tenor*
Linard Vrielink *tenor*
Florian Boesch *baritone*

London Symphony Chorus
London Symphony Orchestra
Sir Simon Rattle *conductor*

There will be one interval

Second only to the 'Spring' Symphony *(see Prom 51)*, *Das Paradies und die Peri* ('Paradise and the Peri') was among the most popular of Schumann's large-scale works during his lifetime – hailed as a piece 'of great genius and power'. Now Sir Simon Rattle and the London Symphony Orchestra and Chorus present the first ever complete performance at the Proms. Part oratorio and part opera, a choral and orchestral cycle that seems to unfold in continuous song, the work tells the story of a Peri – child of a fallen angel and a mortal – who makes a sequence of offerings to the guardians of Paradise in an attempt to gain entry. Lucy Crowe leads an exciting international cast.
See 'Peak Practice?', pages 76–79.

Wednesday 23 August

PROM 50

7.00pm–c10.00pm • Royal Albert Hall

● £14–£62 (plus booking fee')

JOÉLLE HARVEY

Handel Samson

150'

Allan Clayton *Samson*
Jacquelyn Stucker *Dalila*
Joélle Harvey *Israelite Woman*
Jess Dandy *Micah*
Brindley Sherratt *Harapha*
Jonathan Lemalu *Manoa*

Philharmonia Chorus
Academy of Ancient Music
Laurence Cummings *harpsichord/director*

There will be one interval

Our ongoing cycle of Handel oratorios continues with *Samson*. Inspired by Milton's *Samson Agonistes*, Handel created a deeply moving version of the story of the mighty Israelite warrior, imprisoned and blinded by his enemies, but still determined to destroy them. The Israelites' laments are brilliantly contrasted with the jangling joy of the Philistines, Samson's lofty struggles with Dalila's brittle affections. Tenor Allan Clayton and soprano Jacquelyn Stucker lead an all-star cast. One of today's leading Handelians, Laurence Cummings directs the Academy of Ancient Music from the harpsichord. *See 'Body and Spirit', pages 72–75; 'Peak Practice?', pages 76–79.*

Spotlight on ...

Allan Clayton • Prom 50

'I've only sung *Samson* in its entirety once before, years and years ago in South Africa.' Tenor Allan Clayton is looking back on his past history with Handel's epic biblical oratorio, whose title-role he sings on 23 August. 'It's usually terrifying to go back to something like that. Because you know you've done it before, and you open the score and see pencil markings in your own handwriting, but you just don't recognise any of it. So it's been back to basics with it.' But that brings its own rewards, he feels, in terms of reappraising material and perhaps bringing new perspectives.

The oratorio catches Samson after Dalila's strength-sapping hair-cutting: he's been blinded, imprisoned and humiliated. But he's soon to enact revenge on his captors. 'It's easy to forget what a warrior he once was,' explains Clayton. 'But it's there in the music: Handel gives him such strength and majesty in the music he writes for him.'

It's a work that Handel wrote as an unstaged oratorio – the form it takes at its Proms outing – but which has been staged as an opera too. What's Clayton's view on those different performance possibilities? 'I think in Handel's mind it was a dramatic piece. And certainly in terms of my own preparation, I try and inhabit the role just as much as I would if it were an opera. And the economy of being forced to focus just on your voice and the colours you bring, the intensity of your music-making, is another challenge, one that's good for you.'

Spotlight on …
Andris Nelsons
Proms 52 & 55

Riga-born conductor Andris Nelsons is a busy man: Music Director of both Leipzig's centuries-old Gewandhaus Orchestra and the almost-as-historic Boston Symphony Orchestra. It's the latter that he brings to London for a pair of Proms performances this season, but he's pioneering what he calls an 'alliance' between the two ensembles, one of the fruits of which he'll be sharing on 25 August. 'Julia Adolphe's *Makeshift Castle* is one of several works co-commissioned by the Boston Symphony and Gewandhaus orchestras. The BSO and I gave the premiere at Tanglewood last summer, and we were taken by its deeply personal expressivity, subtly shifting colours and bursts of lyricism.'

The other pieces in Nelsons's first Prom this year make for an intriguing contrast: 'Strauss's *Death and Transfiguration* conveys the mind of a man struggling against and then finally accepting his own death, while Prokofiev's Fifth Symphony celebrates the victorious end to a war,' he explains. 'But where there's music, there's always room for interpretations and questions.' Bringing together Stravinsky, Gershwin and Ravel in his second concert (26 August), however, shows 'societal uproar' at the start of the 20th century: 'You feel the turmoil, the change from a neatly ordered life into an explosion of colour and rhythm. All three composers open up a whole new world hidden behind genre definitions like ballet, waltz or jazz.'

Thursday 24 August

PROM 51
7.30pm–c9.40pm • Royal Albert Hall

⬤ £9–£42 *(plus booking fee*)*

CHRISTIAN TETZLAFF

Judith Weir Begin Afresh   c15'
BBC commission: world premiere

Schumann Symphony No. 1 in B flat major, 'Spring'   30'

INTERVAL

Elgar Violin Concerto in B minor   48'

Christian Tetzlaff *violin*

BBC Symphony Orchestra
Sakari Oramo *conductor*

A Spanish inscription on the title-page of Elgar's Violin Concerto reads: 'Herein is enshrined the soul of …..' The identity represented by those five dots remains a mystery as great as that at the heart of the composer's 'Enigma' Variations, and the concerto itself shares much of their wistful, lyrical quality, but with an added dash of heroic bravura. Celebrated German violinist Christian Tetzlaff joins Sakari Oramo and the BBC Symphony Orchestra as soloist. Elgar's musical nostalgia contrasts with Schumann's progressive Romanticism in the youthful 'Spring' Symphony, and the concert opens with the world premiere of *Begin Afresh* by Master of the King's Music Judith Weir. *See 'Peak Practice?', pages 76–79.*

Friday 25 August

PROM 52
6.30pm–c8.35pm • Royal Albert Hall

⬤ £14–£62 *(plus booking fee*)*

ANDRIS NELSONS

Julia Adolphe Makeshift Castle   13'
European premiere

R. Strauss Death and Transfiguration   23'

INTERVAL

Prokofiev Symphony No. 5 in B flat major   46'

Boston Symphony Orchestra
Andris Nelsons *conductor*

The mighty Boston Symphony Orchestra returns to the Proms under Music Director Andris Nelsons for the first of two concerts – human resilience the theme. 'I conceived of it as glorifying the grandeur of the human spirit,' Prokofiev wrote of his Fifth Symphony, premiered in January 1945 at the start of the USSR's successful final offensive against Nazi Germany. The defiant optimism of the finale is mirrored in Richard Strauss's tone-poem *Death and Transfiguration*, in which a dying man gains a musical glimpse of eternity. Jointly commissioned by the BSO and the Leipzig Gewandhaus Orchestra, of which Nelsons is also Music Director, Julia Adolphe's *Makeshift Castle* offers a contemporary meditation on fragility and endurance.

Friday 25 August

PROM 53 • LATE NIGHT ☽

10.15pm–c11.30pm • Royal Albert Hall

⬤ £10–£35 *(plus booking fee')*

IESTYN DAVIES

J. S. Bach
Cantata No. 170, 'Vergnügte Ruh, beliebte Seelenlust'   *24'*

Brandenburg Concerto No. 3 in G major   *10'*

Cantata No. 35, 'Geist und Seele wird verwirret'   *26'*

Iestyn Davies *counter-tenor*

The English Concert
Kristian Bezuidenhout *harpsichord/director*

There will be no interval

Counter-tenor Iestyn Davies – whose 'utterly sublime' singing and 'gorgeous tone' captivated audiences last season – returns with an all-Bach late-night concert. He joins period-instrument group The English Concert (currently celebrating its 50th anniversary) for two of Bach's solo cantatas – both composed in 1726 during his early years as music director at Leipzig's St Thomas's Church. While the lovely *Vergnügte Ruh* gazes towards heaven, *Geist und Seele* marvels at a miracle of creation and God's goodness. The bustling joy of Bach's Brandenburg Concerto No. 3 for strings completes the programme.

Saturday 26 August

PROM 54 ☀

2.00pm–c3.30pm • Royal Albert Hall

⬤ £9–£42 *(plus booking fee')*

ISABELLE DEMERS

Wagner, transcr. Demers
The Mastersingers of Nuremberg – Prelude to Act 1   *9'*

Rachel Laurin Prelude and Fugue in G major   *c6'*
world premiere

J. S. Bach, arr. Dupré
Cantata No. 146, 'Wir müssen durch viel Trübsal' – Sinfonia   *8'*

Coleridge-Taylor
Three Impromptus   *9'*

Reger Chorale Fantasia on 'Ein feste Burg ist unser Gott'   *13'*

Still Elegy   *4'*

Prokofiev, transcr. Demers
Romeo and Juliet – excerpts   *25'*

Isabelle Demers *organ*

There will be no interval

Canadian organist Isabelle Demers makes her Proms debut, putting the Royal Albert Hall's mighty 9,999-pipe organ through its paces. The rigour of Bach and Reger (born 150 years ago) contrasts with lighter pieces by Coleridge-Taylor and William Grant Still and a world premiere from Canadian composer Rachel Laurin. This is all framed with the drama of excerpts from stage-works by Wagner and Prokofiev.
See 'Taylor-Made Sounds', pages 56–58.

Saturday 26 August

PROM 55

7.30pm–c9.45pm • Royal Albert Hall

⬤ £18–£72 *(plus booking fee')*

JEAN-YVES THIBAUDET

Carlos Simon Four Black American Dances   *12'*
European premiere

Stravinsky Petrushka (1947 version)   *34'*

INTERVAL

Gershwin Piano Concerto in F major   *31'*

Ravel La valse   *12'*

Jean-Yves Thibaudet *piano*

Boston Symphony Orchestra
Andris Nelsons *conductor*

Dance – whether it's the whirl of the ballroom or the throbbing rhythms of Black America, the fierce grace of ballet or the shimmy of the jazz club – pulses through this second concert from Andris Nelsons and the Boston Symphony Orchestra *(see Prom 52)*. Jean-Yves Thibaudet is the soloist in Gershwin's Piano Concerto, with its bluesy slow movement and hot, frenzied finale. Ravel's *La valse* dances to the edge of the abyss, while Stravinsky's ballet *Petrushka* projects the earthy rhythms and bold colours of Russian folk music. The concert opens with the European premiere of US composer Carlos Simon's *Four Black American Dances*, drawing on dances that chart the Black American experience from slavery through to today.
See 'Peak Practice?', pages 76–79.

🖥 *Broadcast on BBC TV*

Spotlight on …
Jules Buckley
Proms 48 & 58

Jacob Collier, Laura Mvula, Pete Tong, Quincy Jones, Jarvis Cocker, Anoushka Shankar: the artists with whom British conductor Jules Buckley has collaborated at the Proms straddle genres and forms. And it's a setting that Buckley himself particularly enjoys: 'The Royal Albert Hall has a 360-degree experience for you as a performer. It wraps you up in its mystery from deep in the shadows as you enter. It's a totally magical space where the audience feels so connected to the performers.'

In the second of his two concerts this year, Buckley kicks off a new collaboration with electronic music pioneer Jon Hopkins. 'I've always been an admirer,' says Buckley. 'I remember a particular time when I'd finally fixed my turntable and the first vinyl I dropped on it was Jon's album *Singularity* – it just blew my mind. The pacing and the colours were out of this world. It was a lesson for me in the use of space, and in the careful building and crafting of an idea.'

Buckley and Hopkins are joined by the BBC Symphony Orchestra for the concert, which includes a brand-new commission from Hopkins written specially for the occasion. 'I don't want to give away anything about the new piece, simply because I want the music to speak for itself. Jon, the BBC SO and I aren't attempting to recreate his albums as you might know them. Instead, we're going to try and build a minimalist and mesmeric temple of orchestral colour. I can't give away any more than that!'

Sunday 27 August

PROM 56
7.30pm–*c*9.00pm • Royal Albert Hall

⬤ £18–£72 *(plus booking fee')*

SIR SIMON RATTLE

Mahler Symphony No. 9   81'

London Symphony Orchestra
Sir Simon Rattle *conductor*

There will be no interval

In Mahler's Ninth Symphony the composer – who would not live to hear its premiere – bid 'farewell to all whom he loved'. The words 'Leb' wohl!' ('farewell') are written onto the score itself, transformed into a theme that becomes the heartbeat of the whole work. It's a poignant choice for Sir Simon Rattle's final UK performance as Music Director of the London Symphony Orchestra. Death and life collide in a symphony haunted by loss but urgently clinging to dance and song. The finale, however, looks beyond, closing with a vision of distant hills where the sun is shining.

📺 *Broadcast on BBC TV*

Monday 28 August

PROM 57
7.00pm–*c*9.00pm • Royal Albert Hall

⬤ £14–£62 *(plus booking fee')*

ANNA-MARIA HELSING

Fantasy, Myths and Legends

BBC Concert Orchestra
Anna-Maria Helsing *conductor*

There will be one interval

An evening of orchestral fantasy and adventure featuring classic soundtracks from film, television and gaming's greatest myths and legends. Music from Howard Shore's epic score for *The Lord of the Rings* features, marking 50 years since the death of J. R. R. Tolkien. Among the other symphonic sagas are excerpts from Grammy Award-winner Lorne Balfe's score for the TV adaptation of Philip Pullman's *His Dark Materials* and Ramin Djawadi's award-winning *Game of Thrones* score, as well as music from the *Harry Potter* films and Studio Ghibli's popular animations. The BBC Concert Orchestra and its Principal Guest Conductor Anna-Maria Helsing offer a programme for all the family to enjoy.

📺 *Broadcast on BBC TV*

Every Prom live on BBC Radio 3 and available on BBC Sounds

Tuesday 29 August

PROM 58
8.00pm–c9.30pm • Royal Albert Hall

● £10–£52 (plus booking fee')

JON HOPKINS

Jon Hopkins with the BBC Symphony Orchestra and Jules Buckley

Jon Hopkins

BBC Symphony Orchestra
Jules Buckley conductor

There will be no interval

British composer Jon Hopkins – whose work has been nominated for Grammy, Mercury and Ivor Novello Awards – makes his BBC Proms debut with the world premiere of a 22-minute psychedelic drone epic for orchestra, choir and piano. Alongside this are reinterpretations of pieces from three of his critically acclaimed albums – *Immunity*, *Singularity* and *Music for Psychedelic Therapy* – re-imagined to form what Hopkins calls a 'group sonic meditation for 5,000 people'. A collaboration with the BBC Symphony Orchestra and Creative Artist-in-Association Jules Buckley, this atmospheric Prom focuses on the meditative and emotional side of Hopkins's musical output, leading you on a powerfully immersive journey.

Wednesday 30 August

PROM 59
7.30pm–c9.45pm • Royal Albert Hall

● £18–£72 (plus booking fee')

PAAVO JÄRVI

Beethoven Overture 'The Consecration of the House'   *12'*

Tchaikovsky Violin Concerto in D major   *33'*

INTERVAL

Dvořák Symphony No. 9 in E minor, 'From the New World'   *40'*

Augustin Hadelich violin

Tonhalle Orchestra Zurich
Paavo Järvi conductor

Switzerland's longest-established orchestra, the Tonhalle Orchestra Zurich, makes a welcome return to the Proms under Music Director Paavo Järvi with a concert of classical greats. Following a 'fantastically engaging and uplifting' performance of Dvořák's Violin Concerto last season, Augustin Hadelich is also back again as the soloist in Tchaikovsky's concerto – brilliant outer movements framing the tender Canzonetta. If Tchaikovsky's concerto speaks of romantic heartache, then Dvořák's 'New World' Symphony channels aching homesickness in the nostalgic Bohemian character barely concealed under a new veneer of Americana. The concert opens with Beethoven's overture *The Consecration of the House*, originally written for the opening of a new theatre in Vienna. *See 'Peak Practice?', pages 76–79.*

Spotlight on ...

Augustin Hadelich • Prom 59

'I've been playing Tchaikovsky's Violin Concerto since I was 12, and it quickly became one of my favourite pieces.' But a long history with such a cherished work brings its own dangers, explains Augustin Hadelich, who performs it on 30 August. 'There can be old habits that get in the way, or even the accumulated baggage of violin tradition. Of course, you can't just unhear what you've heard, or forget how you played it before. But you can go back to the score and think about what exactly the composer wrote and what he may have intended. As I went through that process, I ended up loving the piece even more.'

Nonetheless, it's still a piece to be grappled with, as Hadelich explains. 'Technically, it's one of the most challenging works of the 19th century. Tchaikovsky wanted to create a violin concerto in which the solo part would be very virtuosic – it's full of difficult fast passages, chords and double-stops – and also harmonics. At the time it was written, there were few violinists who could play it well, but violin technique has always evolved alongside the challenges that composers pose to violinists.'

And that exuberant virtuosity might just have been designed to demonstrate the prowess of a particularly beloved violinist. 'It's been speculated that Tchaikovsky had a romantic affair with Yosif Kotek, for whom he wrote the concerto. To me, this piece was written by a man who is happily and passionately in love.'

Spotlight on ...
Vladimir Jurowski • Prom 60

'It's our job as performers and interpreters to bring music to the world, and let the world take it from there.' With Thomas Adès's Piano Concerto the centrepiece of his Proms performance on 31 August, conductor Vladimir Jurowski is reflecting on the importance of a wide repertoire. 'I feel strongly that all music – new or old, from whatever tradition or background – must be performed and supported. If you relegate new music, then you'll only be preaching to the converted.' Adès's music has its complexities, but it speaks strongly to Jurowski. 'Thomas is an extraordinary musician – his music is challenging to put together, and there's great pleasure in the dexterity of the writing, but there's also reason and intent behind the difficulties.'

Jurowski concludes his Prom with another composer he's passionate about. 'I feel a deep connection with Rachmaninov – a Russian artist who spent long periods in Europe and the USA – in particular his works composed in "exile", such as the Third Symphony. It's a fascinating balance, infused with 20th-century modernity, but redolent of the traditions of his roots.'

Jurowski brings the Berlin Radio Symphony Orchestra, where he's been Chief Conductor since 2017. 'It's important to me to bring the Berlin musicians to make their Proms debut in their centenary season. We're one of the oldest orchestras in Germany – founded just a few years before the wonderful BBC Symphony Orchestra!'

Thursday 31 August

PROM 60
7.30pm–*c*9.45pm • Royal Albert Hall

● £14–£62 *(plus booking fee')*

KIRILL GERSTEIN

Weill Kleine Dreigroschenmusik *20'*
Thomas Adès Piano Concerto *22'*

INTERVAL

Rachmaninov Symphony No. 3 in A minor *39'*

Kirill Gerstein *piano*

Berlin Radio Symphony Orchestra
Vladimir Jurowski *conductor*

Rachmaninov's 150th-anniversary celebrations continue with the composer's yearning Symphony No. 3. 'Only one place is closed to me,' Rachmaninov wrote after his exile in the USA, 'and that is my own country, Russia.' Following in the virtuoso tradition of Rachmaninov is Thomas Adès's Piano Concerto, performed here by Kirill Gerstein, who gave the 2019 premiere. The work's sardonic brilliance finds an echo in the suite from Kurt Weill's *Die Dreigroschenoper* ('The Threepenny Opera'), with its famous 'Ballad of Mack the Knife'. Coming after last week's visitors from Boston (where the Adès concerto was premiered), tonight we welcome the esteemed Berlin Radio Symphony Orchestra – 100 this year – making its Proms debut under Chief Conductor since 2017, Vladimir Jurowski. *See 'Welcome Back, Mr Rachmaninov', pages 14–18.*

Friday 1 September

PROM 61
7.30pm–*c*9.40pm • Royal Albert Hall

● £9–£42 *(plus booking fee')*

AARON AZUNDA AKUGBO

Valerie Coleman Seven O'Clock Shout *6'*
Coleridge-Taylor Four Novelletten *23'*
Haydn Trumpet Concerto in E flat major *16'*

INTERVAL

Perkinson Sinfonietta No. 1 – Rondo (3rd mvt) *7'*
Beethoven Symphony No. 4 in B flat major *34'*

Aaron Azunda Akugbo *trumpet*

Chineke! Orchestra
Anthony Parnther *conductor*

Following their performance of Beethoven's Ninth Symphony last season, the award-winning Chineke! Orchestra – Europe's first majority Black and ethnically diverse orchestra – returns with the composer's elegant and joyous Symphony No. 4. Full of song and celebration, Haydn's sunny Trumpet Concerto joins music by pioneering Black British composer Samuel Coleridge-Taylor and Valerie Coleman's pandemic anthem *Seven O'Clock Shout*, as well as the irresistibly rhythmic Rondo from the Sinfonietta No. 1 by African American composer Coleridge-Taylor Perkinson, who was named after his British precursor. *See 'Taylor-Made Sounds', pages 56–58.*

▭ *Broadcast on BBC TV*

Saturday 2 September

PROMS 62 & 63 ☀
3.00pm–*c*4.45pm & 7.30pm–*c*9.15pm
Royal Albert Hall

⬤ £10–£52 *(plus booking fee*)*

NICHOLAS COLLON

The Rite by Heart

A dramatic and musical exploration of
Stravinsky's *The Rite of Spring* *c*40'

INTERVAL

Stravinsky The Rite of Spring
(performed from memory) 33'

Actors to be announced

Aurora Orchestra
Nicholas Collon *conductor*

The ever-innovative Aurora Orchestra returns
to the Proms for its greatest challenge to date:
a daring performance by heart of Stravinsky's
iconic ballet *The Rite of Spring*. The premiere of
The Rite in 1913 was the scandal that sounded
the beginning of modern music – a riot onstage,
as well as off. Get under the skin of the piece
that shook the music and ballet worlds with its
stamping, jagged rhythms and modern
harmony. Join Nicholas Collon and the Aurora
Orchestra as they dramatise the work's origins,
set the scene of its notorious concert premiere
and, finally, perform the entire ballet from
memory. *See 'Peak Practice?', pages 76–79.*

📻 *Prom 63 broadcast live on BBC Radio 3*

Sunday 3 September

PROM 64
4.00pm–*c*9.20pm • Royal Albert Hall

⬤ £14–£62 *(plus booking fee*)*

MICHAEL SPYRES

Berlioz The Trojans 235'
*(concert performance; sung in French with
English surtitles)*

Alice Coote *Cassandra*
Michael Spyres *Aeneas*
Paula Murrihy *Dido*
Lionel Lhote *Coroebus*
Adèle Charvet *Ascanius*
William Thomas *Narbal*
Ashley Riches *Panthus*
Beth Taylor *Anna*

Monteverdi Choir
Orchestre Révolutionnaire et Romantique
Sir John Eliot Gardiner *conductor*

There will be two intervals

Few musical spectacles are bigger or more
overwhelming than Berlioz's *The Trojans* – the
five-act grand opera, retelling the story of
the fall of Troy and the doomed love of Dido
and Aeneas, that the composer saw as the
pinnacle of his career. By turns monumental
and heartbreakingly intimate – a cinematic epic
before its time – the vast score reshapes Virgil's
Aeneid with unprecedented dramatic scope
and intensity. Sir John Eliot Gardiner brings
a lifetime's love of Berlioz to the music, with
the help of an outstanding cast that includes
'phenomenal' American tenor Michael Spyres.
See 'The Trojans', pages 48–51.

Spotlight on …
Alice Coote • Prom 64

'I become a different singer when I perform
Berlioz, I think,' says Alice Coote. 'There's
something huge, something grand about
his music, and also a kind of intimacy.' It's
a contrast played out clearly in the role
of Cassandra that Coote sings in Berlioz's
epic opera *The Trojans* on 3 September.
'Cassandra is a visionary, but she's also a
woman, a human being.' And the insights
that the character brings, Coote feels,
make her a particularly relevant figure
for our own times. 'She's almost an
embodiment of mistrust. She's basically
saying that life isn't safe. Can we trust a
higher power, or the people around us?
Everyone around her says everything is
going to be OK, but she feels that it's not
and that nobody will listen. She's certainly
a large part of me: I think we all feel like
nobody's listening to us and we see things
going wrong in so many different ways.
It's an uncomfortable thing to say, and
to sing, but that's the challenge of it.'

Coote is joined in that challenge by the
Orchestre Révolutionnaire et Romantique
and its founding conductor Sir John Eliot
Gardiner, with whom she's collaborated
on several recent performances. How
important is that sense of familiarity for
the performance itself? 'It's beyond 100
per cent. Music is based on trust, and it
feels like he places enormous trust in
me, so I know I can trust him in return.
It's a wonderful feeling, and I know he'll
do anything for the spirit of the music.'

Spotlight on …
Sarah Hicks
Proms 66 & 67

'The song "Cigarettes and Chocolate Milk" was my first exposure to Rufus Wainwright's music, and I remember being immediately captured by his voice and the classical sensibility of his music. I love when songwriters are able to create, in just a few minutes, an entire little world for the listener.' US conductor Sarah Hicks is reflecting on what she finds inspiring about Rufus Wainwright. He's a best-selling 'pop' artist as well as a composer of two operas and several other smaller works. 'I've always viewed him as an artist who uses the styles and sounds that resonate and are meaningful for him. He's beyond categories, and I feel like labels are a disservice most of the time anyway.'

Wainwright and Hicks first collaborated in 2017 with the Minnesota Orchestra. They come together again as she conducts two concerts of his music with the BBC Concert Orchestra on 5 September, with orchestral versions of two iconic albums, *Want One* and *Want Two*. '*Want Two* is a much darker album, and in some ways more orchestral. But, while they may be different, they're still in Rufus's voice, both literally and figuratively.' Hicks casts her net widely as a conductor, leading collaborations with pop, rock and rap artists as well as music for film and gaming, alongside classical performances. 'I apply the same rigour and commitment to any music I conduct – the joy I find in music-making lies simply in the experience I'm creating for the audience.'

Monday 4 September

PROM 65
7.30pm–*c*9.00pm • Royal Albert Hall

● £9–£42 *(plus booking fee*)*

SEMYON BYCHKOV

Bruckner Symphony No. 8 in C minor (1890 version, ed. Nowak) 84'

BBC Symphony Orchestra
Semyon Bychkov *conductor*

There will be no interval

Bruckner described the finale of his Symphony No. 8 – the last he would ever complete – as 'the most significant movement of my life'. It's the culmination of a career, perhaps even of an era: music of 'blazing calm' and impossible grandeur in which the shattering terror of the opening finally finds not just resolution but transcendence. Semyon Bychkov conducts the BBC Symphony Orchestra in a work whose vastness grows out of a sequence of musical fragments shored against the ruin of humanity itself.

Every Prom live on BBC Radio 3 and available on BBC Sounds

Tuesday 5 September

PROM 66
7.30pm–*c*8.45pm • Royal Albert Hall

● £14–£62 *(plus booking fee*)*
Want Both ticket offer†

RUFUS WAINWRIGHT

Rufus Wainwright
Want Symphonic – Want One

Rufus Wainwright
BBC Concert Orchestra
Sarah Hicks *conductor*

There will be no interval

Multi-award-winning singer-songwriter and composer Rufus Wainwright returns to the Proms with his signature brand of 'Baroque pop' for the first of two concerts on the same night *(see Prom 67)*. Wainwright's album *Want One* – released 20 years ago and praised by critics for 'taking his lush, orchestrated pop to staggering new heights' – draws on everything from opera to cabaret, *chanson* and jazz. Hear it as never before, in the world premiere of these symphonic arrangements for the BBC Concert Orchestra. Wainwright says he is 'excited to bring these songs to a new level with all-new symphonic settings. There is nothing more exciting than singing in front of a huge orchestra.'

†*20% off your second ticket when you book for both Want One and Want Two.*

Tuesday 5 September

PROM 67 • LATE NIGHT ☾
10.15pm–c11.30pm • Royal Albert Hall

● £14–£62 *(plus booking fee')*
Want Both ticket offer†

RUFUS WAINWRIGHT

Rufus Wainwright
Want Symphonic – Want Two

Rufus Wainwright

BBC Concert Orchestra
Sarah Hicks *conductor*

There will be no interval

Rufus Wainwright's second Prom tonight reunites the boundary-breaking singer-songwriter with the BBC Concert Orchestra for *Want Two* – his 'stunning' and 'heady' follow-up to *Want One*. The two releases, says Wainwright, 'are maybe the most epic of my albums. They are the two sides of a coin, or better, my personality: the male and the female, the knight in shining armour and the innocent maiden, ecstasy and restraint, glory and doom, decay and creation, the mature and the child.' *Want Two* blends alt-rock and French song, glossy pop music and even an Agnus Dei into a kaleidoscopic musical trip that gleams and grooves, in the world premiere of these symphonic arrangements for the BBC Concert Orchestra.

†*20% off your second ticket when you book for both Want Two and Want One.*

Wednesday 6 September

PROM 68
7.30pm–c9.35pm • Royal Albert Hall

● £10–£52 *(plus booking fee')*

THOMAS GOULD

Lera Auerbach Sogno di Stabat Mater   12'

Corelli Concerto grosso in F major, Op. 6 No. 2   10'

Tippett Fantasia concertante on a Theme of Corelli   20'

INTERVAL

Max Richter Recomposed: Vivaldi – The Four Seasons   40'

Britten Sinfonia
Thomas Gould *violin/director*

Hear Vivaldi's *The Four Seasons (see Prom 4)* through fresh ears, as the Britten Sinfonia and violinist Thomas Gould give the Proms debut performance of Max Richter's rhapsodic *Recomposed* – a heady blend of acoustic and electronic sounds that throws 'molecules of the original Vivaldi into a test tube … and waits for an explosion'. Trace the evolution of Baroque music through a concert that opens with Lera Auerbach's reimagining of Pergolesi's *Stabat Mater* of 1736 and a Corelli *Concerto grosso* published around 20 years earlier, then releases the composer's music into Tippett's sonic hall of mirrors, before finally arriving at the present day with Richter's 21st-century reinventions.

Spotlight on …
Thomas Gould • Prom 68

Is it by Vivaldi or is it by Max Richter? Or is it by both? Richter's compelling 21st-century reimagining of Vivaldi's *The Four Seasons* poses fundamental questions about authorship that also spill over into performance. 'The first time I played it, it took some getting used to,' admits Thomas Gould, soloist in the Proms performance on 6 September. 'Max has left some of Vivaldi's movements virtually untouched, but changed others almost beyond recognition – so, playing the piece as a whole, you're aware of dipping in and out of different worlds.' How does Gould respond to its collision of musical styles? 'It's a fascinating piece. It strikes me as a good balance between reverence for the original and quirky, playful reinvention. It definitely packs an emotional punch, too, for audiences and performers – I always feel quite wrung-out by the time I reach the end of "Winter".'

Also being performed is another piece that takes inspiration from earlier music, Tippett's *Fantasia concertante on a Theme of Corelli*. 'Both composers pay homage to old masters without ever losing their own voices, but they get there through different means. Tippett seems to be looking at Corelli's music through a microscope, relishing the opportunity to write out his own ornamentation on Corelli's theme in detail. Richter gazes up at Vivaldi through a telescope, guiding us on a celestial and spiritual tour through *The Four Seasons*.'

Spotlight on …
Raphaël Pichon • Prom 69

'Mozart's *Requiem* is a really popular piece, so I'm happy to come and offer an unusual angle on it. I think it will be an evening about memory, and also about Mozart's own amazing destiny.' Mozart famously left his *Requiem* unfinished when he died in 1791. It's an unconventional conception of the work that conductor Raphaël Pichon and his Paris-based ensemble Pygmalion bring to the Proms on 7 September, interspersing its movements with a diverse collection of other works by Mozart. It's all with a purpose, however: 'We need a dialogue with the past, with the roots of the *Requiem*'s music. It's as though Mozart is having a discussion with himself, and with his own imagination.' Pichon cites the composer's Kyrie in D minor as an example. 'It's one of the first choral pieces Mozart ever wrote. And it's very similar to the famous opening of the *Requiem*. For me, it's almost as if everything was there already: it's as though the *Requiem*, which is Mozart's last expression and will exist for eternity, had been there for ever too.'

Pichon is using the familiar completion of the *Requiem* by Mozart's pupil Franz Xaver Süssmayr as his starting point: 'It's the most convincing completion – it's mostly Mozart's own work anyway,' he explains. But his intention is to challenge our very familiarity with the piece. 'We've heard it so many times that we might even be a bit tired of it. But we need to listen to it again, closely, and in a philosophical way.'

Thursday 7 September
PROM 69
7.30pm–*c*9.00pm • Royal Albert Hall

⬤ £14–£62 *(plus booking fee')*

ERIN MORLEY

Anon. Plainsong 'Christus factus est' 3'

Mozart
Requiem (compl. Süssmayr) 48'
interspersed with:
Masonic Funeral Music 6'
Kyrie in D minor, K90 3'
Thamos, King of Egypt – 'Ne pulvis et cinis' 4'
Five Solfeggios – No. 2 3'
Quis te comprehendat 4'
Two Church Songs – No. 2: 'O Gottes Lamm' 3'

Anon. Plainsong 'In paradisum' 3'

There will be no interval

Erin Morley *soprano*
Sara Mingardo *mezzo-soprano*
Laurence Kilsby *tenor*
Alex Rosen *bass*

Pygmalion
Raphaël Pichon *conductor*

Raphaël Pichon and his exciting ensemble Pygmalion present an alternative vision of Mozart's *Requiem*, famously left incomplete at the composer's death. Tonight's reimagining swells the popular completion by Mozart's pupil Süssmayr with additional pieces to create a compelling alternative sequence. *See 'Music for the Soul', pages 68–71.*

Friday 8 September
PROM 70
7.30pm–*c*9.50pm • Royal Albert Hall

⬤ £10–£52 *(plus booking fee')*

DOMINGO HINDOYAN

Honegger Rugby 8'
Rachmaninov Piano Concerto No. 3 in D minor 43'

INTERVAL

Gabriela Ortiz Clara 17'
UK premiere

Bernstein Symphonic Dances from 'West Side Story' 24'

Nobuyuki Tsujii *piano*

Royal Liverpool Philharmonic Orchestra
Domingo Hindoyan *conductor*

His Proms debut in 2013 was praised for its 'charming liquid naturalness' and 'delicious clarity'. Now Japanese pianist Nobuyuki Tsujii returns as soloist in Rachmaninov's demanding Piano Concerto No. 3. The lush sprawl of Rachmaninov is framed by the hormone-fuelled rhythmic energy of the Symphonic Dances from Bernstein's *West Side Story* and the musical contact sport of Honegger's tone-poem *Rugby*. The UK premiere of Mexican composer Gabriela Ortiz's Clara Schumann-inspired *Clara* completes the programme. The Royal Liverpool Philharmonic Orchestra is conducted by its Venezuelan-born Chief Conductor Domingo Hindoyan. *See 'Body and Spirit', pages 72–75.*

Saturday 9 September

PROM 71
7.00pm–c10.20pm • Royal Albert Hall

(BBC Last Night of the Proms logo)

⬤ **£32–£115** *(plus booking fee')*

LISE DAVIDSEN

SHEKU KANNEH-MASON

Last Night of the Proms 2023

Programme to include:

R. Strauss Don Juan 20'

Coleridge-Taylor,
arr. S. Parkin Deep River 5'

Bruch Kol Nidrei 12'

James B. Wilson 1922 c5'
BBC commission: world premiere

Wagner
Tannhäuser – 'Dich, teure Halle' 3'

Mascagni Cavalleria rusticana –
Easter Hymn; Intermezzo 10'

Verdi Macbeth – 'Nel dì della
vittoria … Vieni! t'affretta!' 8'

Kálmán The Gypsy Princess –
'Heia, heia, in den Bergen ist mein
Heimatland' 3'

arr. Wood Fantasia on British
Sea-Songs 7'

concluding with:

Arne, arr. Sargent Rule, Britannia! 3'

Elgar Pomp and Circumstance
March No. 1 in D major ('Land of
Hope and Glory') 8'

Parry, orch. Elgar Jerusalem 2'

arr. Britten The National Anthem 2'

Trad., arr. Paul Campbell
Auld Lang Syne 2'

Lise Davidsen *soprano*
Sheku Kanneh-Mason *cello*

BBC Symphony Chorus
BBC Symphony Orchestra
Marin Alsop *conductor*
There will be one interval

Two great names in classical music come
together to host the biggest musical party of the
year. Cellist Sheku Kanneh-Mason and soprano
Lise Davidsen join conductor Marin Alsop and
the BBC Symphony Orchestra and Chorus for an
evening including opera arias, a spiritual, a world
premiere and all the traditional favourites by
Arne, Elgar and Parry. *See 'Taylor-Made Sounds',
pages 56–58; 'Peak Practice?', pages 76–79.*

🖵 *Broadcast on BBC TV*

**Every Prom live
on BBC Radio 3
and available on
BBC Sounds**

'Proms at' Chamber Concerts

Saturday 15 July

PROMS AT LONDONDERRY ☀
2.00pm–c4.00pm • Guildhall, Derry

For ticket prices and booking fees, visit bbc.co.uk/promstickets

William Byrd: England's Nightingale

Sacred and secular choral music by William Byrd and his pupils, including:

Byrd
O Lord, make thy servant Elizabeth *3'*
Sing joyfully *3'*
Great Service – Nunc dimittis *5'*
Ave verum corpus *4'*
Laudate Dominum *3'*
Optimam partem elegit *3'*
Mass for Four Voices – Agnus Dei *4'*

Stile Antico

There will be one interval

Early music vocal ensemble Stile Antico explores the many facets of William Byrd – England's greatest Renaissance composer and a musical chameleon – in his 400th-anniversary year. We meet the obedient Protestant courtier, the devout Catholic, the influential master and the accomplished country gentleman enjoying music in his old age. *See 'Servants of the Church and State', pages 96–99.*

Sunday 30 July

PROMS AT ABERYSTWYTH ☀
2.00pm–c3.45pm • Aberystwyth Arts Centre/Canolfan y Celfyddydau

For ticket prices and booking fees, visit bbc.co.uk/promstickets

Programme to include:

Gibbons
The silver swan *2'*

Weelkes
Come, clap thy hands *2'*
The nightingale, the organ of delight *2'*
The ape, the monkey and baboon *2'*

Ligeti Nonsense Madrigals *14'*
Sarah Rimkus My heart is like a singing bird *6'*
Judith Weir Madrigal *3'*

and madrigals by Italian Renaissance composers

The Gesualdo Six
Owain Park *director*

There will be one interval

A journey through five centuries of madrigals, from English Tudor composer Thomas Weelkes (celebrating his 400th anniversary this year) and Orlando Gibbons to contemporary composers Judith Weir and Sarah Rimkus. *See 'Hungary's Caterpillar', pages 20–23; 'Servants of the Church and State', pages 96–99.*

Every Prom live on BBC Radio 3 and available on BBC Sounds

Sunday 6 August

PROMS AT DEWSBURY ☀
3.00pm–c5.00pm • Dewsbury Town Hall

For ticket prices and booking fees, visit bbc.co.uk/promstickets

Rachmaninov, arr. R. Wallfisch
Vocalise *6'*
Pejačević Cello Sonata *28'*
INTERVAL
Lara Weaver A Thing That Holds *8'*
Rachmaninov Cello Sonata *35'*

Laura van der Heijden *cello*
Jâms Coleman *piano*

Former BBC Young Musician of the Year Laura van der Heijden and pianist Jâms Coleman present a programme of 20th- and 21st-century music for cello and piano. A waft of incense and the echo of chiming bells hover around Rachmaninov's Cello Sonata, a work suffused with the mystical spirit of Russian Orthodoxy. A spiritual journey in sound becomes a spatial one in Lara Weaver's *A Thing That Holds* – an exploration of the cello as a vessel that contains and releases. This season's spotlight on Croatian composer Dora Pejačević continues with the composer's muscular Cello Sonata, with echoes of Brahms and Mendelssohn running through its melody-filled movements. The concert opens with Rachmaninov's lyrical *Vocalise*. *See 'Welcome Back, Mr Rachmaninov', pages 14–18; 'Countess and Composer', pages 52–55.*

Sunday 27 August

PROMS AT TRURO ☀
2.00pm–c4.00pm • Hall for Cornwall

For ticket prices and booking fees, visit bbc.co.uk/promstickets

Schubert Piano Quintet in A major, D667, 'Trout' 40'

INTERVAL

Coleridge-Taylor Nonet
in F minor, Op. 2 27'

Gershwin, arr. T. Poster
songs 12'

Kaleidoscope Chamber Collective

The Kaleidoscope Chamber Collective – a 'sparky, shape-shifting ensemble of starry young musicians' – makes its Proms debut. Schubert's 'Trout' Quintet celebrates the expressive power of each individual instrument with its ebullient, characterful writing – music of unclouded joy and delight. The sun also shines through Samuel Coleridge-Taylor's richly melodic Nonet, captivating with its warm-hearted opening, song-like slow movement, wicked Scherzo and confident finale. *See 'Taylor-Made Sounds', pages 56–58; 'Peak Practice?', pages 76–79.*

Sunday 3 September

PROMS AT PERTH ☀
2.00pm–c3.45pm • Perth Concert Hall

For ticket prices and booking fees, visit bbc.co.uk/promstickets

Haydn String Quartet
in E flat major, Op. 9 No. 2 19'

Tippett Piano Sonata No. 2 12'

INTERVAL

Shostakovich Piano Quintet
in G minor, Op. 57 36'

Heath Quartet
Steven Osborne *piano*

Pianist Steven Osborne joins the award-winning Heath Quartet for a chamber concert of Classical traditions and reinventions. With its mercurial mood swings and four-movement plan, Haydn's early String Quartet in E flat major anticipates the symphonic stature the genre would soon achieve, while still retaining all its early charm. Shostakovich's Piano Quintet harks back to the chamber music of Haydn and his predecessors, revisiting 18th-century forms and gestures through his own distinctive lens. Originally titled 'Mosaics', Tippett's Piano Sonata No. 2 captures the fragmentary brilliance of that idea – an ambiguous scatter of thoughts that refuse to coalesce into a musical argument.

STILE ANTICO • PROMS AT LONDONDERRY

THE GESUALDO SIX • PROMS AT ABERYSTWYTH

LAURA VAN DER HEIJDEN • PROMS AT DEWSBURY

KALEIDOSCOPE CHAMBER COLLECTIVE
PROMS AT TRURO

STEVEN OSBORNE • PROMS AT PERTH

Proms at Sage Gateshead

The first weekend-long Proms festival at Sage Gateshead – rooted in the North-East

Friday 21 July

7.30pm–*c*9.30pm • Sage One

For ticket prices and booking fees, visit bbc.co.uk/promstickets

Self Esteem

Royal Northern Sinfonia
Robert Ames *conductor*

There will be one interval

As Self Esteem, Rebecca Lucy Taylor has become one of the most engaging voices in British music, combining big, bold choruses with lyrics whose honesty, humour and directness have won the Rotherham-born singer an ever-growing list of fans since the release of her 2021 album *Prioritise Pleasure*. The weekend festival launches with an exciting collaboration with the Royal Northern Sinfonia.

Friday 21 July

LATE NIGHT ☽

10.00pm–*c*11.45pm • Sage Two

For ticket prices and booking fees, visit bbc.co.uk/promstickets

Yazz Ahmed *trumpet*
Arun Ghosh *clarinet*

There will be one interval

Innovative trumpeter and composer Yazz Ahmed and her quartet present a set of intoxicating, psychedelic jazz. Joining her is clarinettist, composer and bandleader Arun Ghosh and his band, bringing hypnotic rhythms and transcendental textures. *Presented with GemArts Masala Festival, with support from Jazz North East.*

📻 *Broadcast live on BBC Radio 3*

Saturday 22 July

7.30pm–*c*9.30pm • Sage One

For ticket prices and booking fees, visit bbc.co.uk/promstickets

DINIS SOUSA

Missy Mazzoli Sinfonia (for Orbiting Spheres)   9'
Mozart Piano Concerto No. 20 in D minor   30'
INTERVAL
Brahms Symphony No. 2 in D major   43'

Kristian Bezuidenhout *piano*

Royal Northern Sinfonia
Dinis Sousa *conductor*

Light and darkness battle it out in this tempestuous programme from the Royal Northern Sinfonia and Principal Conductor Dinis Sousa. 'Black wings are constantly beating above us,' Brahms wrote, encouraging the listener to hear the shadow that melancholy casts over his apparently serene Symphony No. 2. The same uneasy spirit runs through Mozart's Piano Concerto No. 20 in D minor, which shares its stormy key with his opera *Don Giovanni* and his *Requiem (see Prom 69)*. Cosmic order is established in the circling musical orbits and intersecting paths of Missy Mazzoli's hypnotic *Sinfonia*, written 'in the shape of a solar system'.

📻 *Broadcast live on BBC Radio 3*

Saturday 22 July

LATE NIGHT ☽

10.15pm–*c*11.15pm • Sage One

For ticket prices and booking fees, visit bbc.co.uk/promstickets

VOICES OF THE RIVER'S EDGE

Chorus of Royal Northern Sinfonia
Voices of the River's Edge

There will be no interval

Formed for Gateshead's 2022 Prom, the Sage Gateshead's young people's choir Voices of the River's Edge has continued to welcome new members and to make music deep-rooted in North-East communities. This Prom brings them together with the Chorus of Royal Northern Sinfonia and additional massed voices from across the North-East, in a celebration of vocal music that includes a new BBC commission by award-winning composer Kristina Arakelyan.

📻 *Broadcast live on BBC Radio 3*

Sunday 23 July

2.00pm–c3.45pm • Sage Two ☀

For ticket prices and booking fees, visit bbc.co.uk/promstickets

Reginald Mobley *counter-tenor*
Baptiste Trotignon *piano*

There will be one interval

Praised for his 'shimmering' voice, American counter-tenor Reginald Mobley is joined by celebrated French jazz pianist Baptiste Trotignon for a musical journey through the African American spiritual. With songs including 'Sometimes I feel like a motherless child' and 'Nobody knows the trouble I've seen', they trace this powerful music from its colonial origins through to jazz standards and homages by Black composers including Florence Price and Harry T. Burleigh.

📻 *Broadcast live on BBC Radio 3*

Sunday 23 July

3.00pm–c4.15pm • Sage One ☀

For ticket prices and booking fees, visit bbc.co.uk/promstickets

CBeebies: Ocean Adventure

Royal Northern Sinfonia
Kwamé Ryan *conductor*

There will be no interval

All aboard for a fun-filled CBeebies musical ocean adventure for all the family! CBeebies friends JoJo & Gran Gran are on board the Sage Gateshead submarine with a Gran Gran plan, and Andy has his safari sub at the ready. Search for endangered creatures, find out fascinating facts and collect sounds and pictures for your very own musical ocean scrapbook.

Proms at Great Yarmouth

Friday 8 September

6.00pm–c7.15pm • Hippodrome

For ticket prices and booking fees, visit bbc.co.uk/promstickets

ANNA-MARIA HELSING

Programme to include:

Vaughan Williams The Lark Ascending   *15'*

Walton Coronation March 'Crown Imperial'   *6'*

Khachaturian Masquerade – Waltz   *4'*

Sarah Rodgers new work   *c5'*
BBC commission: world premiere

Stravinsky Circus Polka   *4'*

Rodgers, arr. D. Walker Carousel – The Carousel Waltz   *5'*

Nathaniel Anderson-Frank *violin*

BBC Concert Orchestra
Anna-Maria Helsing *conductor*

There will be no interval

A programme of popular orchestral favourites at one of only two remaining permanent circus buildings in the UK. There's theatrical flair from Richard Rodgers and Khachaturian, and big-tent novelty from Stravinsky. Walton provides the ceremony, and Vaughan Williams offers a pastoral interlude among the liveliness.

📻 *Broadcast live on BBC Radio 3*

BBC Young Composer Workshops

Gateshead (July)
London (July/August)
Great Yarmouth (September)

The BBC Young Composer Workshops offer young composers aged 12 to 18 the chance to meet and learn from leading composers, and to take part in a range of musical activities.

There is something for everyone, from experienced composers to beginners curious to find out more. Workshops will take place in Gateshead, Great Yarmouth and London.

For exact dates and further information, visit bbc.co.uk/youngcomposer

Proms young composer workshop, 2017

BBC Concert Orchestra

BBC National Orchestra of Wales

Cerddorfa Genedlaethol Gymreig y BBC

BBC Philharmonic

BBC ORCHESTRAS & CHOIRS

MUSIC FOR EVERYONE

FROM THE HEART

BBC Scottish Symphony Orchestra

SO BBC Symphony Orchestra & Chorus

iPLAYER **SOUNDS**

BBC.CO.UK/ORCHESTRAS

Booking

Online
bbc.co.uk/promstickets or
royalalberthall.com

By phone
on 020 7070 4441 *
*(9.00am–9.00pm, daily,
13–20 May; 9.00am–5.00pm,
weekdays, from 21 May)*

In person
at the Royal Albert
Hall Box Office
*(9.00am–9.00pm,
daily, from 13 May)*

20 April
Create your
Proms Plan online

From 9.00am on Thursday 20 April,
go to bbc.co.uk/promstickets and
fill in your Proms Planner. You must
complete and submit your Plan by
11.59pm on Friday 12 May in order
to make a booking. Creating a Plan
does not by itself result in a booking.

12 May
Book your
Promming Passes

From 9.00am on Friday 12 May,
book your Season and Weekend
Promming (standing) Passes for the
Royal Albert Hall. (These passes are
not bookable in the Proms Planner.)

13 May
General Booking Opens

From 9.00am on Saturday 13 May,
submit your Proms Plan or book online
via bbc.co.uk/promstickets, in person or
by phone. See bbc.co.uk/promstickets
for details of how to book.

Tickets for 'Proms at' concerts will be
available directly from each venue, not
from the Royal Albert Hall. (These tickets
are not bookable via the Proms Planner.)

Royal Albert Hall ticket prices

Seated tickets for all Proms concerts at the Royal Albert Hall fall into one of eight price bands, indicated beside each concert listing on pages 108–139. Promming (standing) tickets are available on the day of each concert for just £8.00 (including booking fee). See opposite for details.

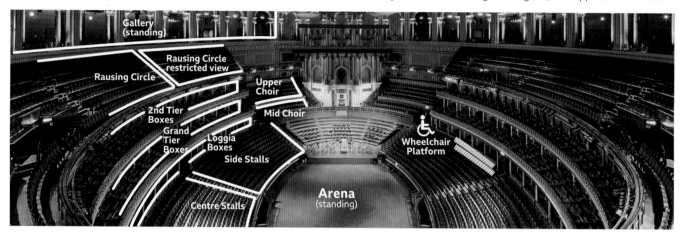

PRICE BANDS	●	●	●	●	●	●	●	●	Promming/ Standing tickets
GRAND TIER BOXES 12 seats, price per seat *	£25.00	£26.00	**£35.00**	£42.00	£52.00	£62.00	£72.00	£115.00	
LOGGIA AND 2ND TIER BOXES Loggia: 8 seats, price per seat 2nd Tier: 5 seats, price per seat	£25.00	£26.00	**£35.00**	£38.00	£48.00	£58.00	£68.00	£110.00	**£8.00**
CENTRE STALLS	£22.00	£24.00	**£33.00**	£35.00	£45.00	£55.00	£65.00	£100.00	
SIDE STALLS	£18.50	£23.50	**£32.50**	£32.50	£42.50	£52.50	£62.50	£95.00	
MID CHOIR	£18.50	£22.00	**£30.00**	£26.00	£30.00	£34.00	£45.00	£75.00	
UPPER CHOIR	£12.00	£17.00	**£22.00**	£20.00	£22.50	£29.00	£38.00	£70.00	
RAUSING CIRCLE FRONT	£12.00	£17.00	**£22.00**	£20.00	£22.50	£29.00	£38.00	£70.00	
RAUSING CIRCLE MID	£15.00	£15.00	**£20.00**	£17.00	£20.00	£24.00	£30.00	£65.00	
RAUSING CIRCLE REAR	£12.00	£15.00	**£20.00**	£13.00	£16.00	£20.00	£25.00	£55.00	
RAUSING CIRCLE RESTRICTED VIEW	£9.00	£9.00	**£10.00**	£9.00	£10.00	£14.00	£18.00	£32.00	

Promming/Standing tickets

Booking fees: a booking fee of 2% of the total value – plus £2.00 per ticket (£1.00 per ticket for the Relaxed Prom, Prom 25) up to a maximum of £25.00 – applies to all bookings (including Season and Weekend Promming Passes), other than those made in person at the Royal Albert Hall. Promming tickets cost £8.00; no additional booking fees apply, whether they are bought online or in person. An optional £1.50 per ticket levy will be added to tickets for concerts at the Royal Albert Hall. *As most Grand Tier Boxes are privately owned, availability is limited.

There is a Prom for every music-lover, whether you're a first-timer or a seasoned regular. To view the whole season at a glance, see the inside front cover. Seats start from just £9.00 (plus booking fee) – and you can Prom (stand) for only £8.00 (including booking fee).

If you cannot use your ticket

Tickets, once purchased, cannot be refunded or exchanged. But, if you cannot use a ticket for any reason and want to try to resell it, we recommend using Twickets – an ethical ticket resale marketplace, enabling concert-goers to buy and sell tickets at no more than their face value.

Promming on the day

The popular tradition of Promming (standing in the Arena or Gallery areas of the Royal Albert Hall) is central to the unique and informal atmosphere of the BBC Proms. Around 1,000 standing places in the Arena and Gallery are available on the day of each concert, for just £8.00 (including booking fee). You can book up to two tickets online on the day of the concert. If you are unable to book online, you may be able to book in person at Door 12 of the Royal Albert Hall, subject to availability. Visit bbc.co.uk/proms for details.

Save money by buying a Season Promming Pass for £250. Whole Season Promming passes also offer priority entry to standing places in the Arena or Gallery throughout the season (excluding Proms 10, 11, 25 and 62) plus great savings on individual ticket prices and admission to the Last Night of the Proms. You can also save money by buying a Weekend Promming Pass. Please see new terms and conditions at bbc.co.uk/proms.

Promming tickets for 'Proms at' venues are available. See bbc.co.uk/promstickets for details.

A limited number of seats either at the back of the Arena or in the Choir or Gallery will be available for those Prommers who are unable to stand for an entire concert. These seats can be booked online. See bbc.co.uk/proms for details.

Online booking

The 'Select Your Own Seat' option is not available via the Proms Planner or during the first few days that Proms tickets are on sale. You will be allocated the best available places within your chosen seating area. It is not possible to book entire boxes online. If you would like to book a complete box, call the Box Office on 020 7070 4441.

18s and under go half-price

Tickets for people aged 18 and under can be purchased at half-price in any seating area of the Royal Albert Hall except for the Last Night. (Not applicable to Promming tickets.)

Great savings for groups

Groups of 10 or more attending Royal Albert Hall concerts can claim a 5% discount on the price of selected tickets (not including the Last Night). For details, call the Group Booking Information Line on 020 7070 4408.

'Proms at' concerts

Tickets for 'Proms at' concerts will be available via each venue from 9.00am on Saturday 13 May. Prices vary for each venue. See bbc.co.uk/promstickets for details.

Last Night of the Proms

Owing to high demand, the majority of seated tickets for the Last Night of the Proms are allocated by ballot, as follows.

The Five-Concert Ballot

Customers who purchase tickets for at least five other concerts at the Royal Albert Hall

are eligible to enter the Five-Concert Ballot. For details on how to enter, see bbc.co.uk/promstickets. The Five-Concert Ballot closes at midnight on Thursday 8 June.

If you require a wheelchair space for the Last Night, you will still need to book for five other concerts, but you must phone the Access Information Line (020 7070 4410) before 9.00pm on Thursday 8 June to enter the separate ballot for wheelchair spaces.

The Open Ballot

Owing to the cancellation of the Last Night of the Proms in 2022, there will not be an Open Ballot this year. Instead, ticket-holders for the Last Night of the Proms 2022 will have another chance to book tickets for this year's Last Night. These bookers will be contacted directly via the Royal Albert Hall.

General availability for the Last Night

Any remaining tickets for the Last Night will go on sale at 9.00am on Friday 14 July by phone or online only. Only one application (for a maximum of two tickets) can be made per household. There is exceptionally high demand for Last Night tickets, but returns occasionally become available.

Promming (standing) at the Last Night

Whole Season Promming Passes include admission to the Last Night. A limited allocation of Last Night standing tickets (priced £8.00, including booking fee) are also reserved for Prommers who have attended five or more concerts (in the Arena or the Gallery). They are eligible to purchase one ticket each for the Last Night on presentation of their used tickets (which will be retained) at the Box Office. For details, see bbc.co.uk/promstickets.

A limited number of Promming tickets will be available on the Last Night itself (priced £8.00 including booking fee, one per person). No previous ticket purchases are necessary.

66 Having a dedicated wheelchair platform makes visiting the Proms so enjoyable and easy. From arrival at the Royal Albert Hall to getting to your 'seat', everything you need is nearby and fully accessible, and the staff at the Hall are so helpful. I am very much looking forward to next season

Antonia Stoneman, Proms concert-goer, 2022

If you have any questions regarding accessibility at the Proms, call the Access Information Line on 020 7070 4410

Access at the Proms

ACCESS INFORMATION LINE
020 7070 4410 (9.00am–5.00pm, weekdays)

Full information on the facilities offered to disabled concert-goers at the Royal Albert Hall is available at royalalberthall.com or by calling the Access Information Line. The Hall has a Silver award from the Attitude is Everything Charter of Best Practice.

All disabled concert-goers (and one companion) receive a 50% discount on all ticket prices for all Proms concerts. To book, call the Access Information Line or purchase in person at the Royal Albert Hall.

Throughout the Proms season at the Royal Albert Hall 12 spaces will be available to book for wheelchair-users and companions on a designated wheelchair platform situated in front of Loggias Boxes 31–33. Depending on the Prom, between 18 and 25 additional wheelchair spaces will be available in the Stalls and the Circle. To book, call the Access Information Line or visit the Royal Albert Hall Box Office in person.

For information on wheelchair spaces available for the Last Night of the Proms via the Five-Concert Ballot, see page 147.

The Gallery can accommodate up to four wheelchair-users.

We offer some accessible seats at £8.00 (including booking fee) in the Arena, Choir and Gallery for Prommers unable to stand. See bbc.co.uk/proms for details.

A limited number of car parking spaces close to the Hall can be reserved by disabled concert-goers; contact the Access Information Line to book.

Ramped venue access is available at Doors 1, 3, 8, 9 and 12. The most convenient set-down point for vehicle arrival is near Door 3. Public lifts are located at Doors 1 and 8. All bars and restaurants are wheelchair-accessible.

Guide and assistance dogs are welcome and can be easily accommodated in the boxes. If you prefer to sit elsewhere, call the Access Information Line for advice. The Royal Albert Hall stewards will be happy to look after your dog while you enjoy the concert.

Transfer wheelchairs are available for customer use. The Royal Albert Hall has busy corridors and therefore visitors using mobility scooters are asked to enter via Door 3 or Door 8 and will be offered a transfer wheelchair on arrival. Scooters can be stored in designated places. The Hall is unable to offer charging facilities for scooters.

To request any of the above services, call the Access Information Line or complete an accessibility request form online at royalalberthall.com 48 hours before you attend. Alternatively you can make a request upon arrival at the Information Desk at Door 6, subject to availability.

Assisted Proms

Three Proms (Proms 10, 11 & 25) will be British Sign Language-interpreted (see opposite). Book tickets for these Proms online in the usual way. If you require good visibility of the signer, choose the Stalls Signer Area when selecting tickets, or request by calling the Access Information Line.

Relaxed Proms

BBC Proms relaxed performances (Proms 11 & 25) are designed to suit individuals or groups who feel more comfortable attending concerts in a relaxed environnment. There is a relaxed attitude to noise and audience members are free to leave and re-enter the auditorium at any point. There will be chill-out areas, where spaces are made for anyone needing a bit of quiet time before or during the performance. For full details, visit bbc.co.uk/proms.

Accessibility at the Proms

BSL
British Sign Language-interpreted Proms

Proms 10 & 11 ('Orrible Opera) • 22 July

Prom 25 (Relaxed Prom) • 3 August

R
Relaxed performances

Prom 11 ('Orrible Opera) • 22 July

Prom 25 (Relaxed Prom) • 3 August

S
Surtitled Proms

Prom 31 (Dialogues of the Carmelites) • 7 August

Prom 43 (Endgame) • 17 August

Prom 49 (Das Paradies und die Peri) • 22 August

Prom 64 (The Trojans) • 3 September

For further information, please visit bbc.co.uk/proms. If you would like to discuss additional access requirements, call the Access Information Line (020 7070 4410, 9.00am–5.00pm, weekdays).

BBC Proms Festival Guide – Braille and large-print formats

Braille versions of this Festival Guide are available in two parts, 'Articles' and 'Concert Listings/Booking Information', priced £4.49 and £4.50 respectively. For more information and to order, call the RNIB Helpline on 0303 123 9999.

A text-only large-print version of this Festival Guide is available, priced £8.99. To order, call Deborah Fether on 07716 225658, or email PromsPublications@bbc.co.uk. (Allow 10 working days for delivery.)

The Guide is also available to purchase as an eBook from Amazon and as both an eBook and ePDF from Bloomsbury. Both formats are compatible with screen readers and text-to-speech software. Visit amazon.co.uk or bloomsbury.com/uk for details.

Concert programmes in large print

Large-print concert programmes can be purchased on the night (at the same price as standard programmes), if ordered at least five working days in advance.

Large-print sung texts and librettos (where applicable) are available with the purchase of a standard programme, if ordered at least five working days in advance. This excludes surtitled Proms, for which librettos are not printed.

To order, call Deborah Fether on 07716 225658, or email PromsPublications@bbc.co.uk. Programmes and texts will be left for collection at the Door 6 Merchandise Desk one hour before the concert begins.

A Royal Albert Hall steward will be happy to read the concert programme to visually impaired visitors. Call the Access Information Line (020 7070 4410) or complete an accessibility request form online at royalalberthall.com 48 hours before you attend.

Booking

Royal Albert Hall

Kensington Gore, London SW7 2AP
www.royalalberthall.com • 020 7070 4441

The Royal Albert Hall of Arts and Sciences was officially opened by Queen Victoria on 29 March 1871. When, in 1867, Victoria laid the foundation stone for the building, she announced that it was to be named after her husband, Prince Albert, who had died six years earlier.

The Hall has hosted 25 suffragette meetings, and many of the world's leading figures in music, dance, sport and politics have appeared on its stage. These include Winston Churchill, Emmeline Pankhurst, the Dalai Lama and Nelson Mandela, as well as various royals and world leaders.

The BBC Proms has called the Royal Albert Hall its home since 1941, after the Queen's Hall was gutted by fire in an air-raid. The Hall has since hosted over 4,500 Proms concerts.

Latecomers
Latecomers will only be admitted if and when there is a suitable break in the performance.

Security
Please do not bring large bags to the Royal Albert Hall. All bags and visitors may be subject to security checks as a condition of entry.

Children under 5
Everyone is welcome at the Horrible Histories Prom (Proms 10 & 11) and the Relaxed Prom (Prom 25). Out of consideration for audience and artists, we recommend that children attending other Proms are aged 5 and over.

Dress code
Come as you are: there is no dress code at the Proms.

Proms merchandise and programmes
Merchandise is available at Doors 6 and 12 and on the Rausing Circle level at Doors 4 and 8. Programmes are on sale throughout the building. Merchandise and programmes are also available online at shop.royalalberthall.com.

South Kensington (Piccadilly, Circle & District Lines); Gloucester Road (Piccadilly, Circle & District Lines); High Street Kensington (Circle & District Lines)

Enjoy a wide range of food and drink from two and a half hours before each concert – see royalalberthall.com

Cloakroom available. A charge per item applies. Cloakroom season tickets are also available *(conditions apply – see royalalberthall.com)*

Wheelchair-accessible *(see page 148 for details)*

Guide dogs and assistance dogs welcome

Promming is easy!

No seats available for your favourite Prom?
Don't give up: get Promming (standing) tickets on
the day for £8.00 (including booking fee). Around 1,000
tickets are available on the day of the concert (maximum
two per person).

How to Prom

Visit bbc.co.uk/promstickets for our guide to Promming
and information on places for wheelchair users and
ambulant disabled concert-goers.

Sage Gateshead • 21–23 July

St Mary's Square, Gateshead NE8 2JR
www.sagegateshead.com • 01914 434666

⇌ Newcastle Central (National Rail; Metro); Gateshead (Metro)

🍸 Bar and restaurant on site

⌂ Cloakroom available

♿ Wheelchair-accessible

🐕 Guide dogs and assistance dogs welcome

Sage Gateshead is an international music centre for the North.
The charity presents music of all genres, creates opportunities
for everyone to make music, works alongside emerging artists
and is a place where communities gather. Its performance
spaces have won several awards and widespread praise for their
design and acoustics. Sage Gateshead's resident orchestra, the
Royal Northern Sinfonia, presents a busy and diverse season of
concerts at the venue. It has deep roots in the North-East and
tours across the region, nationally and around the world.

If you arrive late
To minimise any disturbance, we'll ask you to enter during a suitable
break in the performance.

If you bring a bag in to the building
Any bags might be checked by our security team before you enter the
performance spaces.

Aberystwyth Arts Centre/Canolfan y Celfyddydau Aberystwyth • 30 July

Aberystwyth University/Prifysgol Aberystwyth,
Aberystwyth SY23 3DE
www.aberystwythartscentre.co.uk • 01970 623232

- ⇌ Aberystwyth (National Rail)
- 🥤 Bars on site; food and drink available
- ♿ Wheelchair-accessible
- 🐕 Guide dogs and assistance dogs welcome

Dewsbury Town Hall • 6 August

Wakefield Old Road, Dewsbury WF12 8DG
www.kirklees.gov.uk • 01484 221900

- ⇌ Dewsbury (National Rail)
- 🥤 Bar on site
- ♿ Wheelchair-accessible
- 🐕 Guide dogs and assistance dogs welcome

Guildhall, Londonderry • 15 July

Guildhall Square, Derry BT48 6DQ
www.guildhallderry.com • 02871 376510

- 🚆 Derry (NI Railways)
- 🥤 Bar on site
- 🧥 Cloakroom facilities available on site
- ♿ Wheelchair-accessible
- 🐕 Guide dogs and assistance dogs welcome

Hall for Cornwall • 27 August

Back Quay, Truro TR1 2LL
www.hallforcornwall.co.uk • 01872 262466

≥ Truro (National Rail)

🥤 Bars on site; food and drink available

👔 Cloakroom available

♿ Wheelchair-accessible

🐕 Guide dogs and assistance dogs welcome

Hippodrome, Great Yarmouth • 8 September

St George's Road, Great Yarmouth NR30 2EU
www.hippodromecircus.com • 01493 738877

≥ Great Yarmouth (National Rail)

🥤 Bars on site; food and drink available

♿ Wheelchair-accessible

🐕 Guide dogs and assistance dogs welcome

Perth Concert Hall • 3 September

Mill Street, Perth PH1 5HZ
www.perththeatreandconcerthall.com • 01738 621031

≥ Perth (National Rail)

🥤 Bar on site

♿ Wheelchair-accessible

🐕 Guide dogs and assistance dogs welcome

TURNER VIOLINS

Dealers in Fine Violins, Violas, Cellos, Basses and Bows

Restorations

Expertise

Valuations

1-5 Lily Grove NG9 1QL
NOTTINGHAM
0115 943 0333
Also at Cavendish Square,
London by Appointment

www.turnerviolins.co.uk
info@turnerviolins.co.uk

Whatever you do...
Make Music!

The University of Kent provides a thriving programme of extra-curricular music in the award-winning Colyer-Fergusson Building, open to all students and staff: Chorus, Orchestra, Chamber Choir, Concert and Big Bands and musical theatre. Our Music Performance Scholarships are open to all students, whatever they study. Concerts take place on campus and in Canterbury Cathedral.

For further information

Daniel Harding
Head of Music Performance
E: music@kent.ac.uk
T: 01227 827335
www.kent.ac.uk/music

University of Kent

Watch and listen to Westminster School performances, and learn about Music Awards for entry at 11+, 13+ and 16+.
www.westminster.org.uk

WESTMINSTER SCHOOL

City of London School

Based in the heart of the capital and surrounded by cultural landmarks, City of London School is the ideal place for aspiring young musicians.

- **Scholar mentoring**, coaching and pastoral programme.
- Choral and organ hub, affiliated to **Royal College of Organists**.
- Choristerships to **HM Chapel Royal**, St James's Palace.
- Full orchestral and jazz provision.

- Expert specialist instrumental tuition.
- Strong focus on academic music.
- Impressive concert hall with Steinway piano; riverside teaching and performance spaces.

RCO

TRINITY COLLEGE LONDON
Trinity Champion Centre 2022-2023

cityoflondonschool.org.uk

Christ Church Cathedral School, Oxford

Independent Day School for Boys 3 - 13 & Girls 3 - 5

Flexi-Boarding for Boys 8 - 13

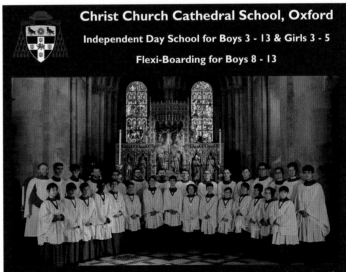

'The choristers' outstanding achievements infuse the entire school', The Good Schools Guide.

All of our Cathedral Choir boarders are awarded bursaries. We have two day boy Choirs: Worcester College and Pembroke College Chapel Choirs.
Book a visit to find out more: registrar@cccs.org.uk // 01865 242561

www.cccs.org.uk // 3 Brewer Street, Oxford, OX1 1QW

CANTERBURY cathedral

Rediscover England's First Cathedral

Kids Go FREE*
until 31 December 2023
*Visitor entry. T&Cs apply

2022
Travellers'
Choice
Tripadvisor

Enjoy a day out 1,400 years in the making

www.canterbury-cathedral.org

HERITAGE FUND

Photo: Bill Hiskett 2014

BENSLOWMUSIC
INSTRUMENT LOAN SCHEME

TAKE YOUR MUSICIANSHIP TO THE NEXT LEVEL

Benslow Music Instrument Loan Scheme is an inclusive and unique UK charity, offering talented young musicians affordable access to high-quality instruments. We have over 800 instruments in our care, ranging from high quality strings to woodwind and brass, available to UK applicants aged 7-25 years in full-time education.

www.benslowmusic-ils.org

@BenslowMusicILS   @BenslowMusicInstrumentLoanScheme   @benslowmusicils

Benslow Music Instrument Loan Scheme, Aston Building, Benslow Lane, Hitchin, Herts, SG4 9RB
Registered Charity No. 313755

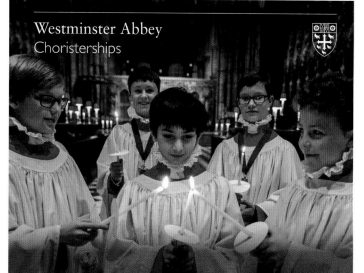

Westminster Abbey
Choristerships

Westminster Abbey choristers receive superb musical training and an outstanding education. Find out more about our world-famous Choir and unique Choir School:
abbeychoirschool.org

Walks and Music at the Gstaad Menuhin Festival
13 - 19 August 2023

Join us in Switzerland to attend four concerts of the Gstaad Menuhin Festival, including a recital of Baroque opera arias by **Cecilia Bartoli** and **Il Pomo d'Oro**. Our 5-star hotel is the epitome of Swiss style and service levels (with meals to match), while a network of cable cars and little mountain railways enables us to enjoy easy walks in superb Alpine scenery.

Kudu Travel • www.kudutravel.com • 020 8150 3367

FREE AND OPEN TO ALL

Tuesday - Sunday and Bank Holidays

10am to 5pm

museumofthehome.org.uk

MUSEUM OF
THE HOME

Produced by
FLAMENCO
FESTIVAL

⊖ Angel
sadlerswells.com

Fire up your summer!

Flamenco Festival London 2023

'Electrifying'
The Times

SADL
ERSW
ELLS

Sadler's Wells in Angel
Sadler's Wells Theatre

with the support of

ARTS COUNCIL
ENGLAND

HAVE YOU GOT COIN OR STAMP COLLECTIONS TO SELL?

CONTACT US FOR A FREE VALUATION

Office: +44 (0)20 3409 1238 · WhatsApp: +44 7485925831

info@harmers.com

HARMERS
OF LONDON
ESTABLISHED 1918

Harmers of London Auctions Ltd
60 St. James's Street
London SW1A 1LE, UK

www.harmers.com

OVER 100 YEARS OF EXPERIENCE AT YOUR SERVICE

St Martin in the Fields
CONCERTS
2023-2024 SEASON
BOOK NOW
Featured artists include:
12 Ensemble | Aaron Azunda Akugbo | Academy of St Martin in the Fields | Avi Avital | BBC Singers
Benjamin Appl | Castilian Quartet | Christopher Purves | Consone Quartet | Darbar Indian Classical Artists
Dunedin Consort | English Baroque Soloists | English Concert | Ex Cathedra | Gavin Bryars Ensemble
eorge Fu | Hugh Cutting | I Fagiolini | John Eliot Gardiner | The King's Singers | La nuova musica | La Serenissima
Ligeti Quartet | Mathilda Lloyd | Michael Collins | Monteverdi Choir | Rachel Podger | SANSARA
St Martin's Voices | Tenebrae | The Carice Singers | The Gesualdo Six | The Jess Gillam Ensemble | The Sixteen
www.smitf.org

Index of Artists

Index of Works

Index of
Works

BBC Proms

Director, BBC Proms David Pickard
Controller, BBC Radio 3 Alan Davey (until March 2023), Sam Jackson (from April 2023)
Personal Assistant Yvette Pusey

Editor, BBC Radio 3 Emma Bloxham

Head of Marketing, Learning and Publications Kate Finch

Business Sanoma Evans (Business Advisor), Tricia Twigg (Business Co-ordinator)

Concerts and Planning Helen Heslop (Manager), Hannah Donat (Artistic Producer), Alys Jones, Jo de Sa (Event Producers), Alison Dancer (Event Co-ordinator), Helen MacLeod (Operations Project Manager)

Marketing Emily Caket (Manager), Chloe Jaynes (Executive), Kiera Lockard (Co-ordinator)

Press and Communications George Chambers (Head of Communications, Classical Music), Jo Hawkins (Communications Manager), Freya Edgeworth (Publicist)

Learning Lauren Creed, Melanie Fryer (Senior Managers), Laura Mitchell, Chloe Shrimpton (Managers), Siân Bateman, Catherine Humphrey (Assistant Managers), Joey Williams, Sharni Edmondson (Trainees)

Music Television Suzy Klein (Head of Arts and Classical Music TV), Stephen James-Yeoman (Commissioning Editor for TV), Livewire Pictures Ltd (Production)

BBC Sounds Philip Raperport (Commissioning Executive, BBC Radio 3 & BBC Proms)

BBC Music Library Tim Auvache, Anne Butcher, Raymond Howden, Alison John, Richard Malton, Claire Martin, Steven Nunes, Alec Pavelich, David Russell, Joseph Schultz

Commercial Rights & Business Affairs Simon Brown, Geraint Heap, Wendy Nielson, Ashley Smith, Bronagh Taylor

BBC Proms Publications

Publishing Manager Christine Webb
Editorial Manager Edward Bhesania
Sub-Editor Timmy Fisher
Publications Designer Reenie Basova
Junior Publications Designer Daniel Hague
Publications Co-ordinator Deborah Fether

Advertising Cabbells (020 3603 7930); cabbells.co.uk
Cover illustration BBC Creative/BBC
Published by BBC Proms Publications, Room 3015, Broadcasting House, London W1A 1AA
Distributed by Bloomsbury Publishing, 50 Bedford Square, London WC1B 3DP

Printed by APS Group

APS Group holds ISO 14001 environmental management, FSC® and PEFC certifications. Printed using vegetable-based inks on FSC-certified paper. Formed in 1993 as a response to concerns over global deforestation, FSC (Forest Stewardship Council®) is an independent, non-governmental, not-for-profit organisation established to promote the responsible management of the world's forests. For more information, please visit www.fsc.org.

In line with the BBC's sustainability strategy, the BBC Proms is actively working with partners and suppliers towards being a more sustainable festival.

ISBN 978-1-912114-14-6

© BBC 2023. All details correct at time of going to press.

Image credits for 'Mood Music' (pages 90–95)

Helen Grime: INTERFOTO/Alamy (jewellery); Ben Lim/Unsplash (bubbling undercurrent); Lyon & Turnbull/Bridgeman (Catterline); Sheng/Unsplash (Scottish landscape); Oscar-Helgstrand/Unsplash (miniature horse); ZUMA Press, Inc./Alamy (Elliott Carter)

Samy Moussa: Geneviève Caron (Moussa); Sean Pavone/Alamy (Bryce Canyon); The Picture Art Collection/Alamy (Coorte painting); NPL – DeA Picture Library/Bridgeman Images (Parmenides); Hemis/Alamy (carnyx); Ivan Kliun (Red Light); Zev Radovan/Alamy (Herodium)

Derrick Skye: Hannah Arista Photography (Skye); Sean Pavone/Alamy (Bridge); Indiapicture/Alamy (tabla); Science History Images/Alamy (sun); Andre Hunter/Unsplash (dancing feet); Ariadne Van Zandbergen/Alamy (African textiles)

Index of Works